Contents

Acknowledgements

Most authors can rarely pin-point the moment at which the seed which eventually blossoms into a book is sown.

In this case, I have no such difficulty. The idea of doing a book on Jack Lynch took root as John Sheehan photographed me talking to the former Taoiseach on Friday, 15 December 1979 in the old Victoria Hotel in Cork.

Ten days previously Mr Lynch had made what Michael Mills of the *Irish Press* had called "the shock announcement" of his resignation.

His meeting with journalists in Cork was his first on-the-record session since then.

It was an impromptu press conference, and during it Mr Lynch talked of doing a book himself.

Over the years since then he has talked several times about this to me and to others. I don't know whether he ever will – but in the meantime this is a modest attempt to fill a void in late twentieth century Irish political history.

This is a the story of a man – a sportsman and a statesman. And it is a story for everyone because in a sense it is a story about ourselves and the times in which we live.

I owe gratitude to all who helped to make it possible. My media colleagues, as always, were supportive and generous with time, with recollections, with advice, and with materials from their own files.

If I single out the following, it is because they have been especially helpful: Michael Mills (now Ombudsman), formerly of the *Irish Press*; Dick Walsh of the *Irish Times*; Chris Glennon of the *Irish Independent*; Sean Duignan, Kevin Healy (now Director of Radio Programming) and Shane Kenny of RTE; Raymond Smith of the *Sunday Independent*; Tim Ryan and John Garvey of the *Irish Press*, and Ray Ryan of the *Cork Examiner*.

In addition, I wish to acknowledge a debt to the late John Wallace of the *Evening Press;* to Sean Cronin of the *Irish Times* in Washington, and Sean Donlon, former Secretary of Department of Foreign Affairs.

I owe a special word of thanks to Vincent Browne of the *Sunday Tribune* for the material from *Magill.*

For help with photographs I am indebted to Des Barry and Norma Cuddihy of the *Cork Examiner;* John Sheehan and Liam Burke of Press 22 and the *Irish Independent* for permission to use photographs they supplied.

John O'Connor of Blackwater Press liked the book at first glance, so to speak, and went for it. His suggestions have made it a better book, as has Ms Anna O'Donovan by her skilful editing.

In the preparation of the book, a number of people spoke to me on the understanding it was for "background', and I have respected this.

To those who spoke to me "on the record", I owe a special word of thanks.

I am particularly grateful to Mr Jack Lynch for granting me a number of interviews, and for replying to written queries. At no stage did he ask to see, let alone endorse, what I was writing.

This, therefore, is his story as told by me. Facts in the political sphere are not always easy to establish; the interpretation of facts is perilous and subjective. All I can say is that this is my version.

In a New York pub in March 1990, I discussed this project with Mr John Hume, MEP, the leader of the SDLP. As we finished our conversation, Mr Hume said: "Jack Lynch deserves a book".

I would go further – he deserves several, given the times that were in it.

This, I suspect, is just the first.

Finally, to my wife, Lil, my thanks once again for her loving support.

For Veronica and John
Two of the Best and the Brightest

Foreword

For the entire island of Ireland it was a time of high drama – and great uncertainty.

The year was 1970, the month May. That same year there were other major news events. On the political front, Answar Sadat replaced Gamal Nassar as President of Egypt. Bernadette Devlin, the 23-year-old MP for Mid-Ulster, lost her appeal against a six-month sentence for incitement to riot.

In the USA, four students, two of them girls, were shot dead by the National Guard during an anti-Vietnam War demo at Kent State University.

On the sporting front Tony Jacklin became the first Briton to win the US Open for 50 years.

In the world of music, The Beatles broke up, ending a creative alliance that might justifiably be said to have changed the world, at least in rock 'n' roll terms.

In literature Alexander Solzhenitsyn, author of *Cancer Ward* and *The First Circle*, won the Nobel Prize, and a slim volume entitled *Selected Poems* by Mary Wilson (wife of the Prime Minister Harold Wilson) caused a stir when it went on sale in Britain.

And in theatre, the uninhibited sex revue *Oh! Calcutta*, devised by Kenneth Tynan, opened in London.

But in Dublin events were unfolding which even now – 21 years on – are not fully comprehended.

Aspects of what has become known as "The Arms Crisis" remain shrouded in secrecy. They have been embellished by rumour, distorted by time, and sanitised by the desire of human beings to be well thought of.

It was a psycho-drama on a grand scale – but drama with grim, Machiavellian undertones. And, like all good drama it had the ingredients of tragedy at its core.

That such tragedy was averted, that the entire island was not plunged into a quagmire of blood and death and civil strife was entirely due to one man – Jack Lynch.

That should never be forgotten.

And for that alone Lynch's place in history is secure.

But what of Lynch the man? What of his motives, his beliefs, his hopes, his vision of life?

Do we yet appreciate what he achieved in 1970? Do we yet understand this Taoiseach who, as a political opponent remarked, was far from the "simple man" he is often portrayed to be?

That same opponent was surely right when he said that Lynch was "more devious and deeper" than the usual public perception of him.

There are sides to Jack Lynch that even today remain difficult to unravel. And there is a dimension to his personality which, arguably, not even the one person who is closest to him – his wife, Mairin understands.

Jack Lynch met President John F. Kennedy just once. That was in June 1963 when Kennedy came to Ireland, and addressed both Houses of the Oireachtas.

In his speech, the President observed that we need not savour the bitterness of the past to discover its meaning for the present and the future.

"For the Ireland of 1963 – one of the youngest of nations and oldest of civilisations – has discovered that the achievement of nationhood is not an end but a beginning ."

They were remarks Jack Lynch would remember.

At the time Lynch was Minister for Industry and Commerce. He was 45 years of age, as was Kennedy, both having been born in 1917.

As far as age and timescale are concerned, they were contemporaries.

The age that created Kennedy was also the age that created Jack Lynch, though they were fashioned by very different cultures.

In Kennedy's case, it was open and pluralist, multi-racial and nondenominational, at least at constitutional level.

In Jack Lynch's case, it was a culture of turbulence, of bitterness, a culture that was narrow, inward-looking and reactionary.

Above all, it was a culture of ambivalence.

Lynch's own recollection of his meeting with the President who was to be gunned down months later in Dallas is not very detailed.

The meeting was brief, their acquaintance fleeting.

I have no doubt that had they had the opportunity to get to know each other better, they would have liked and admired each other very much.

If Kennedy had survived and served a second term in The White House, who knows what the implications might have been for the "Irish Question".

Lynch became Taoiseach in 1966 – at what would have been the midway point of the second term of the Kennedy Presidency.

And that fleeting meeting in Dublin might well have provided a "window of opportunity" to fashion a new initiative on the North, to involve Washington at a much earlier stage, and to alter history.

We shall never know, though the mere thought of a Lynch Kennedy alliance is a tantalising one.

I mustn't tempt fate too much, or push the parallels too far, or look for links and prospects in a "what might have been" situation.

Yet the Lynch-Kennedy link, albeit brief, will forever fascinate.

And if only by virtue of a certain opaqueness of personality, they are intriguing and also difficult subjects for any biographer.

At the core of their lives there is a single episode which is resistive to investigation, hostile to exploration. In President John F. Kennedy's case it was his involvement in the death of Marilyn Monroe in 1962, an involvement rich in conspiracy theories.

In Jack Lynch's case it is the Arms Crisis of 1970 – an event also shrouded in conspiracy.

Verifying the events of Jack Lynch's life is one thing. And it is not difficult. Not most of the time, though there remains that dark knot of 1970.

Like Kennedy, it is Lynch's personality, his motives and his self-understanding that cause the problems.

Even now, in the autumn of his life, his personality remains mysterious.

The facts live, but Jack, lurking behind and in the interstices between them, remains elusive, his secret self intact.

We are in terrain which requires a psycho-historian.

I have tried to penetrate beyond the mask, to reveal something of the man as well as the politician, the sportsman and the statesman.

It is for the reader to gauge the extent to which I have succeeded.

I am fond of Cork, of Ireland, and of Jack Lynch.

But fondness isn't enough. Not nearly enough.

Sometimes we have to get away from our birthplace to see it again, anew, and in some fresh kind of perspective.

I was still seeking that perspective on Cork, on Ireland and, above all, on Jack Lynch when I ended up in the lovely Yugoslav town of Dubrovnik.

That proved to be a happy coincidence, because I learned later that it was while on holiday there that Lynch met a man who arranged his first meeting with Mrs Margaret Thatcher.

Dubrovnik has a lot in common with Cork; a beautiful harbour, quays and boats and old bars where late at night songs of joy and hope, and some of loss and sorrow, are sung.

It also has very friendly people.

In the age of *perestroika*, Yugoslavia, like Ireland, is going through a period of real change, even of turbulence and upheaval.

So it was the ideal place to reflect, to sort out my thoughts, and to write two of the key chapters of this book.

I needed to strengthen my resolve, because history scares us, especially our own.

Its revenants stalk our streets, inhabit our dreams, and help to fashion some of our worst nightmares.

Often we desire to be free of history, and yet we can't be. It has us trapped, holding us in thrall.

History isn't just about public events. It's about primal things like blood and sperm and territory, things at the root of our lives, things which are capable of pushing us into madness or homicidal acts.

It's also about power, intrigue, conspiracy, treachery and, even death itself.

That's why real history is so difficult to capture. It's inside every one of us. We are, in the most profound sense, our own history. And there is a kind of impudence in attempting to relate another's history.

To do it with care, with sensitivity, with – best of all – affection, is one's best defence. With this project, it is certainly my defence.

When you walk through a man's life, even quickly, you carry a heavy responsibility.

There is, first and foremost, a responsibility to the man himself in this case, Jack Lynch.

The truth has its own demands, and one can only fudge or escape them by retreating into what Jean-Paul Sartre called *mal foi* – bad faith.

But can we ever be sure of the truth when we cut through the contours of a man's life, especially when that life is enmeshed in legend, in folk heroism?

Legend has karmic implications, but does it always overshadow or swallow up the truth?

Can the truth be separated from legend? Or can the legend sometimes be no more or no less than the truth?

That's the challenge. I can only say that I have tried to meet it.

T.P. O'MAHONY
DUBROVNIK AND CORK 1990-91

1. A Backward Glance

These days Jack Lynch walks with a pronounced limp, and often with the aid of a stick – the legacy of an injury sustained in 1973 when he hurt his foot while stepping ashore from a boat near his holiday home in West Cork.

The once-sturdy shoulders, which shifted many an opponent off the ball in classic hurling and football encounters, are slightly stooped now.

At 74, the strains of the years in high office are etched in the drawn face, and the hair atop it is thin and greying.

Gone forever are the handsome Hollywood-type looks of a superb athlete who, in his heyday, turned the head of many a beautiful woman.

In the new Glen Rovers Clubhouse at Ballancollie Road on the northside of Cork City a photograph of the famous 1934 team has pride of place over the fireplace in the Members' Bar.

An 18-year old Lynch stands in the second row, flanked by Eamon Carroll and Pa Joe Dorgan.

Looking at it today, one is struck, not just by Lynch's youth relative to the rest of the team, but the sheer splendour of the man.

Seeking a Hollywood parallel, I came up with Gary Cooper – a choice reinforced for me afterwards when I saw Cooper in *The Pride of the Yankees*, the exceptional 1942 film biography of Yankee baseball star Lou Gehrig.

The sporting motif is very apposite, for in looking for clues to Lynch the politician, one must begin with Lynch the sportsman.

Today, looking at Lynch, it calls for no small feat of imagination to bridge the gap between the ageing figure of the nineties and the young, sexy, hunk in that photograph.

For him to gaze on that photograph these days must be a painful reminder, not just of his lost youth, but of the heavy toll exacted by the life which followed his glorious years in the great Gaelic arenas of Ireland.

It is pointless to speculate what might have become of Lynch had he never entered the world of politics.

A man who always knew the value of a shilling, he has been known to muse at odd moments that had he stuck to Law, his first calling, he would now be much wealthier.

Perhaps. But then, as he himself is quick to add, money isn't everything.

And while he himself might have finished up richer, there can be no doubt – on any objective assessment – that the Ireland we live in today would be the poorer had he not entered public life.

If there is much to like about Lynch, there is also much to like about the Ireland which today he looks upon with a certain weariness.

It is the weariness of one who has endured difficult times, hard battles, and trying campaigns – both on and off the field.

It is the weariness of a great player who has played one match too many – a player who has lost his appetite for the game, knowing in his heart of hearts that, finally, its demands are beyond his energies and talents.

Most definitely, it is not the weariness of the disillusioned or the disappointed. And it is tinged, not even to the extent of one whit by bitterness or scorn.

Lynch displays all the outward signs of being at peace with himself. Now entered upon his 75th year, he is in all external appearances content with himself.

If he has regrets – and what man or woman hasn't? – they are marginal, masked and muted, at least to the eye of the observer.

There is no air of wistfulness about him. And for a man who has been through one of the most dramatic, harrowing and bitter periods in modern Irish history, he is remarkably free of rancour and acrimony.

Of his part in that period, he can be remarkably reticent, given the central role which he played. Some will see in this signs of the old reluctance to move centre stage, the tendency which led to his being titled "the reluctant Taoiseach" after he succeeded Sean Lemass in 1966.

Others, less kind, will say his reticence is due to his having no cause for pride, or because he has something to hide.

The truth is much closer to the former rather than the latter.

There was always a genuine shyness and modesty about Lynch and a tendency to underestimate his own abilities.

Even now, he will say that he never saw himself as an "historical figure". Unlike other contemporaries who are in no doubt about the place they want (or believe they deserve) in history, Lynch claims no such status or right.

Is this false modesty?

I think not.

Would a man who felt he deserved a special niche in history leave behind in the archives all State papers when he left office? Would such a man not have kept a diary or notes or arranged for an amanuensis to record his words and deeds for posterity?

Those who know Lynch will say he has never changed. And to see him today, ensconced among old colleagues and old hurlers in a Cork pub, a glass of Paddy in his hand, is to be convinced of the veracity of this view.

Not that that is the whole story. How could it be?

None of us is ever all that we seem in public. We all wear masks; and we all have to live with varying degrees of self-understanding, and even of self-deception.

In Lynch's case, I doubt that he needs to be reminded of the importance of the role which he played in the affairs of the nation, especially in the post-1966 period.

But, because there is a genuine self-effacing quality about the man, he does tend to hide his light under a bushel.

Norma Smurfit, who got to know him through his connections with the Smurfit group of companies, once described him to me as "a nice man".

Of the many adjectives applied to Lynch these days, "nice" is the most common.

In another context, that may seem a limpid tribute, but in the context of Irish society, the word "nice" carries connotations of warmth, acceptability, personableness and decency surpassing the ordinary.

Jack Lynch is a genuinely nice man. That is almost universally acknowledged.

But what of the Ireland he helped to fashion? What of his legacy?

The Ireland he himself surveys is an Ireland still unsure of itself and of its place in Europe and the world.

It is an Ireland still gripped and largely characterised by the culture of ambivalence.

It will be an essential part of the thesis expounded in this book that Lynch played a leading role in changing aspects of that culture, while reinforcing others.

For good or ill, the Ireland of the 1990s bears his mark.

But how do the scales balance out?

History will render the final adjudication.

We are still too close, and the great events of the past quarter of a century are still too recent to allow us to take a disinterested view.

But we can at least risk an interim verdict.

2. Two Prime Ministers

Jack Lynch had two lapses of memory that I know about: the first nearly cost him his career, the second upset (albeit briefly) the harmony of his marriage.

In both cases things worked out fine, though not without some short-term embarrassment.

The public at large knows about his first act of forgetfulness. It concerned a widely publicised episode in 1973 with overtones of espionage, double-dealing and cloak-and-dagger activities.

The second is much more recent, and not very well known.

Those who witnessed it hushed up about it to save the former Taoiseach some blushes.

In fact, it would have made a good item for the gossip columnists and diarists – a species of journalist far more common now than in 1973 though no less unpalatable, I would suspect, to public figures such as Lynch.

Had they been present in the Limerick Inn, a hotel situated on the road between Limerick City and Shannon, on 21 September 1990 they would have been in their element.

The occasion was a gala dinner organised by the Junior Chamber of Commerce in Limerick, and the guest speaker was the former British Prime Minister, Mr Edward Heath.

And who better to invite along to greet him than Jack Lynch, a man with whom Heath first clashed and then subsequently worked with in something approximating to harmony.

That was back in the period between 1970 and 1974, Heath's one and only term as the occupant of 10 Downing Street.

He and Lynch didn't always see eye to eye, which is hardly surprising given the convulsive nature of Anglo-Irish history. No matter. That was the seventies. This is the nineties. And these are two civilised men.

So picture the scene.

The hotel is crowded as the guests, who include a Government Minister, assemble. The Minister is Desmond O'Malley from Industry and Commerce, leader of the Progressive Democrats, an old friend and one for whom Limerick is his political base.

There is a flurry of activity when Mr Lynch and his wife Mairin arrive.

In the foyer they are greeted by the hotel manager, Mr John Fahy, and by the President of Junior Chamber, Ms Mary Harty, and the Chamber's PRO, Ms Noelle O'Neill.

Mrs Lynch, casually dressed, has been looking forward to this evening for some time, and is in particularly good spirits, even more charming than usual.

Jack, on the other hand, who has been troubled by a shoulder injury (sustained some months before when he slipped on wet leaves while walking with Mairin in the Phoenix Park after Sunday Mass) is tense, his face pale and drawn.

Still, he too has been looking forward to the evening, and to the opportunity to renew acquaintances with Mr Heath.

A moment later Mrs Lynch's attention is distracted by two couples coming into the hotel.

To her consternation she sees the quartet are in formal dress.

Her heart drops.

She turns on her husband, unable to contain her surprise and disappointment.

"Jack," she says in a voice tinged with frost, "you never told me that formal attire was required."

The former Taoiseach, pipe in mouth, is disconcerted.

"Mairin, I forgot all about it," he replies with a half smile.

Their hosts exchange embarrassed looks.

By now Mairin is livid.

"Jack, you should have told me, you should have remembered," she remonstrates.

The hotel manager, well used to dealing with emergencies, steps in.

"Don't worry," he tells the Lynches, "we'll take care of things."

Jack apologises.

Mairin is furious.

She turns to Ms O'Neill. "Oh Noelle, I'm so disappointed. I have such lovely clothes, and I would love to have shown them off here tonight."

Jack glances anxiously at her.

She averts her gaze.

At that moment all she can think of is the Cybil Connolly dress she is so proud of. It would have been ideal for this occasion, but it is hanging in a wardrobe in 21 Garville Avenue in Rathgar, Dublin.

Even as she changes into the quite attractive outfit (a black and grey suit with a white, wide-collared blouse) which the hotel staff have managed to find, her sense of hurt is slow to dissipate.

In the world of high public affairs in which she has lived with her husband for 35 years it is an especially minor incident.

Yet that same small incident must have called unpleasantly to mind the turbulent, dramatic and very painful events which punctuated her husband's career at the top of Irish political life.

For Jack Lynch himself the meeting and the subsequent dinner with Edward Heath must have transported him back to a time of great tension and uncertainty in Irish life, to events in which they were both central players.

To onlookers at the reception later in the Castle Room, Jack Lynch and Ted Heath must have looked an odd pair.

One, the silver-haired, silver-tongued product of Oxford, a member of the British ruling class, one-time leader of the Conservative party and a former Prime Minister.

The other, hunched and limping in his borrowed tuxedo and bow tie, plagued by old sporting injuries, is a product of the northside of Cork City, a distinctly working class area.

But he too was leader of his country's main political party, Fianna Fáil, and he too is a former Prime Minister, though he prefers the Irish term "Taoiseach" (Chief).

Jack Lynch and Ted Heath.

An Irishman and an Englishman.

Two Prime Ministers.

Antagonists – once.

The burden of history saw to that.

How could it be otherwise?

In a crowded room they stand together.

Two figures whose great days are behind them. Yet both, precisely because of their past, remain relevant figures today.

During that past, each, in his own way displayed, while in high office, an openness to the future, a willingness to accommodate change, which set each apart from their fellows.

And still in the 1990s – demonstrating that both were not in their time as leaders merely responding to prevailing winds – they show again, in separate and distinctive ways, the same sensitivity to the need for progress, the need to get beyond the old shibboleths, to break free from old mythologies.

On a Friday evening in September 1990, they stand together for photographs in a Limerick hotel.

Yet standing still – in a political sense – was not something both were good at in their political heydays. Something to remember and celebrate.

As Jack Lynch and Ted Heath did.

For the two men there were other reminders of times past, and of the turbulent nature of those times.

For Heath's arrival (in a bulletproof Garda car) there was massive security.

And across from the hotel entrance a group of 17 protesters gathered, carrying placards which read "British Troops Out of Ireland", "No to Heath", "Stop Extradition" and "Remember Bloody Sunday".

Inside, pipe gripped between his teeth, Lynch watched impassively, gripped no doubt by a sense of *déja vu.*

Like Heath, he is no stranger to scenes like this.

When the convoy of Garda cars and outsiders pulled up outside the main door of the hotel, many of the people invited to the dinner as well as regular hotel guests, gathered as the former British Premier, resplendent in formal dress, stepped inside.

For a moment he glanced in the direction of the protesters, some of whom shouted at him.

Then he turned away, walked into the foyer, smiling and waving at the crowd assembled there to greet him.

Lynch transferred his pipe from his mouth to his hand and waited for the Junior Chamber officials to welcome Heath. Mairin was standing to his left and just behind him, the contretemps over the clothes forgotten.

Then it was their turn to greet Heath.

A photographer wanted a picture of the two men together.

Jack Lynch and Edward Heath.

Some would say they are forgotten men. Yesterday's men. Forgotten they are not, though the latter is true as far as it goes.

Heath served as British Prime Minister from 1970 to 1974.

Lynch served as Taoiseach for two terms – 1966 to 1973 and 1977 to 1979.

Their terms of office at the very top overlapped for just three years. Not a long time in the context of Anglo-Irish history, or any other history for that matter.

True.

But in that relatively short time both would accomplish what their predecessors over the previous decades had been unable or unwilling to do, or perhaps even to contemplate.

Both broke the mould – though it was accomplished (achieved) in very different ways, and for very different reasons, on either side of the Irish Sea.

For Lynch the mould was broken out of a sense of conviction.

For Heath it was broken out of a sense of necessity.

Either way, Anglo-Irish relations would never be the same again.

With Lynch and Heath a new era was born, a threshold was crossed, a watershed was reached – and there would be no going back.

In the tumult of events since the significance of what they achieved has been overshadowed if not altogether lost.

Memory is fickle. And sentiment short-lived. But were it not for Lynch and Heath the history of Anglo-Irish relations would be very different in the last decade of the twentieth century and a great deal bloodier.

On any objective assessment of the evidence there can be no doubt at all about that.

And so they sat down to dinner.

And in due course Heath praised the work of Jack Lynch who would have, he added, a special place in Irish history.

And he also showed he was conscious of his own place in history when he said he still regarded the Sunningdale Agreement of 1973 as "the greatest achievement between Britain and Ireland in establishing good relations".

Later there would be liqueurs and brandy and a chance for both men to reminisce.

They would talk about Northern Ireland, how intractable a problem it is proving, and about the need for a political solution – a point repeated by Heath at a press conference in Dromoland Castle the next day, where he stayed.

Both knew they were talking against the background of one of the most extraordinary years in modern European history, the year the Stalinist regimes crumbled in Eastern Europe, the year after the Berlin Wall came down, the year of the end of the two Germanies.

For both, the contemplation of all of this must have been the cause of deep sadness, as well as the cause of great hope.

And for Lynch, in particular, the knowledge that they were speaking within weeks of the achievement of German reunification by democratlc and peaceful means must have weighed on him very heavily, evincing mixed feelings.

"Lost chances and new opportunities", he tells himself.

"The achievement of reunification by democratic and peaceful means" – as he pondered those words he must have felt the old Celtic gods were mocking him, the gods of discord and strife, the gods of blood and iron.

Throughout his life as Taoiseach they have dogged his heels, at times threatening to devour him.

But somehow he manages to hold them at bay.

Perhaps other gods have smiled on him, protecting him from the abyss.

As he sips an end-of-dinner liqueur those words haunt him.

"Democratic and peaceful means . . . "

Was it not this that he strove for with might and main, with cunning and courage, on this island throughout his time as Taoiseach and leader of Fianna Fáil?

Even now he must smile ruefully as he contemplates contemporary events in Ireland against the backdrop of the larger drama being enacted still on the European stage.

And it was all brought back to him in late 1990 by two relatively unimportant events – his forgetfulness about the proper clothes for a dinner in Limerick, and the presence at that dinner, of a man who is now an ordinary backbencher in the House of Commons.

Those minor events caused him to look backward to what has been, and forward to what yet might be.

Let us join him on that multi-directional, multi-dimensional journey, for in so doing we may come to a better understanding not only of Jack Lynch and his times, but of ourselves and our times and the Ireland of the 1990s as well.

An Taoiseach Jack Lynch with the British Prime Minister Edward Heath on the steps of No. 10 Downing Street, London.

3. The Early Years

It is a sultry Sunday in late May in 1990, and outside the main entrance to the City Hall in Cork a number of Gardai are on duty. They stand at the gates at the bottom of the front steps, beneath the busts of two of Cork's most famous sons – Terence McSwiney and Tomas MacCurtain, both of whom served as Lord Mayor.

Inside, in the vast auditorium, another famous Corkman is just finishing an oration on the rostrum.

As the applause dies away, he walks unsteadily along the stage and down the wooden steps to resume his place in the front row of seats.

The master of ceremonies thanks him. And then the applause thunders through the auditorium again as he hails Jack Lynch and assures him that to the people of Cork he will always be the "real Taoiseach".

It is by now a familiar if obviously erroneous tag, and one to which Jack Lynch is well used. He knows it is as much an expression of affection as anything else, though he knows too that it harks back to dark and traumatic days for the Fianna Fáil party and the country.

Today he is able to look back with a certain serenity and detachment on that period. Nothing if not a realist, Jack Lynch recognises that past events are beyond the reach of all of us.

He would think it apt to apply the words from the Rubaiyat of Omar Khayyam:

"The Moving Finger writes; and, having writ,
Moves on: nor all your Piety nor Wit
Shall lure it back to cancel half a Line,
Nor all your Tears wash out a Word of it."

Jack Lynch is not a sentimentalist. Although he refuses to see himself as a shaper of history, he knows he was the right man for his time, the leader the country needed at a time when all of the island could have been plunged into another bloody and bitter civil war.

"He kept his head, and so enabled all of us to keep ours," is how his fellow Corkonian, Senator John A. Murphy, Emeritus Professor of Irish History at UCC, describes the essence of Lynch's role in the highly dangerous years of 1969-70.

The pressures on him were great, much greater than anyone outside of Government realised.

He remained steadfast when lesser men might have gone for the more dramatic option of invading the North.

And it didn't end there.

In fact, that was just the beginning.

And it isn't over yet.

Jack Lynch is 74 now, and inclined to make the odd joke about advancing years.

After that speech in the City Hall, for instance – the occasion was "A Call to Arms", a ceremony to pay tribute to retired members of the National Army – he sat in the Lord Mayor's office, a place once graced by McSwiney and MacCurtain, and joked with the then incumbent Councillor Chrissie Aherne, about his health.

In response to Pearse Wyse, a former Lord Mayor and Fianna Fáil colleague (now with the Progressive Democrats), he said: "I'm as well as can be expected at the hospital gates."

On being told by another admirer that he was "looking well", he glanced briefly at the glass of Paddy in his hand, and commented: "There are three stages of manhood – adulthood, middle-age, and you're looking well!"

Later he looked across at a splendid silver model of the *Sirius* (a paddle steamer which made history in 1838 when she completed the first transatlantic crossing from Cork to New York) in a glass-case alongside the Lord Mayor's desk.

"When I was on the board of Irish Distillers, I suggested to the other directors that they might make an appropriate gift to the City Hall, something for the Mayor's room, and we came up with that . . ."

Someone wanted to know if he was still a director.

He shook his head. "I'm nearly off everything now," he replied with a wry smile, eyeing the glass in his hand. "Old age, you know."

It wasn't always so.

The Jack Lynch story begins in a small, narrow laneway, a laneway without a name which intersects Exchange Street at the foot of one of Ireland's best-known landmarks.

Here, in the shadow of St Anne's Church, Shandon, in Cork City – John Mary Lynch was born on 15 August 1917.

The house still stands today, though it is now a ruin. A proposal in 1985 – by a Fine Gael TD (Bernard Allen) strangely enough – that Cork Corporation should purchase and restore it got all-party support, and in August 1986 it was bought for £16,000.

It is a modest two-storey building, abandoned many years ago as a place of habitation, other than for crows and mice from the nearby cemetery.

Down all the years the laneway hasn't changed much. It still has a shabby, grotty appearance.

It serves as a pedestrian walkway which had the reputation in a less permissive age of being a lovers' haunt.

It was never known as anything other than "Bob and Joan's" – the name being derived from two statues on either side of the lane.

Tales of unrequited love circulated about the couple the statues (which still exist) were said to represent.

No doubt, that was fanciful. But even now, in the nineties, a vaguely romantic aura continues to cling to the place.

And some of that must also have surrounded Jack Lynch in his youth, especially when he began to enjoy sporting glory.

During the first of the three General Elections between 1981 and 1982 (when he put in a token appearance on the hustings), Lynch sat with a group of reporters in a pub called "The Chimes", near the famous old pepperpot tower, and recalled his early years.

With a father from Bantry, and a mother from just east of Cork City, he had been reared, as his friend Eamonn Young once said, in "an atmosphere rich with the national traditions of the hills of West Cork and the echoing streets of older Cork". Both left their mark.

"Because my father was a tailor, we could always claim to be reasonably well-dressed, though nothing extravagant. Our clothes were usually hand-me-downs. My mother's training as a seamstress made her fussy about our clothes and appearances. I suppose I learned a certain fastidiousness in that regard from her.

"With six of us in the house and all going on to secondary education, it wasn't easy. A couple of us won secondary school scholarships, so that helped out a lot.

"There was never any sign of wealth in the house, but the quality of life was good.

"We didn't have a very exciting youth. Any half-days we got we went out hurling, usually up to the Fair Field at the top of Fair Hill.

"Then sometimes we'd go to what we called the fourpenny hops – film matinees – in The Palace in MacCurtain Street. That would be on wet half-days."

Today, as in Lynch's time, Shandon is a working-class area of Cork, dominated by the Protestant Church of St Anne. Locally, its tower is still affectionately referred to as the "four-faced liar" – not out of antipathy to Cork's Protestant population it is explained – but because its four clocks often disagreed.

His father, Daniel Lynch, was a tailor who came to Cork from Bantry.

Christened John Mary, Lynch was born the fifth son (one of them died before Jack was born) of Dan and Nora Lynch. There were also two girls, both younger than Jack.

Dan Lynch came from a farming family at Baurgorm, south of Bantry, and when he married Nora O'Donoghue, from near Glounthane, just east of Cork City in 1908, he was working as a tailor.

His bride was a seamstress, and she continued as such after their marriage, helping to augment her husband's earnings.

"That was a much needed supplement to my father's earnings," recalls Jack. "In those days he wasn't always able to get a full week's work. Even though he was regularly employed, his employers didn't have sufficient work. He was often on short time.

Lynch describes his father as a tall dignified-looking man, quiet and modest in all his doings.

"He liked a drink occasionally, and was interested in sports.

"My memory of him is as a strict but fair father. I was regarded as the wild boy of the family and, therefore, came into conflict with him more often than did my brothers, but we had a good father/son relationship.

"He took particular interest in my sporting career, and was often quietly critical of my performances, but always in a helpful way.

"I remember once, after a match I had played for Glen Rovers, him commenting: 'You were rather lackadaisical today', which was quite true on the occasion and, coming from him, a stern rebuke."

Jack was the fifth son, his brothers being Theo, who became a schoolteacher and a key figure in St Nicholas GAA Club (the sister club to Glen Rovers); Charlie, who joined the priesthood and became parish priest of Ballinlough (in Cork City), and Finbar, who worked as a civil servant, but retired from it to take up a civilian job in Cobh.

Theo, who died in October 1985, was also a capable hurler, and was my teacher in Blackpool NS for a couple of years.

His nickname among the boys was "Baggy", and we all knew who his brother was.

He talked only occasionally and sparingly about his brother, then and later, but there was no mistaking the quiet pride he felt in Jack's achievements on and off the playing field. In an interview with Dick Cross for the *Sunday Independent* in March 1978, he spoke of Jack.

"As a boy, he always showed courage, daring and toughness in character. But his temperament was always very even. He was never arrogant or aggressive for its own sake, but was willing to give as he got.

"Jack had a number of natural advantages in life. Study came easy to him, and he had exceptional physical stamina to match it.

"I remember when he was a civil servant and was studying Law at the University. He would come in for his tea and study from seven to midnight, and then get up early in the morning to study again before going to work. At the same time, he was playing hurling and football. I don't know how he did it," Theo admitted.

Father Charlie, who died in February 1986, celebrated the Requiem Mass for Jack's great friend and sporting colleague, Christy Ring in April 1979 at Ballinlough Church in Cork City where he was parish priest.

His two sisters, Rena, the eldest, and Eva, are still living in Cork.

The former married Gerard Dunne, principal of the Cork School of Commerce (their son is Cathal Dunne, well-known composer and singer of popular music).

Eva married Dr John Harvey, who died 20 years ago.

Although in later years Jack was known as the quiet-spoken, pipesmoking man from Cork, as a boy he was the "wilder" of the family. His eldest brother Theo once recalled that "he was always getting up to some devilment and, because he was the youngest of the four boys, always getting away with murder at home."

Eamonn Young makes a somewhat similar assessment: "The boy who grew to young manhood may have been at times quiet, like his late father. But Jack, with his brothers and friends camping in

Crosshaven, swimming in the Baths and in the rivers, or training over bushes to win the hurdles in the school sports, was a gay, bright young lad, full of fun and mischief, enough to cause his poor father to wonder if his youngest boy would 'go to the dogs' and end up in the gutter."

There was little real fear of that happening.

If the young Jack was clever, the young Jack was also blessed with more than a fair share of common sense.

"He was a lively fellow," remembers Young. "Among his friends at parties, in a bunch where singing and music were an important part of light-hearted relaxation, Jack's baritone voice in 'Rose of San Antoine' or 'Bould Thady Quill' was a favourite."

The family home was situated almost in the middle of a graveyard behind St Anne's which was a favourite playing area for local youngsters.

The laneway runs through a cemetery behind the famous church, and even today it is with some amusement and much truth, that Lynch claims to have been "born in a graveyard".

It was a small rented house, and a family named Drennan had it after the Lynch family left. That was in 1934 when his mother died.

While they were there, the address was always simply "St Anne's, Shandon".

But remind him that, according to his brothers, he was the bane of the old sexton's life and he will smile ruefully.

The sight of the old man chasing the youthful, loose-limbed Lynch among the headstones was not uncommon.

The old Cork Butter Market, which was close to the Lynch home, made a passable ball-alley, and the street featured many a tussle among the young hurlers who used the Market's doorposts as a goal.

Apart from playing hurling in the streets, young Jack also swam during the summers at Crosshaven, and "Hell Hole" near Inniscarra, and raced on his bicycle against the old Muskerry tram.

He was a fine swimmer as well as a 120 yards hurdler. And today he claims he "would be dead from old injuries" were it not for his thrice-weekly swims at the Fitzwilton Club in Dublin, where he has lived since 1952 at 21 Garville Avenue, Rathgar.

From this background, not at all unusual for the northside of Cork, came the man who was destined to carve an unrivalled niche for himself in the annals of the Gaelic Athletic Association.

The long thin legs of John Mary Lynch first took him to the nearby convent of Peacock Lane. It's on record that he went home on his first day, at the luncheon break, thinking that was that for the day!

He was with the nuns at St Vincent's for two years, before moving to the North Monastery CBS, where he spent eleven years and came under the influence of such noted men as Brother Malone, Brother Lawlor, Brother Moynihan – who later became Brother Provincial of the Southern Province of the Christian Brothers and who was affectionately known as "Tango", Brother McConville, who was in charge of the Technical School there, laymen John and Dan Moore and Pat Callahan.

"We were comfortable enough for the time," according to Fr Charlie, the third of the boys to be born. He served as a curate and parish priest in the city until his death in 1986.

"There was always enough on the table, and we were well-dressed with our father a tailor."

Sport was the family's constant talking-point. "Politics", confirmed Fr Lynch, "were hardly ever discussed."

Confirming this years later, Jack Lynch told the *Irish Times* in January 1959: "I haven't any idea what my father's politics were".

Lynch's mother died when he was still a teenager (her death occurred in the autumn of 1934), and his aunt – who had six children of her own – took the family into her care.

Of his years in the North Monastery CBS he says today that he learnt "how to speak Irish, a working knowledge of Latin, and how to get by in English".

The North Mon. was famous for another reason – it was a hurling nursery, and it was here that Lynch began to hone his talents with the camán.

The first real sadness to mark his life was the death of his mother on the very day she was expected home from hospital. He was 17 at the time, and her passing deeply affected him for years afterwards.

"My mother was a quiet person and, naturally, I was close to her when growing up. I was absolutely shattered when she died unexpectedly, when I was in my early teens. She had gone into hospital because of what we believed to be a minor ailment, and we were expecting her home the day that she died. She had been fairly healthy up until then, and had been in hospital for only a week or two.

It also forced the breaking up of the family home. They went to live with his aunt, Mrs Statia O'Reilly, his mother's sister, initially at 5 Vernon View on the South Douglas Road, on the other side of the River Lee.

But this was too far from the schools they were attending, so they moved back to the northside, to 22 Redemption Road.

"There were more than a dozen of us living in that house, but it was, nevertheless, a very happy home," he recalled years later.

His best friend as a schoolboy was the late Michael Twomey, whose family had a grocery business in Shandon Street.

Other contemporaries were Tadgh Carey (later to become President of UCC); Leo Skentelberry, who became Ambassador to Argentina and Australia, and Tadgh Carroll, later Secretary of the Department of Labour.

Jack Lynch left school in 1936. His Leaving Certificate marks were not high enough to earn a scholarship. But he also sat several other exams, including teacher training, clerical officers, the Agricultural Credit Corporation, and the ESB.

He got all of those, and so had a choice of career.

It came down, at that stage, to either a career as a schoolteacher or a civil servant. He chose the latter.

His first job was a temporary one with the Dublin District Milk Board of which a man named Seán Ó Braonáin had charge. This was significant because Ó Braonáin was a top official with the Civil Service Hurling Club, and he persuaded Lynch to play for them.

When the Civil Service examination results came out that year (1936), he opted for the Service and joined the Cork Circuit Court Staff in December. He regularly filled the post of acting registrar and developed a keen interest in the law and legal procedures.

This led him to study for the Bar at UCC for two years before transferring to Dublin, a transfer that was made easy by his sporting connections. There he was attached to the District Court Clerks' Branch, and this facilitated his attendance at lectures at the King's Inns.

His next move was to the Department of Justice proper where he became private secretary to the Secretary, while still keeping up his law studies.

Faced with the choice of continuing in the Civil Service or practising law, the story is that he tossed a coin and law won.

He probably would have gone anyway. "To be quite honest with you, the Civil Service as a career got me down." Strangely enough, later on that story of the coin tossing was to be applied, erroneously, to the circumstances in which he first entered politics.

That was the following year (1946) when Fianna Fáil sounded him out about a forthcoming by-election.

His time in politics had not yet come. In his pleasant way, he took the sting out of his refusal by saying: "Maybe next time. Next time was nearer than he thought, and the 1948 election which put Fianna Fáil out of office after 16 years put Jack Lynch into Leinster House where he was to remain for 34 years. My own father, Denis "The Sheriff" O'Mahony (who stood as a candidate for the Labour Party in the local government elections of the 1940s) recalls meeting Lynch on the day of the count in Mannix's Bar behind the Church of the Annunciation in Blackpool.

"We all knew he was going to be elected by a comfortable margin, but he kept looking for reassurance. Party workers from all sides were in the pub, and he kept going around asking were they sure he was in. I was the first to tell him he had made it, but I had no idea then what lay ahead."

Thereafter, the name of Lynch would be synonymous with Blackpool, in both sporting and political contexts.

Blackpool is a suburb of Cork City, colourful, vibrant and deeply tribal.

Situated north of the Lee, it is flanked by hills, and nurtures within its environs, a distinctive breed of Corkonians who lay claim – like their Roman counterparts in Trastevere – to being the true representatives of the city.

The place is famous for its deep pride, its passion for hurling, and its love of bowl-playing, pigeon-racing, draghunting, and pub-singing.

Its women, who are second to none, have been immortalised in several local ballads. Even in the changed circumstances of the 1990s, they play a significant role in maintaining the robust community spirit which, in good times and in bad, is one of the area's dominant characteristics.

With its Shandon chimes, its network of narrow streets and lanes, it remains even today a tightly-knit, closely interwoven community.

Here you will find rich gossip, creamy pints, dishes of tripe and drisheen, stories of great sporting feats, tremendously strong loyalties and an enduring pride.

Lynch was a product of what the late John Healy once called a "village culture". And the "village" of Blackpool simply regarded itself not only as special, but as the best.

Didn't it, after all – according to the locals – produce the best hurlers and bowlplayers? Weren't its women, whether up against the Sunbeam wall (as a well-known Cork song has it), or in its cosy lanes, a class apart?

"Sweet Blackpool" has always been a place apart, a place noted for an extensive folklore, based, for the most part, on the achievements of local exponents in all spheres of sport.

Something of the flavour of the place is well captured in this verse of a song composed by Val Dorgan (a good Glenman):

"Oh, old Blackpool I dread ye,
You'll never set me free.
At any time in any place
You'll claim my loyalty.
And right or wrong, you're right by me,
Great women and great men.
They are the heart of sweet Blackpool.
And the Spirit of the Glen."

Little wonder that in a sub-culture such as this that Lynch became a totem-figure. To be one of these totem-figures is to have a special place in the communal consciousness. And this is one very potent reason why a man like Lynch had such extraordinary appeal in Blackpool in his heyday.

In the words of Tim Pat Coogan: "Lynch is an Irish folk-hero".

And nowhere was his status higher, nowhere was there more intense pride in him, than in Blackpool.

It is only in this milieu of passionate loyalties and a burning pride in the local boy who had made good which can explain the sobriquet "the real Taoiseach" – a title which continues to be used today.

And it is only in this cultural context, with its heightened sense of being a place apart, that an extraordinary *Cork Examiner* frontpage article in 1977, could describe Lynch, in hyperbolic prose, as "King of Ireland"!

To understand Cork, to feel its heartbeat, one must experience Blackpool. It is, and remains, a place like no other.

Lynch himself would almost go so far as to say it is a state of mind. And, as if highlighting the unimportance of boundary, he once told me that he always felt he was in Blackpool when he crossed the Lee at the North Gate Bridge.

This is Jack Lynch's own place, and over the years, even when he occupied high office, he was nowhere more relaxed, happier or at his ease.

In 1966 when, on becoming Taoiseach, he made a triumphant return to Cork, the first place he headed for was the Glen Rovers Hurling Club in Blackpool.

A reporter, sent by one of the Dublin papers to cover the homecoming, could not understand why the new Taoiseach would settle for such a place, thinking a civic reception in the City Hall more appropriate.

"Why did you come here, Mr Lynch?" he asked, totally ignorant of the new Prime Minister's intimate relationship with Blackpool.

A slightly uncomprehending Taoiseach was taken aback for a moment.

Then he recovered, and replied: "Sure in the name of God where else would I go to?"

It was left to a local party worker to explain to the Dublin journalist just exactly what Blackpool meant to Jack Lynch.

Much more recently he illustrated this in his own inimitable way by relating how in 1953 he approached the manager of what used to be the Munster and Leinster Bank to organise a loan of £10,000 to build a new clubhouse for Glen Rovers.

"He asked me what arrangements I proposed to make by way of collateral. I replied: 'The people of Blackpool are my collateral.'"

To appreciate the regard in which he is held, and the nature of the affection felt for him there, one should really be present for one of his (nowadays all-too-rare) visits to Blackpool.

"Sure, he's one of our own," they'll tell you down there when you ask about him or his enormous appeal and popularity.

And here among his own, "Jack" – only journalists like myself ever called him "Mr Lynch" or "Taoiseach" in Blackpool – puts aside the guarded and guarding watchfulness which in the past often conveyed the impression of gaucherie and uncertainty in public.

And only this most 'Corkonian' of Cork places could have inspired the extraordinary *Cork Examiner* frontpiece in June 1977 (to which I referred earlier).

Penned by Tim Cramer, a good Blackpool man, it carried the heading "It's a Toast to 'The King'".

And because it expresses so well the regard in which Jack was held, I will quote some of it: "IN THE PUBS of Blackpool last night, they were prepared to crown Jack Lynch as King of Ireland. And with more than double the quota to his credit, so well they might.

"They would tell you triumphantly, between sips: 'Now they know who the REAL Taoiseach is'. Few would blame them. They were savouring their moment of triumph, and they had every right to do so.

"For by any political standards, this was an extraordinary performance, even allowing for the charisma of the man. Let there be no mistake about it; the Fianna Fáil victory, the amazing political turnabout, was entirely due to one man. This was a personal triumph for Mr Lynch, and it is being widely and rightly recognised as being so ....

"Not even Mr Lynch could have anticipated such an extraordinary swing to him and to his party.

"But, somehow, against all the odds – and the political pundits will agree that the odds were stacked against the former Opposition – this former Cork hurler, this former Taoiseach, this man of many battles, this son of Cork, this man of charm and distinction, has managed to prove once again the validity of the old saying about the old dog for the hard road.

"So last night in Blackpool they were gathering the makings of the bonfires, and they were out hunting for tar barrels. For nothing is more certain than the fact that when Jack Lynch comes home to his native city, he will receive a welcome that Parnell himself, the 'uncrowned King of Ireland' would have envied.

"The difference, they will tell you in Blackpool, is that Jack is already crowned!"

Long before that stunning electoral success put Jack Lynch into the political sections of the history books, he had made his indelible mark in other spheres.

In 1946 Lynch made sporting history. That year Cork beat Kilkenny in the All-Ireland Senior Hurling Final by 7-5 to 3-8.

And with that victory Lynch attained the singular distinction of playing in six All-Ireland Finals in a row, and being on the winning side in all six.

But something else happened in 1946 – something which was to change his life and ensure that in another arena he would also make history.

That "something" was the political "bug" which bit him that year. And that arena was politics.

The road that would eventually lead to the unprecedented success of 1977 was already beckoning.

The journey had begun.

4. Sporting Glory

On the evening of 20 November 1990 Jack Lynch could be found doing two of things he loves most – sipping a glass of Paddy whiskey and talking about hurling.

The location was the hospitality room of the Beamish & Crawford Brewery on the South Main Street in Cork City. And the occasion was the launching of a book by journalist Raymond Smith entitled *The Greatest Hurlers of Our Time.*

And not the only surprise of the night was the fact that, although Lynch had agreed to formally launch the book in response to an invitation from Smith, he himself was not included in Smith's list of the 21 "greatest" hurlers.

The irony was not lost on Jack himself, nor on most of the other famous hurlers who had gathered for the occasion.

I happened to be present that night, and I asked him how he felt about his omission from the list.

He smiled coyly. "These things are always subjective, aren't they? But there are some there who would not meet my definition of hurling greatness."

Others present echoed similar sentiments. By any standards, the omission of Lynch was astonishing. And in retrospect, one would have to say that it took some chutzpah ("neck" they would say in Cork) for Smith to invite Lynch having, in effect, snubbed him.

It also tells you something about Lynch that he accepted readily in the circumstances.

But then generosity towards opponents has always been one of his characteristics – both in hurling and in politics.

Let us turn the clock back over half a century.

The setting is Croke Park. The year is 1939. And in Europe, Hitler's armies are on the march.

Jack Lynch was wet, haggard and depressed. Cork had just lost what would forever after be remembered as the "thunder-and lightning" All-Ireland hurling final.

It was 3 September, and the war drums which had been silent since 1918 were beginning to beat again across the European mainland.

In the crowded Cork dressing-room no one was thinking about that.

"Don't worry," said one of the team selectors to the disconsolate Lynch. "There will be another day."

Lynch, uncertain, looked up. "I wonder will there . . . ?"

He need not have worried.

Although it did not seem so then, a glorious chapter in the annals of the GAA lay ahead.

It all started in 1935.

In his fifth year in secondary school, he was chosen for the Cork senior team in a League match against Limerick. He was pitted against no less an opponent than great John Mackey. "Everything must have gone all right for me," he recalled, "for I stayed on the Cork team until 1950".

The following year, while still at school, he was on the championship side.

He recalls: "I think it was recognised fairly early on that I had ability as a hurler and, frankly, I took advantage of this for missing an occasional class, as I used to have allowances made for me by teachers who were convinced I was otherwise preoccupied, which may not always have been the case.

"My older brothers, Theo, Charlie and Finbar, had joined Glen Rovers at an early age and I did likewise. There I came in contact with one of the great father-figures of the Glen, Paddy O'Connell, who took a special interest in my progress, suggesting to me that I had some potential."

Paddy O'Connell held up Mickey Cross, the Limerick half-back, as the player to emulate.

Jack Lynch learned well. He was one of the few Glen Rovers players to collect eight successive Cork county medals, starting in 1934.

During the famous four-in-a-row All-Ireland Hurling Finals of 1941, 1942, 1943 and 1944, he made another bit of GAA history (in 1944) when he played three games in the one day.

He turned out with the Civil Service in the Dublin hurling league in the morning and, in the afternoon, figured with Munster's hurlers and footballers in the Railway Cup championships.

Incidentally, he was on the winning side in all three. "I came on to the Cork senior hurling side during one of the county's leanest eras in the sport. Cork had won the 1931 All-Ireland title, but Limerick dominated hurling in Munster for most of the rest of the decade.

"I played with the Cork minors in the early thirties, but unfortunately Cork were also then eclipsed in the minor sphere by Tipperary. My first game with the senior team was in the 1935-36 season in the National League campaign against that famous Limerick side of that era."

Towards the end of the thirties, players like Willie Campbell, Alan Lotty, Jim Young, Sonny Buckley and Paddy Donovan came into the side.

Cork won the Munster Championship in 1939, but were beaten by Kilkenny by a single point, scored in the last minute of the Final in Croke Park. That game was played in atrocious weather conditions. The other disaster was the outbreak of World War II on the same day, 3 September.

Although beaten by Limerick the following year in the Munster Final, Lynch felt Cork had an All-Ireland winning combination, especially with the advent of another Buckley (Din Joe) and Christy Ring.

"Ring was one of the most accomplished hurlers of all time, and I would omit the qualification were I not to know I would be accused of bias.

"He had supreme confidence in his own ability, refusing to be taken off a marker who may have been getting the better of him, feeling that he would turn the tables sooner or later. And so, too, he often did with a remarkable burst of sheer excellence that would turn the course of a game.

"He was by no means a mere hurling robot. He had a fine intelligence and marvellous perception. His contribution to Cork hurling and especially to the club, Glen Rovers, over 35 years as player and selector, was outstanding.

"That defeat by Limerick in the 1945 Munster Final was the only defeat suffered for two seasons by the team and, therefore, when we came to face Dublin in the All-Ireland Final of 1941 we were firm favourites.

"The team was a fine balance of young and experienced players. I played practically all my games for Cork at midfield, although I started at left half-back and played a few times at right half-forward.

"Towards the end of my career, when I was slowing down, I was moved to full-forward. I was at mid-field for all the All-Ireland Finals (three against Dublin, one against Antrim), including our first victorious one in 1941."

Cork played only one championship match before reaching the Final that year. That was again against Limerick and this time Cork won easily by 8-10 to 3-2.

Because of an outbreak of foot and mouth disease, the Munster Final was postponed, and Cork were nominated to represent the province in the All Ireland.

In a strange quirk, Tipperary beat Cork in the Munster Final after Cork had won the 1941 title.

"I was playing well in that 1941 Final before first, being injured and then, being forced to leave the field. However, Cork won by a huge margin – 5-11 to 0-6 – and Cork was set on a remarkable course which was to yield four All-Ireland titles to the hurling side in five years.

"Dublin were our opponents in the 1942 Final again. We had beaten Limerick by 2-14 to 3-4 in the Munster Final, and this time we beat Dublin by the less convincing margin of 2-14 to 3-4."

In those days there were enormous transport difficulties because of the war. As in the previous year, in 1942 several cycling parties set out from Cork on the Saturday before the Final, stayed in Portlaoise that night, and cycled on to Dublin the following day.

Cork met Antrim in the 1943 Final and of the 48,000 people in Croke Park that day at least 30,000 were hoping for an Antrim victory because of the fillip that would give the game in the North.

It was a disappointing final, largely because Antrim were suffering from stage fright and Cork ran out easy winners by 5-16 to 0-4.

In 1944 Cork were going for their fourth title in a row which would have established a unique record. They beat Tipperary 1-9 to 1-3; Limerick by 4-6 to 3-6 and Galway 1-10 to 3-3 in what were all very tough games on the way to the Final. Nine of that Cork side had, by now, won three All-Ireland medals, including Lynch, and they were a very experienced side. The Final was perhaps the easiest match of the championship that year with Cork winning over Dublin by 3-13 to 1-2.

"We failed to get out of Munster in 1945, being beaten by Tipperary who went on to beat Kilkenny in the Final. However, I was fortunate in having another string to my bow that year in being on the Cork football side.

"I had played football with the North Mon. in college competitions, and later with St Nicholas, a sister club to Glen Rovers. Football, however, was a very secondary interest for me as indeed it was to Cork city in general at the time. There didn't seem to be much prospect for Cork football in Munster then because of the pre-eminence of Kerry.

"However, the breakthrough came in 1943 when we beat Kerry on a wet day in the Cork Athletic Grounds in the Munster Final. We were beaten in the semi-final that year by Cavan."

The Glen star transferred to Dublin shortly after this to continue his bar studies at the Kings Inns and he played football with Civil Service when they won their first Dublin senior title.

"Through playing football with the Civil Service, I began, really for the first time, to take football seriously and play in the company of players to whom football was their only sporting interest. I think this helped me greatly in the game and, because of this, I got onto the Cork side which beat Cavan in the 1945 All-Ireland Final.

"Cork owed their victory then to the fact that the team was backboned by the county champions, Clonakilty, and had in it great footballers like Eamonn Young, Jimmy Cronin, the late Weeshie Murphy, Caleb Crone, Mick Tubridy and Derry Beckett."

Back came the hurlers in 1946 and won yet another All-Ireland, beating Kilkenny in the final by 7-5 to 3-8, enabling Lynch to attain the distinction of playing in six All-Ireland Finals in a row and being on the winning side in all six.

"Indeed, I blame myself for failing to make that record seven for we reached the hurling final again in 1947, this time to lose to Kilkenny by a single point. I had the opportunity of equalising the game twice in the closing minutes, but hit wide on both occasions."

For Lynch it was to be the end of a glorious era.

"My last competitive hurling game was the Munster Final in Killarney in 1950 when Cork were beaten by Tipperary. My last football game was for St Nicks against the Army in the Cork County Championship of 1951. I was then a Parliamentary Secretary.

"I did play one other game with Cork however. I attended an inter-parliamentary conference in Ottawa in 1952 and came home via New

York. There I was persuaded by a former Glen Rovers man, Paddy Barry, to turn out for the New York Cork team. I was very unfit and overweight and was stiff and sore for weeks afterwards."

Therein lies a tale, told to me by Barry himself not so long ago in the splendid surrounds of the new Glen clubhouse, sitting under a large framed photograph of Lynch with the famous Glen team of 1934. That game was at Gaelic Park, and Barry, affectionately known as "Chancer", had difficulty persuading Lynch to play.

"The Cork team in New York were playing a tough Galway side the next day, and I told Jack we needed him.

"In the end he agreed to play, but only on the understanding that it would be just for the first ten minutes.

"Jack started well and settled in quickly, and he played so effectively that we kept him on for the entire hour, and in the end he won the game for us."

In the course of the tough exchanges Lynch also took a hard knock.

"Afterwards, he said he was feeling a bit sore, but we all put it down to the fact that he hadn't been training for a bit and was out of condition."

The truth emerged the following day when the future Taoiseach set sail for Cobh on board a Cunard liner.

"He was still feeling the effects of the game in Gaelic Park, and was having a very painful journey home by boat. It was only when he was finally persuaded to consult the ship's doctor that he found out what was wrong," recalled Paddy.

After a brief examination, the doctor delivered his verdict: "You have three cracked ribs!"

"I was in bed for most of the trip by liner back to Cobh," says Lynch. "What a way to finish a career!"

Paddy said it was typical of Jack Lynch that the GAA Board in New York never heard another word about it.

"I only found out myself a good deal later," he admitted.

That was the end for Lynch: the curtain had finally come down on a marvellous playing career, a career in which he established a record that will never be surpassed.

"Like most other players, I have marvellous memories of my playing days, of team mates and opponents and of incidents on and off the field."

One playing field in particular holds very special memories for him: Semple Stadium in Thurles.

Indeed, for most GAA fans Thurles and hurling are synonymous and particularly so Thurles and Munster Final day. At the centenary All-Ireland Hurling Final of 1984, he recalled his great days there, though like others he was apprehensive about the decision by Congress to stage the 1984 event in Thurles.

"I was worried mainly about accommodation difficulties at the stadium, but I think whatever doubts I had were emphatically dispelled at that year's Munster Final when close to 50,000 spectators were accommodated adequately and stewarded efficiently.

"Cork were favourites that day, but in the end were lucky to get away with the title, and almost literally 'stole' victory from Tipperary.

"My earliest memory of Thurles was a game in the early thirties when Cork played against Limerick. I saved, scraped and cajoled the five shillings necessary to finance me for the day – a half-crown for the train excursion fare from Cork, 1/6 for a meal before the game and a shilling to get into the match.

"My two companions were Jimmy O'Donoghue, a first cousin, and Mick Healy. All three of us, from Shandon, succeeded in working within our budget. I don't think we had any spending money left for ice-cream or apples, but it was an expedition successfully accomplished.

"My next visit to Thurles was a few years later when I was just out of my teens in 1936. I was playing for the Cork seniors. Clare beat us by about seven goals. If I may mix the metaphor, this was the nadir of Cork's period in the doldrums in the thirties.

"We came back in 1939, most of the team having matured and learned many lessons out of a succession of defeats, and that season we beat a great Limerick team which had reached its zenith three years before (when winning the All-Ireland crown under the captaincy of Mick Mackey), and was still a powerful force in hurling."

Apart from Mackey, that team also had Paddy Scanlon, Timmy Ryan, Jackie Power, McMahon and, of course, Mick's brother, John Mackey. Although he was missing from that 1939 game, Limerick in those years also had Paddy Clohessy at centre-back.

"What a team to play and beat," recalled Lynch, "especially when Mick Mackey was then the player who had captured the imagination of the hurling public. On his right in a powerful attack was his brother John, for whom I had always a great admiration as a player. No wonder we were cock-a-hoop for the 1939 Final in which we were unexpectedly (for us anyway) beaten by Kilkenny in what is now called the 'Thunder-and-Lightning' Final.

"Much the same Cork team as that which took Munster honours in 1939 was back in Thurles – give or take a few changes – over the next few seasons, back with a fair degree of success.

"The very next year, however, Limerick, with new young stars like Jim McCarthy, Dick Stokes and Tony Herbert, edged us out of it by two points and went on to win the 1940 All-Ireland title."

Although this period saw Cork win their four-in-a-row All-Irelands, they were beaten twice by Tipperary – in 1941 and in 1945 when Tipperary put an end to Cork's bid for five-in-a-row.

"I'll never forget that 1941 match in Limerick as the late Bill O'Donnell ran rings around me."

For Lynch, no pitch in Ireland compares with Thurles as a hurling venue. "Its maximum dimensions, beautiful Golden Vale sod, and perfectly-trimmed grass were always a joy to play on. That is, once you got over the colly-wobbles or, as someone put it, the 'confessional pain' stage. But it was impossible for a player not to feel like that before a Munster Hurling Final in Thurles."

There was the build-up at home to begin with, where training in "the Park", the old Cork Athletic Grounds (now Pairc Uí Chaoimh) would be attended by hundreds of supporters.

And in the days immediately preceding the match itself, everyone a player met in the street, in the workshop or on the farm asked: "How will you do on Sunday?"

Today, with a rueful smile, Lynch admits that he never learned how to answer that question properly.

This was all part of the build-up to the electric atmosphere one experienced on entering the Square in Thurles on the day of the Final.

"The visiting teams had to get there early, in time to relax and have a cup of tea before the game. But you couldn't relax in the hotel. You found yourself moving out into the Square and the crowds.

"And of course the tension wasn't eased by the huge crowds and more questions as to 'how will you do?' or enquiries about some player's injury."

There is one story Lynch likes to tell about a famed Cork forward in the twenties and early thirties who, having endeavoured to "relax" by walking around the Square, was advised by a team selector, Fr Eddie Fitzgerald, to come and have the customary cup of tea before the team changed in the hotel for the match. The answer he got was: "Is it tay, Father, and we playing Tipperary?"

In those days, and for three or four decades afterwards, "plain teas" and "meat teas" were the order of the day at Munster Finals in Thurles.

"It wasn't all tea or cold meat, however. Many a Thurles pub that did not regularly stock Beamish or Murphys stout made sure that they had adequate supplies of each brew for the discriminatory Cork palates.

"It was all good fun and entertainment, no rowdyism or vandalism. Everybody who went to Thurles went primarily to see good hurling and enjoy themselves afterwards".

It wasn't just Thurles, of course. It was Limerick, Killarney, Cork and Croke Park too.

Peadar O'Brien, *Irish Press* GAA Correspondent, is very proud of the fact that Jack Lynch and he have something in common. "His first appearance for Cork in an All-Ireland Senior Hurling Final was also my first time at a game of such major importance."

Their paths were to cross on many occasions at other big match events.

"Unlike many others, he always had time to offer his opinions on a game – even if Cork lost. Even in his native city I cannot remember him being referred to as Mr Taoiseach. It was always 'Jack'!"

The broadcaster Michael O'Hehir says that Lynch's style of play, his sporting attitude, and his spirit which he instilled into colleagues were as much the success story of Jack as those All-Ireland medal and national League awards that he has treasured".

O'Hehir, an indispensable feature of the GAA scene for decades, remembered in December 1983 (when Lynch was elected to the Texaco Hall of Fame) another side of the great Corkman:

"He was always gracious and considerate, and had time for everyone."

Val Dorgan, who played with Glen Rovers in the fifties, and who covered GAA games for years for the *Cork Examiner,* knew Lynch well.

"An Adonis-like figure, he had a graceful style, total dedication, and an innate sense of fair play. But nobody took liberties with Lynch.

"He will always be a legend in GAA folklore, and is particularly venerated by the fanatical supporters of Glen Rovers."

The year Lynch became a TD – 1948 – he found that there was no escape from politics, not even on the playing field. Jim O'Neill, who played with another Cork club, Sarsfield, was on the Cork selection for a game against Tipperary in the Cork Athletic Grounds. O'Neill was just married, and was anxious to get a house in the Millfield area of Blackpool.

He told me the story over a pint. "Josie Hartnett was late getting to the grounds, and one of the selectors said: 'Put O'Neill on, he's the best we have'.

"I was picked at right half-forward, and I spoke to Jack before the game about the house. 'I'll make a note of the details after the game,' Lynch said.

"I saw Josie Hartnett coming in just as the game started, so I thought I'd be taken off after ten minutes. In the meantime, I got two of the best points I ever scored, and I stayed on. Afterwards Lynch took the details. A week later I got a call from him. 'Go down to so-and-so and collect the key . .'

"When I met him the next time I thanked him, and he said: 'It's good to do something that turned out right.' From that day on until he retired he got my vote.

"As a player, he had everything – skill, speed, size and strength. And if you wanted to play it dirty, he'd handle that too."

A man who played alongside Lynch in the 1945 All-Ireland Football Final against Cavan – Eamonn Young – remembers him as a fast, strong and clever footballer.

When it came to hurling, Young says Lynch was essentially a stylish player. His brother, Jim, who partnered Lynch in the famous four-in-a-row, agrees.

"He could play well, facing the ball or doubling on it. Very dependable both on the ground and in the air, he was steady with both hands and this, added to strength, speed and imperturbability made him a champion performer," says Eamonn.

"Reflexes faster than normal, a mature shrewdness and an ability to keep cool, allowed him not only to see what way the tide was flowing, but to take advantage of that flow by adjusting his own play or suggesting changes.

"Never one for spirited exhortations, he led more by example than word. But anything he had to say was said in that quiet determined level-toned voice which became so familiar to the entire nation later on."

In the January 1967 issue of *Gaelic Sport* there is a famous photograph of Lynch cutting through the Tipperary defence to score a great goal. Eamonn Young has a vivid memory of that score:

"There was a momentous duel with Tipperary in 1949 when Cork drew the first game in the Munster Championship, and went on to lose the replay.

"It was towards the end of the drawn game that a big forward with powerful hips and shoulders brought the sliothar thirty yards and slapped it to the net for the vital goal. Jack Lynch wasn't done yet!"

Former GAA President, Con Murphy, who played on the famous Cork teams of the forties with Lynch, agrees about Jack's ability to lead by example.

"Lynch always displayed leadership qualities as a player. He was, in fact, the last of the real captains in the sense that he took responsibility for what went on out there on the field. He took decisions and made the necessary changes as the game went on. And there was never any doubt about his toughness."

Eamonn Young reckons Lynch's involvement in sport played a significant part in shaping his character – character that would be tested in tempestuous circumstances both on and off the field.

Sitting in a cosy pub in Cork with his brother, Jim, in the summer of 1991, Young summed it up: "Team games train one's character on very desirable lines. Jack Lynch gave a lot to games; they did a lot in moulding him".

Paddy "Chancer" Barry, who worked with TWA in New York for over 20 years, has fond memories of visits to the Big Apple of the two most famous men associated with his old team, Glen Rovers – Christy Ring and Jack Lynch.

"It is generally agreed that Ring was the greatest hurler ever, and he was indeed a genius. But Lynch was also a great player and had leadership qualities, on and off the field, which in my view set him apart."

Paddy played with both men during his ten years with the Glen from 1932 to 1942. And he was also associated through marriage with a pub – Molly Howe's in Blackpool – which was a Glen "institution" until it closed in the late sixties to make way for new developments in the area.

Jack Lynch was a regular caller there, even after his playing days were over. It was situated just around the corner from the original Glen clubhouse on Bird's Quay. And since this was literally a house, Molly Howe's was always the place the Cup was brought to after the team's many successes in the County championships.

Lynch often went for a few drinks there with Barry and others.

"I admired Ring as a player," Barry told me, "as we all did, but I always had, and still have a special regard for Jack Lynch. Over the years, even when he became Taoiseach, he never changed. He was still the same Jack that I always knew."

And on the playing field Paddy says that the late Mick Mackey told him one day that as far as Limerick were concerned, it was Lynch rather than Ring that they always worried about.

"Like most other players," says the man still known as the 'real Taoiseach' in Cork, "I have marvellous memories of my playing days, of team mates and opponents, of incidents on and off the field.

"Inevitably, I made friendships all over the country and this, I suppose, helped me in the political sphere afterwards.

"I think I learned from hurling and football a discipline and a self-control; how to be part of a team and how to cope with both victory and defeat.

"All players acquire these qualities in time, if they are to survive. And they are qualities that apply well to life outside sport."

Especially, as we shall see in Lynch's case, to politics.

Hurling Action in the Munster Hurling Final against Tipperary

5. Lynch, Ring and Mackey

On a bleak March day in 1979 two old foes stood beside an open grave in a small country churchyard in East Cork.

In the little village of Cloyne the two were part of a huge crowd which had gathered to pay their last respects to the man widely regarded as the greatest hurler of all time – Christy Ring.

The two men – Jack Lynch and Mick Mackey – stood bareheaded in St Colman's Cemetery as the final prayers for the dead were recited by Most Rev. John Ahern, the Bishop of Cloyne.

The vast crowd – commentators said it was between 50,000 and 60,000, making it the biggest funeral in Cork since that of Tomas MacCurtain in 1920 – stood hushed and numbed.

Many great hurlers were there that day, old foes and old team-mates of the man known throughout the length and breadth of Ireland simply as "Ringey".

I was wedged just inside the gate of the cemetery, standing with other reporters next to Tony Reddan and Tommy Doyle, members of the great Tipperary teams of 1949-54.

Mackey was close by, his massive frame unmistakable, as Lynch, on the other side of the grave, stepped forward and began his eulogy.

Speaking, as Val Dorgan recorded in his book on Ring, "in a voice unsteady with emotion", Lynch wondered what more could be said and written of Ring.

"But more and more will be said and written of him as long as young men will match their hurling skills against each other on Ireland's green fields.

"As long as young boys swing their camáns for the sheer thrill of the tingle in their fingers of the impact of ash on leather, as long as hurling is played, the story of Christy Ring will be told – and that will be forever."

Lynch had loved Ring. If that sounds far-fetched or exaggerated, or offends against certain sensibilities, then so be it.

It was nevertheless true.

"As long as the red jerseys of Cork, the blue of Munster, and the green, black and gold of Glen Rovers – colours which Christy wore with such distinction – as long as we see these colours in manly combat, the memories of Christy Ring's genius and prowess will come tumbling back in profusion.

"We will relish and savour them for we will hardly see their likes again. And men who are fathers and grandfathers now will tell their children and grandchildren, with pride, that they saw Christy Ring play.

"The story will pass from generation to generation, and so it will live . . ."

Of his many achievements on and off the field, of which he was justifiably proud, Lynch, arguably, was proudest of all, of the fact that he was instrumental in enticing Ring to Glen Rovers – the Blackpool club of which they were the brightest stars.

It was a story he told over and over, and there was no hiding the simple unalloyed pleasure he took in recalling how that came about.

That pleasure was matched only by the pleasure Lynch found in re-living and re-telling Ring's great deeds.

"Even before half of his playing days were over, his feats and his skill were legendary. If these skills were inherent, as they were, they were enhanced by his sheer dedication to the game of hurling that he loved, and by his constant aspiring to improve his playing of it – if, indeed, that were possible.

"If, in the course of a match or a season, we thought we had seen the ultimate in what constituted a complete hurler, Christy was always able to produce or perform an even greater '*gaisce*', a new feat of hurling magic of which only he was capable.

"He had consummate belief in his ability, and that ability was consummate. "

Lynch, and many others present, were visibly moved as they bade farewell to the greatest hurler of all time.

After the funeral, Mackey – regarded by many as Ring's only real rival for the title of "the greatest" – said he wanted to visit the Glen Rovers club in the heart of Blackpool.

The pressmen got to know of it, and some of us followed him on the journey from Cloyne to the northside of Cork city.

Mackey was standing at the bar when we arrived, surrounded by players and officials.

One of those present was Dr Jim Young, a man who had played with Ring and Lynch for Cork against the great Limerick teams of the two Mackey brothers, Mick and John.

Some of us were told afterwards that when Ring's coffin was being taken from the Church in Ballinlough, Young was standing shoulder to shoulder with Mackey.

When the coffin passed, Young turned to Mackey, tapped him in the chest with a bony finger, and said: "Now you are the greatest".

Years later, sitting in a pub in Ballinlough in Cork city, Young, smiling wryly, confirmed that story to me.

Someone in the clubhouse presented Mackey with a Glen tie. As we pressed forward to shake his hand, someone else referred to the famous Justin Nelson photograph taken during the 1957 Cork Tipperary championship encounter.

The photograph shows Ring, his right arm in a sling, leaving the field behind one set of goalposts. Mackey, who was an umpire that day, is standing, white-coated, by the posts and is saying something to Ring who is glancing, none too happy, in his direction.

It is one of the most famous of all GAA photographs. And one of the most talked about.

"Can you remember what you said to Ring?" someone asked Mackey.

The Limerickman, grim-faced, a faraway look in his eyes, shook his head.

"Naw. 'Twas nothing important."

The curiosity remains, and will always be there.

Here were hurling's two superstars. What was said?

The question, as Jack Lynch concedes, is as much a tribute to Mackey as to Ring.

Perhaps only Lynch himself, in similar circumstances, would excite as much, or nearly as much, curiosity.

In a pub in Murroe, Co. Limerick, once, Paddy Grace of Kilkenny told me he considered that Mackey was better than Ring.

Lynch, he added, wasn't far behind.

As a Blackpool and a lifelong follower of the Glen, I baulked at his evaluation of Mackey *vis-à-vis* Ring.

I said I preferred the comment once made in the old Cork Athletic Grounds by the great Kilkenny player, Jimmy Langton.

He had come to watch a Co. Kilkenny League game, and Ring, now in the twilight of his career, was playing that day.

We gathered around Langton.

"What do you think of Ring?" a voice asked.

"Look at him now while you have him because there will never be another like him."

Much later I told the story to Jack Lynch.

"Yes. Well, they'll say as Corkmen we're not objective when it comes to Ring. But Langton is right. Ring's excellence will never be surpassed."

Not surpassed – but did Mackey in his heyday match it?

That remains one of hurling's great perennial questions.

On 13 September 1982 Mick Mackey died. And in another great GAA funeral he was buried in Castleconnell.

Jack Lynch was not present; Mairin had injured her arm that morning. But his tribute to the great Ahane man was characteristic:

"I am deeply saddened at the passing of Mick Mackey. Even though he had been gravely ill for some time, his death comes as a shock to me and, I am sure, to all his contemporaries as well.

"He was a tough opponent, and no matter how hard that granite body of his hit one, he did it with resoluteness and yet he never lost his sense of humour.

"Above all, he was a magnificent hurler. In his heyday he had no peer. His skill and his sportsmanship will be an example for generations of hurlers to come."

Lynch went on to say that there were never better games than those between Cork and Limerick in the Munster championship in the late 1930s and early 1940s.

Mick Mackey was always a dominant character, and a doughty and fair opponent whether on the winning or losing side.

"He will always be compared with Christy Ring. As to who was the better is an argument that will probably never be resolved – each in his peak almost a decade apart.

"With Christy and now Mick gone, we have lost, in my opinion, the two greatest hurlers and hurling personalities of all time," added Jack Lynch.

Lynch had been magnificent in the titanic battles with Limerick in the 1939-44 championships. Now, on the occasion of Mackey's funeral, he was nothing if not tactful in skirting the obvious question: was Mackey better than Ring?

But what did he really think?

At the end of a long interview in 1990 in the Imperial Hotel in Cork, as we relaxed over drinks in the bar, I asked him, rather tentatively, the question he has steadfastly refused to answer over the years.

"How would you compare Ring and Mackey – which was the greater?"

He studied his pipe for a moment before replying. "I have always refrained from comment on that," he reminded me. "I played with Ring and I played against Mackey. So let me put it like this – I would rather play with Ring than against him."

That was all he said. It was enough.

The eulogy that sad, sad day in Cloyne had said it all.

Others, of course, have pronounced on this.

Paddy Downey of the *Irish Times*, in the context of what I regard as the finest piece ever written on Ring (it was entitled "Here Comes The King" and was commissioned for the *Spirit of the Glen*) dealt with it in the following way:

"It may seem politic to say in a Glen Rovers publication that Christy Ring was the greatest hurler of all time. To leave it unsaid, for that reason, would be a denial of a fact that has been established, I believe, by the considered opinion of men of sound judgment who saw all the great players of the century.

"Mick Mackey, too, has his advocates, and the difference between these two giants can have been only marginal in several aspects of their game.

"But I have heard it argued, reasonably, clinically, emphatically and, to me, convincingly, that Ring possessed the wider range of skills, developed them through sheer, spartan dedication to the point of perfection, and applied them for club, county and province with more consistency and greater reward than his famed Limerick rival."

No doubt, the argument will go on.

For Lynch there is immense satisfaction in the knowledge that not alone did he count both Ring and Mackey as friends, but he graced the same playing fields and the same great occasions with them.

It came as no surprise, therefore, in 1984 when Lynch was chosen along with Ring and Mackey as members of the *Sunday Independent*

/Irish Nationwide/GAA Hurling Team of the Century, selected by a special panel after the *Sunday Independent* had carried out a national poll of its readers in the GAA's Centenary Year.

That team was as follows: Tony Reddan (Tipperary), Bobby Rackard (Wexford), Nick O'Donnell (Wexford), John Doyle (Tipperary), Jimmy Finn (Tipperary), John Keane (Waterford), Paddy Phelan (Kilkenny), Lory Meagher (Kilkenny), Jack Lynch (Cork), Christy Ring (Cork), Mick Mackey (Limerick), Jimmy Langton (Kilkenny), Jimmy Doyle (Tipperary), Nick Rackard (Wexford), Eddie Keher (Kilkenny).

What of Lynch and Ring?

When Ring died Lynch was quoted as saying: "We were very close friends as well as being colleagues together on the hurling field over many a year".

Lynch loved Ring, as I said earlier. There is no doubt of that.

I have a very clear recollection of one amusing incident involving Lynch and Ring in the old Glen Field on the edge of Kilbarry.

Lynch's playing days were over at the time. Indeed, I'm fairly certain he was a Parliamentary Secretary, which would make it the early fifties at least.

However, on a visit to Cork he had made his way to see how his old clubmates were doing as they prepared for another championship.

In particular, he had come to see Ring.

After an hour or so, as the evening shadows drew in, a halt was called to the training, and the players made their way to the dressingroom.

In those days, this was nothing more than a corrugated iron shed, measuring perhaps 20 x 8 feet and situated in one corner of the ground.

It had no conventional windows – that is to say, no glass. But it had two open frames to let in air and light, each measuring perhaps 4 foot square. At night they were secured by hinged wooden covers.

Lynch and Ring, chatting intently, were among the last on the field. And as they walked down the touchline, Ring, in the famous green, black and gold of the Glen, Lynch immaculate in a dark suit, they collected stray sliotars.

The dressing-room was on the opposite side of the ground, and as they came to a point directly opposite it, Lynch threw out a good-humoured challenge to Ring.

"I'll bet you half a crown you won't put three sliotars through one of those windows."

Ring, without another word, placed three sliotars side by side. And then, in that free-taking style of his that sent electricity through the packed thousands in Thurles, Limerick, Killarney and Croke Park, he bent, lifted and struck the three balls through one of the windows with unerring accuracy.

The only problem was that the players inside suddenly found themselves bombarded by mini-missiles!

And as the balls rattled against the corrugated sheeting at the back of the dressing-room, creating an almighty din, one of the Glen players (my recollection is that it was Josie Hartnett), still half-naked, ran out of the place in a fury.

With fist raised, and eyes blazing, he informed two of the greatest hurlers of all time that they were "madmen" – a descriptive term greeted by the future Taoiseach and the Cloyneman with hoots of laughter!

Others will have their own memories of the special friendship between Lynch and Ring.

But what of them as players?

I am reminded of the tribute the late Padraig Puirseal, for many years GAA correspondent of the *Irish Press*, paid to Lynch the day after he became Taoiseach.

"I saw Jack Lynch win every one of his All-Ireland and Railway Cup medals," wrote Puirseal.

"In my view, he had few equals and no superior as the most accomplished all-round hurler of his time."

Strangely enough, or perhaps it is not so strange, it is only in Blackpool that you will hear it occasionally said that some players would pick Lynch before Ring.

Paddy "Chancer" Barry, who played on Glen teams with both of them, told me that, while he didn't doubt Ring's genius, he would pick Lynch ahead of him for his "leadership qualities".

Interestingly enough, in his excellent book *Ireland 1912-1985: Politics and Society*, Professor Joseph Lee of UCC speculates that these same qualities may have been undermined by the death of Ring in 1979. In this instance, of course, he is talking of Lynch's leadership in the political sphere, in what was to be his last year as Taoiseach.

"He seemed increasingly bored by politics, deftly though he had played the party game when the humour was on him. It may even be that the sudden death at the age of fifty-eight in March 1979 of the legendary hurler Christy Ring, with whom Lynch had shared in many a memorable victory in the red jersey, and at whose funeral, Lynch was visibly distraught, left its mark on him."

Professor Lee is right; Lynch was badly shaken by Ring's death.

And he may also be right when he speculates that the tragedy may have lessened Lynch's appetite for politics.

What is beyond dispute, however, is that that appetite started to go long before Jack's great friend collapsed of a massive heart-attack outside the School of Commerce on Morrison's Island on the afternoon of 2 March 1979.

One final sad incident, a poignant coda, is worth recording. I give Val Dorgan's version, contained in his very fine 1980 book *Christy Ring*.

"Earlier in the day the State car of the Taoiseach, Jack Lynch, stopped at Brian Boru Bridge (in the centre of Cork city) to buy an Evening Echo. It was the street news vendor who told him of Ring's death. 'Oh no, it can't be true!' was Lynch's reaction."

In the next day's *Examiner* reporter Larry Lyons (who has since died) led off his piece with the incident. And, as Dorgan recalls: "It was the story most people remembered in the thousands of words written afterwards ...."

Jack Lynch with Mrs Kitty Mackey, widow of the famous Mick Mackey, – pictured at the Sunday Independent/ACC GAA awards in T.C.D. – 1987.

6. Dáil Éireann

But for an element of chance Jack Lynch might have entered Dáil Eireann in 1948 as a Clann na Poblachta deputy. And the subsequent history of that institution, of the Fianna Fáil party and of the Nation might have been very different.

He acknowledges there are some myths about his early career in politics, several of which have stuck to this day.

One of these is that he was first approached by Fine Gael in the 1946 Cork by-election to be their candidate.

The other is that he tossed a coin to decide between Clann na Poblachta and Fianna Fáil.

"That is not true," says Mr Lynch. "There was no coin tossing on the issue of going forward as a candidate."

But it is true that an approach was made to him by Sean MacBride's Clann na Poblachta.

"Without hesitation I said 'no'. I had always had great feeling for Dev. I was conscious of him being a marvellous, romantic figure.

"The facts are that I was approached by the Brothers Delaney Fianna Fáil Cumann in Blackpool, Cork to fight the 1946 by-election caused by the resignation of William Dwyer.

Incidentally, the Cumann was named after two brothers from Dublin Hill who were killed during the Civil War.

"I had only recently been married, and I had started practising at the Bar. I was not at that time an active member of Fianna Fáil."

The Cumann members who called to the small flat in which Jack and Mairin lived on Summerhill at the time were Maurice Forde, Pat McNamara, Bill Barry and Garret McAuliffe.

Lynch declined their offer.

"An additional reason for my turning down the offer of the Brothers Delaney Cumann was because a friend of mine, 'Pa'

McGrath, who had been a lifelong member of Fianna Fáil was seeking the nomination, and I wasn't going to stand against him.

"I told the Cumann that maybe I would stand for the party the next time.

"And next time was the General Election of 1948 when the party was defeated and the Coalition Government was formed."

The 1946 election was an historic election because it was at the time Sean McCaughey, an IRA man, died in prison while on a hunger strike.

General Tom Barry was a candidate. So was Michael O'Riordan, who had been in the North Mon. during Lynch's time, and who stood as a candidate for the Communist Party. Fine Gael and Sinn Féin also had candidates in the field.

Lynch helped out on the canvass, and made his first political speech at Blackpool Bridge, on the same platform as Frank Aiken.

The result was a great victory for 'Pa' McGrath and the party.

It was undoubtedly the circumstances of 1946 that gave legs to the story that Lynch was a reluctant TD. Later it would even be said that he was a reluctant Taoiseach.

Lynch himself maintains he was not really that reluctant a candidate.

Yet to the question – why did Jack Lynch enter politics? – there is no neat answer. There was an "accidental" element about it.

Mrs Lynch hinted at this one time when she said her husband's career owed something to being on the right corner of the right street at the right time.

Chance. And opportunity.

Asked once about this, his old friend "Gus" Healy, who served as a Cork TD for many years, and also as chairman of the Parliamentary Party, replied:

"He was a sportsman and he was intelligent, and he represented the new generation we wanted to bring into politics. The majority of the Party were from the old IRA, and we wanted to set a good example to young people."

The situation in 1946 was governed by his personal circumstances.

He anticipated that at a later time he would be asked to stand as a Fianna Fáil candidate.

Meanwhile, he wanted to avail of the opportunities he had to prepare himself for the Dáil if he was eventually elected.

He had been called to the Bar in 1945.

"At the Bar I was an ordinary run-of-the-mill barrister doing company actions, road accidents and rent cases. It was great training, and if I had not gone into politics, I would have stayed at the Bar and I would have specialised in some particular branch of the profession.

"As a barrister one sees all the vicissitudes of human life just as a TD does, but in a different way. There can be no doubt that practising at the Bar is very useful training for one who wishes to take up politics as a career."

He said once that this is why political parties often prefer barristers as members of their group.

In an interview with the *Sunday Press* in February, 1973, Mr Lynch recalled his early commitment to the party of which he eventually became leader.

"I never even considered any other party but Fianna Fáil. I remember at the age of about 15, I carried a banner through the streets of Cork in a procession during the 1932 general election campaign. I was walking beside Eamon de Valera's carriage at the time. From that time, I formed a great admiration for Mr de Valera.

"Later I formed an admiration for Sean Lemass, for whom I had great respect.

"But even as a youngster, because of Dev I felt that one day I might be asked to stand as a Fianna Fáil candidate for the Dáil."

Prior to the 1948 General Election his chance came when the Blackpool Cumann approached him again. This time he allowed his name to go forward.

He couldn't attend the convention because of a law dinner on the same night. And it was during the meal in the Metropole Hotel that he was informed that he had been selected.

Still clad in his dinner jacket, he went to the Courthouse to accept the nomination.

Strangely enough, he had not formally joined Fianna Fáil at the time of being nominated.

Walter Furlong, 'Pa' McGrath and Sean McCarthy were also selected, and that night Lynch joined the Cumann.

Dev came to Cork for the final rally in 1948, and that's when Lynch met him for the first time.

"I had a reverential awe of him, but at that meeting I found him very human."

Years later he spelled out what Dev meant to him. The occasion was the launching of a book, *De Valera and His Times* at UCC on 12 October 1983.

Before a distinguished gathering, Lynch declared: "I am a lifelong admirer and supporter of Eamon de Valera, his ideals, his philosophy and his policies and will be as long as I live."

He took issue with one essay in the book in which it was asserted that when Dev departed from active politics in 1959 he left Irish society very much as he found it.

"To suggest that Eamon de Valera did nothing to change Ireland is something that I must challenge . . .

"Reference is often made to his speech in 1943 about looking into his heart to know what the Irish people thought – that it was an indication of the man's arrogance.

"I am certain that it was no sign of arrogance, but the belief of a man who, because he identified with the basic philosophies of the Irish people, thought he could express them as well as any man.

"No 'arrogant' or 'vain' man could have sustained the support and loyalty of the majority of the Irish people as expressed in the most democratic way over four decades, nor, above all, could he have sustained the support, love and dedication of a noble, learned and good-hearted woman like Sinéad, Bean de Valera, for almost three quarters of a century . . ."

This tribute would be formulated later, but even in the 1940s, it was clear that Dev was Lynch's only political hero.

Now, after 16 years in power, Dev and Fianna Fáil had to adjust to being in Opposition.

Lynch's comment on this is a gem of an understatement, bearing in mind that he is talking about a Leader and a party which had come to believe that they had a divine right to govern.

"Naturally, the party took a while to acclimatise itself to these new circumstances."

Victory in the 1951 Election brought promotion for the affable Corkman.

Dev created a new position, Parliamentary Secretary to the Government, and asked Lynch to fill it.

The meeting with Dev to accept the appointment was Lynch's very first time in the Taoiseach's office.

He didn't realise it then, but his feet were already on the first rung of the ladder that would enable him to make this office his own, 15 years later.

In between he would serve as Minister for the Gaeltacht for four months in 1957; Minister for Education 1957-59; Minister for Industry and Commerce 1959-65; and Minister for Finance 1965-66.

In 1977, after becoming Taoiseach again, Lynch admitted after his triumphant homecoming to Cork, that when he first entered politics in 1948 he did not think the "end of the road" would come like this.

"If I did, I probably would not have started at all."

One of the most remarkable features of the Jack Lynch story is the manner and apparent ease with which he was promoted, the steady climb up the ladder – all the more remarkable given his public image as a "reluctant" man of power.

Senator Maurice Manning, who is also lecturer in politics at UCD, has dwelt on this.

"Jack Lynch had the reputation of being a reluctant politician, and yet he has invariably been in the right place at the right time.

"He was reluctant to enter politics at all in 1948, but once in, he easily won a seat in spite of having no family background in politics.

"He was reluctant to accept office in 1951 and again in 1957 because he was building up his legal practice and only agreed after persuasion from de Valera.

"As a Minister he was neither radical nor spectacular – merely competent, common-sensical, and reasonably hard-working – yet he moved effortlessly up the ranks, and in 1965 was appointed Finance Minister in Sean Lemass's Cabinet.

"When Lemass retired in 1966 Lynch at first refused to compete for the succession, and it was only when the party looked as though it would tear itself apart that he let his name go forward – after which he was an easy winner."

Manning, like other commentators, has latched onto a puzzling aspect of Lynch's political career.

He is very aware that political opponents have contended that this reluctance on the part of Lynch was but a clever pose, a public mask that hid acute ambition and cunning.

But the picture of Lynch as a kind of Richard III figure is surely wide off the mark.

"The case seems to be," says Manning, "that Lynch never had any blind personal ambition, rarely wanted power badly enough to think it worth fighting for, and had been to some extent diffident about his own abilities.

"Once in power, however, he showed remarkable skill and toughness in holding on to it."

Lynch's promotional career within Government, the steady climb from Parliamentary Secretary through successive senior

Departments, also undoubtedly indicated the continuous approval and support of both de Valera and Lemass.

But after 1966 he was out from under the shadow of his predecessors.

On the final rung of the ladder, he would find himself on his own. How did he perform on the lonely pinnacle of power?

Hugo Young's judgement of James Callaghan after the latter succeeded Harold Wilson as Prime Minister in 1976 is applicable to Lynch.

"He shone in none of these Departments, but it was soon the general opinion that as Prime Minister of Great Britain he performed much better than the sum of his past."

Nevertheless, as Brian Farrell has stressed, he was to find out that a Taoiseach who succeeds without a General Election has only limited influence.

Even after his election in place of Lemass, it was clear that factions had formed, and some ambitious Ministers regarded him as a mere caretaker.

Lynch was to find out the hard way that he could not hope to make his mark on the Cabinet immediately. And, in fact, the initial Lynch Cabinet registered only minimal changes from the previous line-up in the last Lemass Administration.

That fact alone was to prove a recipe for trouble.

Jack Lynch and the late Erskine Childers

7. Minister - Yes!

Competent, cool, efficient – but hardly dynamic – that's how Jack Lynch is mainly remembered from his days as a Minister.

He was not an innovative Minister, nor one who felt the need to buck the system.

His terms of office handling the portfolios for the Gaeltacht (March-June 1957), Education (1957-59), Industry and Commerce (1959-65) and Finance (1965-66) were smooth and, for the most part, hassle-free.

This was as much by design as accident. In style, Lynch was far removed from the flamboyance of one of his predecessors in the Department of Education, the late Donogh O'Malley. Lynch would never even dream of calling together local newspapers on a weekend visit to his constituency and "leaking" plans for a free school transport scheme – even before it had Cabinet clearance.

His ministerial career began on St Patrick's Day 1957, when he got a phone call instructing him to ring Dev. The latter offered him Education, and also asked him to hold the Gaeltacht portfolio, which he did for a few months before Michael Moran was appointed to the Cabinet as Minister for the Gaeltacht.

The promotion came at a time when Lynch was seriously considering concentrating on a legal career, having returned to the Cork Bar when Fianna Fáil were defeated in the 1954 General Election.

"I told Dev I liked the Bar and was beginning to feel that I had a good career there. However, as I hadn't got a family, I felt I wasn't risking too much by going back into politics full time.

"My wife would very much have preferred me to stay at the Bar, but I felt I had an obligation to accept the offer once it was made. I was, of course, flattered to be offered a Ministry at all."

Lynch admits that Dev liked him a lot. And he learned from the master. "One of his traits I noticed particularly, was his meticulous attention to the words he used in public speeches. I used to help him on his speeches from 1948-49 and I learned a lot about the need for precision in speech from Dev."

Years later this would be remembered by opponents and commentators who had to attempt an exegesis of what came to be known in some quarters as "Lynchspeak".

In office prior to 1966, the Corkman's achievements were rarely newsworthy.

As Minister for Education he was responsible for removing the marriage ban on women teachers.

Justifying this, the Catholic Bishops had argued that it was "unseemly" for school-going children to behold the spectacle of pregnant women in class.

"As far as I was concerned, school kids would merely regard pregnant teachers as 'fat women'," said Lynch.

He also pushed through a major building project at the training college in Drumcondra, and at third level he established a Commission to review accommodation, resulting in a considerable increase in university grants.

In June 1959 Eamon de Valera resigned his office as Taoiseach at the end of 42 years in politics, and subsequently became President, beating Sean MacEoin.

"I wasn't involved in Dev going to the Park," Lynch recalls.

"And there was really no question but that Lemass would succeed him. I never detected any animosity against Lemass in Cabinet"

Even before the latter moved into the Taoiseach's office, he told Lynch he wanted him to take over as Minister for Industry and Commerce.

"His first words when I entered his office were 'I want you to sit at this desk.'"

Lynch was none too keen but, as he said, "I suppose I had little choice. "

He was to remain at Industry and Commerce for six years, during a time when enormous changes were taking place in Ireland's industrial life.

The policy of protectionism, which Lemass had pioneered, was giving way to freer trade. And it was in this period also that Ireland first applied for EEC membership.

"Incidentally, our application reached Brussels before the British one did. However, de Gaulle vetoed the British application and ours lapsed as a consequence."

When the Labour party came to power in Britain in 1964, Lynch played a leading role in negotiations which led to the Anglo-Irish Free Trade Agreement which was signed in 1965.

At Industry and Commerce, Lynch was responsible for handling all labour matters, and he was constantly called into the settlement of strikes.

"There was a number of occasions when I was called back from holiday because of strikes, and my wife and I lost a few holiday deposits during that period."

His first real brush with controversy at Cabinet level also occurred during this period. In 1964 Paddy Smith resigned as Minister for Agriculture in protest against what he saw as capitulation to the trade unions, provoking a mini-cabinet crisis.

"Although I disagreed with his views at the time, he was representing a growing tension between the industrial and agriculture sectors as the industrial one boomed under the expansionary Fianna Fáil policies, and the agricultural sector lagged behind."

Later, as Taoiseach, Lynch would face his first real test when the National Farmers' Association (NFA), afterwards to become the IFA, staged a series of massive protests.

After the 1965 General Election, Lemass moved Lynch to the Department of Finance – a move which gratified the latter because, implicit in it, in his eyes, was a signal that he had done well at Industry and Commerce.

"But the promotion sent other signals as well. It fuelled speculation that I would be the successor to Sean Lemass as Leader of Fianna Fáil and as Taoiseach."

In Finance, Lynch came into daily contact with the Secretary of the Department, and one of this country's most outstanding civil servants, Ken Whitaker, with whom he already had a very good relationship.

In November 1990, in a review of a book entitled *Planning Ireland's Future: The Legacy of TK Whitaker*, Lynch paid generous tribute to the role played by the latter in "one of the most important political economic periods of our history".

Whitaker's famous study "Economic Development" formed the basis for the White Paper published in November 1958, ever since known as the "First Programme for Economic Expansion".

This was to serve as the basis for the economic growth of the sixties and early seventies, and justifiably earned him the description of being "the brains behind the economy of a new Ireland".

Throughout 1966 the speculation about a successor to Lemass, who was having some health problems, continued, with Lynch being increasingly talked about.

"Quite early on, as the speculation mounted, my wife and I discussed the prospect, and we concluded definitively that I should make it clear from the outset that I would not be a contender for the position.

"We had found that our family life had already been greatly disturbed by the demands of public office, and we were both anxious to minimise this as much as possible.

"Ministerial life didn't leave much time for private life, and we knew that being Taoiseach would leave even less time."

Quite apart from these considerations, Lynch had genuine difficulty visualising himself assuming the mantle of the likes of Eamon de Valera and Sean Lemass.

"They were both towering figures in my mind, and the thought that I could adequately fill their place seemed to me the height of presumption."

But the die was cast; his fate was being determined by whatever gods rule over that realm of human endeavour known as "politics".

And when Lemass resigned in November 1966, Jack Lynch became the new Taoiseach.

As a Minister, he was remembered with affection by those who worked with him, though there are varying views of his talents.

"He liked to clear his desk each day, and not allow a backlog of paper to build up," according to one civil servant. "But he was very low-key, and went out of his way to avoid confrontation rather than to invite it."

His loyalty to his two leaders – first Dev and then Lemass – was unquestioned, though it also appears to be the case that the awe in which he held them had an inhibiting if not a stultifying effect on him.

This was apparently true to such an extent that there is no evidence that Lynch ever became entangled in Cabinet infighting, or kicked over the traces in pursuit of some particular policy objective.

Jim Dukes, who worked as his Departmental secretary in Education, remembers him as a "superb administrator", but adds that he was not an "ideas man".

It is also said of Lynch that he never lost his temper. "I think a man who loses his temper in a discussion puts himself at a disadvantage," he once said.

Unlike some of his colleagues, he did not believe in the "spoils system", and it is said that during all his time in office no relative of his benefited directly from any action of his.

On a mid-morning train from Cork to Dublin on 13 May 1991, Dick Walsh of the *Irish Times* – returning from the annual conference of the Progressive Democrats in Cork – delivered a mini-dissertation on the contrasting styles of Eamon de Valera and Sean Lemass in Government.

"Dev gave a lot of rein to his Ministers around the Cabinet table. He allowed discussion, and let each man have his say. But he rarely entered a Cabinet meeting without having his own mind made up. And when everyone had had his say, he would then announce his decision – which had been known to him all the time anyway.

"Lemass was different. Dialogue around his Cabinet table was genuine. He was interested in what others thought. He listened. He wasn't at all autocratic. Unity of purpose was important to him, but he didn't believe it had to be an imposed unity. And when he gave people a job to do, he expected them to get on with it."

According to Walsh, this was also very much Lynch's style when he took over in 1966.

"His *modus operandi* was much closer to Lemass's than to Dev's... "

A somewhat different picture is painted by Brian Farrell, though the difference relates to Lemass rather than Lynch:

"Lynch preferred the concept of the Cabinet as a team to the more brilliant solo runs favoured by Lemass."

Professor Joe Lee's overview of the Lynch "style" is instructive, and serves as a guide to much of his future behaviour:

"Lynch was instinctively a temporiser. Having no strong views himself on most things, he preferred to lead from behind, and to let policy 'emerge'.

"It was not that he could not act when his back was to the wall. He would show that he could, to the discomfiture of the doubters. But he was not a natural pacemaker. He preferred to move from a consensus position . . . "

8. Taoiseach 1966

The story is probably apocryphal, but it is said that Sean Lemass, in contemplating a leadership contest between Jack Lynch and George Colley in 1966, commented: "Either way it's going to be petticoat power".

The assumption is that Lemass was acknowledging that both Lynch and Colley were married to strongminded – some would say, domineering – women who would be the power behind the throne.

Given what we now know about the role of Nancy in the Reagan White House from 1980 to 1988, such a view seems neither exaggerated nor disconcerting.

That is, of course, providing it has a basis in fact. I'm assured that Lemass never actually said it, though I doubt that that can be proved. Jack Lynch himself remembers things differently. And subsequent events overwhelmingly support his version. "When I told Mairin that I was the new Leader and Taoiseach, she cried. And all she could say was: 'Why do you want to take on that burden?'"

Throughout the years that followed, years of strain, of tension, and of drama, she was enormously supportive. But no one was more relieved than she was when her husband resigned as Taoiseach in December 1979, and finally left active politics in June 1981.

"There will be no tears," she said on 5 December 1979 when the word flashed around Leinster House that he was standing down as Taoiseach.

And she meant it. The years between 1966-79 had been traumatic ones for the country – and for the Lynches themselves. And if there were no tears at the end, there were certainly plenty of occasions for tears in between.

On the morning of 10 November 1966 things were different. It was a day of joy, of pride, and of celebration. Jack had reached the pinnacle of political life in the Irish Republic. In those heady hours after his endorsement by the Dáil and the drive to Aras an Uachtaráin to receive his seal of office from President Eamon de Valera, life must have seemed all silver lining.

The clouds, some of them very dark indeed, were hidden away in a distant, unknowable future.

Mairin Lynch was asked by reporters in Leinster House what she thought of it all.

"I honestly never thought it would come to this. My mind was a total blank. All I could think of was – Jack is sitting in Mr Lemass's place."

Was Mr Lynch really as shy as he was reputed to be?

"It is not really shyness. It is more an internal reluctance to push himself forward. But when he makes up his mind to do something there is no going back, no recrimination. His decisions always stand."

The emergence of Lynch in succession to Sean Lemass, who served as Taoiseach from 1957 to 1966, and who resigned on grounds of health, surprised many people.

At that stage, the image of the "reluctant politician" had fixed itself firmly in the public mind.

But some insiders saw it differently. One such was James Dukes (the father of the future Fine Gael leader, Alan Dukes), who served as Lynch's private secretary at the Department of Education from 1957 to 1959.

He says he wasn't one bit surprised.

"Jack was the first politician of the new generation to make it to the top. We knew he was the star. Dev thought very highly of him, and liked him very much. Lemass must have too."

Lynch wasn't quite the "dark horse" people made him out to be at the time.

A senior member of the Government is said to have been asked at dinner one night who were the young hopefuls of Fianna Fáil.

"Well," he said, "there's Lynch, and there's . . . Lynch, and . . . "

Whether true or not, it's indicative of the quality of Jack Lynch.

And when he was hesitant about allowing his name to go forward, Lemass sent for him.

"Why me?" asked Lynch.

"Look around," replied Lemass. "Who else have I got?"

The background to the leadership contest of 1966 was recalled for me by the man who became the successor to Lemass and Dev.

"About seven weeks before he eventually retired, this would have been about mid-September 1966, Sean Lemass called me into his office and enquired if I was interested in succeeding him as Taoiseach. I told him emphatically that I was not, and he seemed to accept it.

"Some weeks later, however, he called me into his office again, this time in the company of Charlie Haughey and George Colley, and again he told us that we should be thinking about the future leadership of the party.

"I reminded him of my previous interview with him when I said that I was not interested. I cannot precisely recall the response from the other two, but they seemed to indicate that they were interested.

"It was following this latter meeting that the 'succession stakes', as the press called it, really hotted up. Press speculation was rife. There was constant discussion about it in the party rooms, but I steadfastly remained apart from it all and repeated my lack of interest on several occasions when approached.

"Apparently, a group of old backbenchers went to Lemass at the stage when Neil Blaney became a candidate. They were worried that the party would be damaged by division and dissension. They strongly pressed the case for getting me to stand as the sole candidate, saying that I had clear majority support within the party, over and above the other candidates anyway.

"The point was also made that I had stayed aloof from the fray, that I was not a divisive force within the party, and that my varied and relatively long ministerial career had suggested that I would be suitable. Some saw me as a via media."

Despite the warnings, Lemass's final decision to retire came rather suddenly. He despatched a telegram to America, where George Colley was on an industrial promotional tour, and advised him to come home.

It was at this stage that a group of backbenchers went to Lemass and pressed him to urge Lynch to go forward as a candidate.

One of the ironies here is that the group included Tom McEllistrim of Kerry who, 13 years later, was to play a prominent part in the plot by a small group of TDs to replace Lynch with Haughey.

The outgoing Taoiseach finally managed to persuade Lynch to stand in the interests of party unity.

Looking back now, Lynch can see a pattern in the way Lemass pushed him forward, but at the time he attached no great significance to it.

"Once or twice when I was making a speech in the Dáil he came in to listen and complimented me later.

"He asked me to take his old job in Industry and Commerce even before his formal promotion as Taoiseach was announced. Even though I was not conscious of it, he was pointing me in some direction."

When Sean Lemass stepped down as Taoiseach in 1966, Jack Lynch was the overwhelming choice as his successor, easily defeating George Colley in the leadership contest.

That happened in November 1966. And Lynch won by 57 votes to 21.

"The ballots were collected in an old cardboard shoebox," he recalls today with a chuckle. "So much for technology!"

His emergence came as a surprise to some people, people who expected that Charles Haughey, Neil Blaney or Colley would be chosen.

"There were other ambitious people around, and some people had them picked for the job."

On Friday, 11 November 1966, Jack Lynch was elected as Taoiseach in Dáil Éireann by 71 votes to 64.

At the age of 49 he became the "youngest Taoiseach" (the key words in the *Cork Examiner's* headline the next day) in the history of the State, and also the first Corkman to hold the office.

In the public gallery Mrs Lynch, in a blue costume and autumn brown, turban-type hat, watched her husband thanking the House for his election.

In handing over the reins of power, Sean Lemass uttered prophetic words.

"It is a great privilege for me to propose Deputy Lynch as Taoiseach. I believe he has the qualities of intelligence and integrity and the capacity to work which will enable him to become a great Leader and Taoiseach. Time will prove this to be so."

Other voices, no less prophetic, were also raised.

Deputy Gerard Sweetman of Fine Gael warned that a "couple of knives" were being "sharpened for him down on his left".

Another Fine Gael member, Paddy Lindsay, sounded a similar warning.

"He certainly possesses the integrity; he certainly possesses the capacity to secure everyone's goodwill. There is only one area where I would fear for him, that is that his gentle nature, which I hope is not as gentle as we think it is, will easily submit to pressures. . . "

And glancing down pointedly at the Fianna Fáil front bench, Deputy Lindsay left no doubt as to where those pressures might come from:

"And all along that side . . . there is a gathering of gentlemen whose capacity for intrigue and pressure is unmatched..... "

That doughty warrior, James Dillon, picking up on earlier reports that Lynch had described himself as the "via media" during the leadership contest in Fianna Fáil, sought to turn this around.

"Now what is a "via media" in politics? It is expendable. As soon as the knives have been sharpened, as soon as the assassinations have been consummated, they hope, as the *Guardian* said, 'to send that decent man to the Park'. Then the battle will begin ...."

But all of that lay ahead.

Lynch, of firm composure, contented himself with some words in praise of his predecessor, saying that no man had left a greater mark on the progress of the nation than Sean Lemass.

"He has set the highest of standards because these were the only standards he knew and aspired to. I shall do my best to attain these standards."

The satisfaction and the pride was not confined to the Fianna Fáil benches.

Brendan Corish, leader of the Labour Party since 1960, paid the new Taoiseach a warm tribute.

"Jack Lynch has always been a very affable, kindly, courteous and courageous man."

More importantly, Corish sensed a new departure.

"We may see some significance in this new era in that for the first time in 35 years there sits, in the seat of the Taoiseach, a person who was not actively engaged, nor could he be, in the events of 1922 or the five, six or seven turbulent years that followed.

"I hope this appointment of one such as Deputy Jack Lynch is a sign that we are at last becoming politically mature . . . "

There was understandably parochial pride as well, even across party lines.

Sean Casey of Labour, a deputy for Cork City like Lynch himself, was quick to point out that "it would be wrong to present any picture other than that the people of Cork generally, irrespective of politics, irrespective of sport, of class or of creed, all rejoice in the selection and election of Deputy Jack Lynch as Taoiseach".

Another Cork City deputy, Stephen Barrett of Fine Gael, got in his somewhat two-edged say:

"I formed the same opinion of him as most people in Cork have – that he is a man of decency and integrity – two qualities which can be quite an incapacity in dealing with some of the Front Bench he has presented to the House this afternoon. . ."

One deputy, Sean Dunne (Lab) of Dublin, obviously found the repetition of references to Lynch's "integrity" a bit overdone. And there was gentle laughter when he interjected: "He has so much integrity that he has it for export!"

In Cork there was widespread rejoicing.

And when he returned there in triumph into Blackpool, tar barrels blazed in front of the Glen clubhouse, and old men pressed forward to shake the hand of the man who was now Captain of the Nation.

Tom MacSweeney, now RTE's correspondent in Cork, witnessed the scenes.

He wrote: "The people of Cork made this a memorable occasion. They turned night into day with brilliant lights, blazing tar barrels and fireworks, for this was an occasion of occasions, a Corkman had become Taoiseach and he was coming home ....

"Jack was coming home, Jack the Taoiseach . . .

"The excitement reached fever pitch as the time of his arrival at the Grotto at Blackpool, drew near . . . "

"In his first speech in Cork as Taoiseach, Mr Lynch said he was proud to be the successor to Mr Lemass and the second successor to Eamon de Valera.

"He spoke in Irish and English and said he remembered that when Mr de Valera came to Cork in 1932, he was one of the small boys who carried a lighted torch alongside his lorry.

"'And let you all know that there were no other political beliefs in my young mind at that time, though it is said that there were,' he added, to tremendous cheering....

"Mr Lynch made a particular appeal to everyone to take an interest in politics. 'Political parties are the cornerstone of our democracy, and by taking an interest in them you will not alone be helping, but will strengthen public life.

"'I appeal particularly to the younger people amongst us in this regard. If you enter politics now, you may end up like me – but don't let that deter you....'"

One lovely incident was witnessed that night by Eamonn Young, who played with Lynch on the victorious Cork football team in 1945.

Jack climbed up on a makeshift platform across from Molly Howe's pub in Blackpool. He didn't have the benefit of a microphone and a PA system, and not possessing an Ian Paisley-type voice for public speaking, a lot of what he had to say wasn't heard by many in the large crowd.

"Two teams of schoolboys in the colours of the Glen and St Nicholas formed a victory V in front of the clubhouse and sang 'A Nation Once Again'.

"Visibly moved, the Taoiseach's words were inaudible from where I was, back in the crowd.

"'What's he saying?' said one old-timer.

"'Yerrah, what's he saying?' replied his pal, 'only that he's glad to be home and he'd play for the Glen in the morning if he could'.

It was the stuff of which memories are made.

Jack Lynch signed the Franco/Irish Cultural Agreement in Paris on November 4 1967

9. *Annus Mirabilis*

For Jack Lynch and Cork, 1966 was an auspicious year – an *annus mirabilis*. In Croke Park in September of that year, in a game charged with emotion, the Cork senior hurlers ended a 12-year spell in the wilderness by beating Kilkenny in the All-Ireland Final.

Below me in the stand as the McCarthy Cup was hoisted aloft by the jubilant captain, Gerald McCarthy, I could see various VIPs and personalities from the worlds of sport and politics and the Church. There was no sign of Jack Lynch. For once on the first Sunday in September he was absent from Croke Park.

"I had booked a holiday to Greece, and the dates clashed, inadvertently as far as I was concerned. As Mairin and I walked up to The Parthenon in Athens I looked at my watch. It was about three o'clock. And I said: 'Just about now the lads are running out onto the pitch in Croke Park.' Mairin turned to me. 'Here we are at the very birthplace of western civilisation, and all you can think about are the Cork hurlers in Croke Park. Jack Lynch, you're a philistine!'"

Fixed in my mind's eye, as I reflected on Lynch's absence, was an image of a meeting only months before, in the heart of Blackpool between Jack and Christy Ring. As the two chatted, onlookers gazed with rapt attention at two of Ireland's folk heroes.

Two months later another image fixed itself indelibly in my mind – an *Irish Press* photograph of Sean Lemass shaking hands with Lynch in Leinster House, congratulating him on his succession to the leadership of Fianna Fáil and the office of Taoiseach. In the background George Colley, the unsuccessful challenger, stood forlorn and dejected.

Later in the Dáil, amid great applause after he had been formally elected as Taoiseach by 71 votes to 64, the redoubtable Martin Corry could be heard shouting "Another All-Ireland, Jack!"

Cork had two tumultuous homecomings that year. First, it was the hurlers' return. The late Jerry O'Sullivan of Glen Rovers – a hurler much admired by Lynch – once told me how he looked down into Patrick Street with tears in his eyes at the vast sea of faces as the lorry carrying the team turned around Paddy Barry's corner.

Jack Lynch had known that experience as well – no less than six times, all in succession between 1941 and 1946. But in November 1966, the joyous homecoming was for him alone and was a political rather than a sporting occasion. Cork welcomed him back as Taoiseach. And on the northside the bonfires blazed.

He was to say, many years later, he never could cope with public adulation. "I always wanted to get on with my work quietly and without fuss."

But in 1966 the fuss and adulation was only just beginning for the man who would ever afterwards be known in the City which came to love him, and beyond, as the "real" Taoiseach.

Lynch's great friend, Gerry O'Mahony, who served for many years as his press officer in Cork, recalls the 1966 reception. "It was tremendous. And, of course, there was a lot of pride involved.

"Cork people right across the spectrum were proud that one of their own had made it to the top political office in the country."

According to Professor John A. Murphy of UCC, no leader of an Irish Government has been so well-liked. "De Valera and Haughey polarised emotions. Lemass was more highly-regarded than well-liked. Jack Lynch was loved."

Professor Murphy recalls emerging alongside Lynch from St Mary's Cathedral in November 1982, after the funeral Mass for Bishop Cornelius Lucey. "I was struck by the enormous affection which the huge crowd outside had for Lynch even then, when he was gone from politics. It was an acclamation of one of their own, but it was utterly natural on his side and theirs . . . "

Pressed to explain what Dick Walsh of the *Irish Times* has described as Lynch's "magnetic electoral appeal", Professor Murphy says it has a lot to do with the "big brother syndrome – the feeling that he could be trusted absolutely, and that he would look after things. You felt he'd mind the house for you."

Jack himself, with typical modesty, has a more mundane explanation: "People in Cork are tremendously loyal to the people who try to help them and serve them."

The trusting side of Lynch's own nature could and did land him in difficulties from time to time. Bobby Molloy, now with the PDs, was made Minister for Defence by Lynch in 1977. "He let his Minister get on with the job. In fact, he could be trusting to a fault. He was absolutely honest himself, and expected it from his colleagues as a matter of course. History now knows that that trust wasn't always reciprocated."

To some this was Lynch's 'Achilles heel'. His enemies tried to exploit it. His friends sometimes unwittingly misled him because he too readily reposed trust in them.

The two examples most often cited are the 1977 election manifesto (he took much on trust from Martin O'Donoghue), and the battle for the succession after his resignation in December 1979, when he trusted George Colley's figures suggesting that he (Colley) would defeat Charlie Haughey.

All that came later. During the interim he was to get caught up in drama and tragedy of an order and magnitude unimaginable in 1966. As Lynch in that year, at the age of 49, assumed his onerous responsibilities, nobody could have foreseen that within three years Ireland, North and South, would be in crisis.

Did we but have in our midst a real visionary, he or she might have been able to look to the wider world and to see there, signs, faint stirrings, pale foreshadowings of portentous events to come. But we possessed no such person.

On the domestic front in 1966 the prevailing mood was one of complacency. Fianna Fáil had been in power for 15 years, and in the North the Unionist hegemony seemed fixed, assured and unshakable.

Soon, very soon, much of that was to change – and change in a much more dramatic, radical and bloody fashion than Lynch or his contemporaries could have anticipated.

Within a short time a passage from the W.B. Yeats poem "The Second Coming" would seem apposite:

"The best lack all conviction, while the worst

Are full of passionate intensity."

But only fleetingly.

Surface appearances were deceptive. And the best – in this case Jack Lynch – would yet carry the day, though not without considerable pain, trauma and controversy.

Jack Lynch with Garret Fitzgerald and Frank Cluskey

10. The Lynch Charisma

It was a dull day in late July in 1991, and among the many thousands who came to Cork for the Cutty Sark Tall Ships' Race were Jack and Mairin Lynch. The city's quays were thronged when the Lynches decided to take a walk about to see some of the splendid vessels at close quarters.

Accompanying them were their old friends, Ted and Gretchen Crosbie. As they mingled with the crowds more and more attention focused on Jack.

"It was just amazing," recalled Ted Crosbie, who is the chief executive of the *Cork Examiner* and who also played a leading role in organising the Cork phase of the Tall Ships' Race.

"His appeal continues right across the board, and I'd wager a few pounds that he'd get 84 seats again tomorrow if he were still in politics." The scenes on the quays conveyed their own message, testifying to the lasting charisma of Lynch.

"People always felt safe with Jack," observed Ted Crosbie.

One fan hailed the grey-haired, balding figure, and told him that to the people of Cork he would always be "the real Taoiseach".

It is by now a familiar, if erroneous, tag, and one to which Jack Lynch is well used. He knows it is as much an expression of affection as anything else, though he knows too that it harks back to a time of drama and trauma for the Fianna Fáil party.

Today he is able to look back with a certain serenity and detachment on that period.

Nothing if not a realist, Jack Lynch recognises that past events are beyond the reach of all of us.

But he also knows enough about history to realise that we are never free of its tentacles.

Jack Lynch is not a sentimentalist. Although he refuses to see himself as a shaper of history, he knows in his heart that he was the right man for his time, living proof of the old dictum that a nation can be blessed in its gravest trials with its greatest leaders.

Lynch was the leader the country needed at a time when much, if not all of the island could have been plunged into bloodshed and civil war.

"He kept his head, and so enabled us to keep ours," is how his fellow Corkman, Professor John A. Murphy, expressed the essence of Lynch's role in the dark dangerous days of 1969-71.

Even now, few realise how close we were to catastrophe. The pressures on Lynch were great, far greater than anyone outside of Government appreciated.

He remained steadfast when lesser men might have gone for the more dramatic option.

And it didn't end there.

In fact, that was just the beginning.

And it isn't over yet.

What was the secret of the Lynch charisma, and of his enormous popularity?

The feeling that Jack Lynch was an ordinary man who got caught up in extraordinary events is still widespread today, not least among those who were never convinced Lynchites.

But is that all there is to it?

The human psyche holds the key to the qualities of leadership which have broad, popular appeal.

That and timing. Or, more precisely, the socio-political conditions prevailing at a particular time.

Cometh the hour, cometh the man.

Invariably so, as history teaches us.

As the fashioning of this chapter began, I was listening to Barbara Dickson's version of "The Skye Boat Song" on RTE radio, a song most of us learned in school.

"Speed, bonnie boat, like a bird on the, wing
Onward, the sailors cry.
Carry the lad that's born to be King
Over the sea to Skye . . . "

No doubt, to a republican like Jack Lynch the concept of kingship is alien.

Nevertheless, the Gaelic blood in his veins, or his Gaelic genes, might well cause this concept to resonate within his being with not-so-foreign vibrations.

There was a time not so long ago on this ancient island when kingship was accepted – and Kings (and some Queens, as well) were the natural leaders.

It was part of the order of things, the natural order.

And Jack Lynch has a very strong sense of order and of symmetry.

He was a King of sport, and in time he became a King of politics.

The first crown came naturally to him, and he wore it as if to the manner born.

He was reluctant to accept the second crown, though, unlike Caesar, he did not once, never mind thrice, refuse it publicly.

Yet, once accepted, he wore it uneasily for a time.

His critics and his enemies (the two are not the same) would go further and claim that he wore it unfittingly.

But there is a huge corpus of evidence against them, as well as the witness of thousands upon thousands of citizens of this land.

Yet the truth remains that Lynch was a reluctant King of politics.

He sensed, certainly Mairin Lynch sensed, that the crown would bring with it many thorns.

And so it came to pass.

Was he a lad born to be King – the man to rule in the Kingdom of politics?

Destiny determined it so. But destiny had good material to work with.

"The truly extraordinary man," it has been written, "is truly the ordinary man."

And that saying could have been tailor-made for Jack Lynch.

People from all walks of life and all backgrounds, on meeting Jack Lynch, even and especially now, are struck and immediately impressed by his "ordinary" demeanour.

And therein lies much of the "secret" of his appeal as a politician.

In a brief discussion on Jack Lynch in the early part of 1991 with Eamon Dunphy, the latter remarked that he always found Lynch to be "a genuinely decent man".

It was only later I recalled that Dunphy, writing after the 1984 All-Ireland Hurling Fmal, where Lynch was given a standing ovation by the crowd, remarked on the "ordinariness of the man as a source of extraordinary popularity".

That All-Ireland, in the centenary year of the GAA, was played in Thurles, where the Association was founded. And the emotion which swept through the huge crowd that day, when Lynch was introduced to the attendance before the start of the game, was almost palpable.

His "ordinariness" can be illustrated by numerous incidents.

One of the ones I like best was related to me by Donal Musgrave, now News Editor of the *Cork Examiner*, but a reporter with the *Irish Times* at the time.

"I was walking up Sun Valley Drive to an election count at the Parochial Hall in Gurranabraher, when this car pulled up, and somebody called my name.

"I walked over and there was Jack Lynch in his official car, as Taoiseach, offering me a lift to the count centre.

"What other Prime Minister would instruct his driver to stop the State car to offer a lift to a provincial journalist?"

I was told another story about Lynch canvassing in the Blarney Street area of Cork during the 1977 General Election campaign.

Some Labour Party people were also canvassing and were a few doors behind Lynch. One old woman told them straight out she was going to vote for Jack Lynch, and not to be bothering her.

They wanted to know why, and pressed her for a reason. "Sure, he has a lovely face," she told them.

As one of them said afterwards, "It's hard to compete with that!"

At another level, Tom Garvin, the political scientist, pointed out that Lynch was "a very unfanatical politician, with a markedly consensual style".

He was a personification of the view that the best leaders have been unifiers, conciliators, consensus-seekers. They use their power, but they remain awed by it.

Another well-known academic, Professor John A. Murphy, said people felt safe with Lynch, and, what's more, they felt while he was in charge the country was safe as well.

Michael D. Higgins echoes this: "With Lynch, there was a great sense of security in the country. People felt safe with him. He also had an uncanny gift for remembering names."

There is a danger, if one reflects on that surge of emotion that day in Thurles in 1984, that one might begin to consider that a residue of what, in an anthropological sense, would be called "magical qualities" attach themselves to Lynch.

The reality is much more mundane, even banal. With Jack Lynch what you see is what you get.

The problem is, of course, that what you see is a good deal less than the whole truth.

As he was a hurler, Lynch was also a very cagey politician, and a most dexterous one.

It may well be the case now – as I believe it is – that he does not miss the chessboard of power.

But while he played on it, he was a most formidable opponent.

Paddy Cooney, who was Minister for Justice in the Cosgrave-led Coalition Government of 1973-77, once described Lynch to me as "pleasant and courteous". But he added, "He was not a simple man. He was rather more devious and deeper than many people realised."

Lynch was good at dissembling his feelings.

Emotionally, he never gave much away.

After the 1971 Árd Fheis, that occasion of bedlam and bad blood and near violence in the RDS, someone who knew Lynch but could not be present, asked a friend, who had been there, how Lynch had coped.

"The place was going wild, delegates were shouting, different factions were abusing each other, there was an enormous din, but Jack just sat there, puffing on his pipe, cool as a breeze."

The other person smiled knowingly. "When you've been through as many Munster Finals as Jack has been through, you're not going to get upset or be put off by a bit of shouting and roaring."

Of his decency, there was never any doubt. Former Fine Gael TD Paddy Lindsay put it well when he said: "Lynch was always willing to help a lame dog over a stile".

A journalist had this to say: "Jack will be remembered as a gentle, humane, civilised Taoiseach who was, in many ways, too good for his party. . . "

There will always be unanswered questions about the secret of Lynch's appeal.

Television undoubtedly helped. It magnified his "ordinariness", brought his qualities of goodness and integrity into the living-room, made him one of the family – and elicited sympathy for him when the Brian Farrells of the cathode tube were deemed to be giving him a hard time in the studio.

"Sure, poor Jack – wouldn't they leave that nice man alone," was a not uncommon response in many a household.

In an earlier, pre-television age he might not have been as effective, because it remains the general view that he was not an impressive public speaker.

After one of his first appearances on a political platform, an old-timer in Fianna Fáil shook his head. "He won't even draw the dogs," he remarked.

But Lynch learned fast.

In John A. Murphy's words, "He had the common touch incomparably".

The shift since the sixties, not just in Ireland but in other democracies as well, towards Presidential-style politics and electoral campaigns suited Lynch.

In these type of situations image and chemistry can be of overwhelming importance.

Many years after Lynch had departed from the political stage, the Fianna Fáil TD for Dublin West, Liam Lawlor, talked about the importance of image.

"The single most important aspect in Irish politics is the face on the poster, the leader's face. The party's hopes and aspirations are entwined with leadership, and I say to the party this issue overshadows all other considerations."

The Lynch image was good, positive, clean, manly, fair, trustworthy and sound.

The vibes emanating from it touched a chord in people who were not even Fianna Fáil supporters or voters.

Was Lynch lucky?

Yes, more than no.

In politics as in sport, the winners tend to have luck on their side. The ball runs for a winning team; they tend to get the breaks.

So also with politics.

On the other hand, Lynch would no doubt argue that, in both sport and politics, the good player, the good performer and the good team, tend to make their own luck.

There is that – and more. Always more. And indefinable.

Perhaps Con Houlihan's observation comes nearest the truth: "We all need father-figures".

Lynch was one of the nation's great father figures. And if not a father-figure, then an uncle-figure, because he projected that warm, avuncular image which made us all feel protected and wanted and safe.

It worked only part of the time, of course.

But when it worked it was pure magic.

Jack Lynch with Dr James Kavanagh – Auxiliary Bishop of Dublin

11. A Fan in the White House

Sport meant a lot to Richard Nixon, as it did to Jack Lynch. One day in The White House – the year was 1971 – while officials waited, the US President attempted to explain the rules and techniques of American football to the Irish Prime Minister.

That same Prime Minister – Nixon had difficulty with the Irish word "Taoiseach" – might well have made a good quarterback or running back.

So said the President of the United States to aides afterwards.

"He's quite a guy," he told Henry Kissinger.

And he was right about Jack Lynch.

At the time the compliment wouldn't have meant much to an Irish audience. But these days – thanks to television – the name of Joe Montana or Bo Jackson is almost as well-known as that of Kevin Moran or Larry Tompkins or Nicky English.

Back in early 1971 – when Lynch first met Nixon in Washington – the names on both sides of the Atlantic would have been different.

The previous All-Irelands (September 1970) in hurling and football had been won respectively by Cork and Kerry, powered by players like Ray Cummins, John Horgan and Willie Walsh (for Cork), and John O'Keeffe, Mick O'Connell and Mick O'Dwyer (for Kerry).

Over in the States in 1971 the Dallas Cowboys and the Baltimore Colts battled for the Superbowl title. And among the headliners in American football that year were names such as O.J. Simpson, Roger Staubach and Joe Namath.

Sport was a common thread running through the relationships Lynch had with the six American Presidents he met – Kennedy, Johnson, Nixon, Ford, Carter and Reagan.

It mattered most to Kennedy, coming as he did from an intensely competitive family where winning – in whatever arena – was paramount.

JFK's father, Joseph Kennedy, once remarked that "second best is a loser".

And that was very much the Kennedy philosophy.

It wasn't Lynch's – ever, which is not to say that winning didn't matter to him.

It did – but not at any price.

On the hurling and football fields he never took an opponent out deliberately, but he knew how to look after himself. If an opponent tried the dirt on him, he usually came off second best.

His Glen and Cork team-mate, Dr Jim Young, says Lynch was the fastest big man he ever met.

"He had some punch. I think he could have made it as a heavyweight boxer. He was a natural athlete."

The late Donal Foley, who was news editor of the *Irish Times*, used to tell the story of the day he played for Waterford against Cork, when he was marking Lynch.

When the first ball came between them, Foley pulled across Lynch. The next time the ball came in, Lynch pulled up Foley's hurley, skinning all his knuckles.

Con Murphy, former President of the GAA, and Lynch's colleague on two All-Ireland winning Cork teams in the 1940s, once told me of an incident in a game between Cork and Limerick.

John Mackey was playing full-forward on Murphy, who was fullback for Cork. Lynch was having a "blinder" at centrefield, and Mackey decided to go out and do something about it.

Five minutes later he came back into the square with a bloody nose.

"What happened you?" asked Murphy.

"Lynch hit me," replied Mackey.

"What happened?"

"He told me I had no business out around the middle of the field."

"Serves you right," said a smiling Murphy.

Even when his own playing days were over, sport continued to play a big part in Lynch's life.

Paddy "Chancer" Barry recalled how Lynch once kept one of the most powerful men in the United States – the Postmaster General, Jim Farley – waiting, because he wanted to see a hurling match in Gaelic Park, New York.

"Getting an appointment with Farley was a big deal, but he had to change it for Lynch because Jack refused to miss the match. The people around Farley could hardly believe it."

And on another occasion the British Prime Minister, Edward Heath, had to re-schedule a meeting with Lynch because of an All-Ireland Final.

Sean Donlon, who worked closely with Lynch when he was in the Department of Foreign Affairs and later as Ambassador to Washington, said Heath and the officials at 10 Downing Street wanted Lynch to travel to London on the first Sunday in September.

But Jack refused. "Tell them there's an All-Ireland Final on, and that I'll travel on the Monday."

It may surprise some to learn that Lynch admired Nixon. In fact, Nixon, more than any of the other American Presidents he met, impressed him.

In this context, Kennedy doesn't really count, because Lynch never really had a chance to get to know him.

They had that one brief meeting in Dublin in the summer of 1963; that was all.

Had that awful day of 22 November 1963 not happened, things might have been very different.

A Kennedy White House would have suited Lynch. He would have felt at home there.

Ireland and sport would have been the twin over-lapping themes. What an ambience that would have created!

And what stories might have been told in the Oval Office!

"Ring's *gaisce* in 1946 . . ."

"Excuse me, Taoiseach, but what is a *gaisce* . . . ?"

It was never to be.

Nixon, Kennedy's adversary in 1960, struck up a quick and genuine relationship with Lynch.

Standing in the Rose Garden in the grounds of The White House on the eve of St Patrick's Day 1990 – waiting for President George Bush to receive a bowl of shamrock from the then Minister for Defence, Brian Lenihan – Sean Cronin, the US correspondent for the *Irish Times,* confirmed this to me.

"Nixon is a great lover of spectator sports, and admires sports figures. Among leaders of Governments I don't know of one who matches Jack Lynch as an athlete. Nixon referred to this in a dinner speech, once. That was a genuine feeling on Nixon's part."

Cronin said he felt Nixon's inordinate admiration for outstanding athletes was due to the fact that he himself was a puny, sickly youth at school, and not very good at sports.

"He was a bit of a weakling. Consequently, he tended to hold superb athletes in very high regard, and to have a lot of respect for them.

"He was very well briefed on Jack Lynch. And so the rapport between them was very good almost from the first moment they met.

"Nixon genuinely liked Lynch and had time for him because of his prowess at sport – that wouldn't have been true of any other leader. They talked about sport a lot."

Lynch's regard for Nixon, on the other hand, was based on other things.

"His grasp of world affairs was better than any other President's of the ones I have met, that is," says Lynch.

"And he also had a better understanding of the Irish situation, both in terms of historical background, and what was currently happening."

Lynch, who went through his own Armsgate – admits to being puzzled by Nixon's handling of the Watergate scandal.

"I think if he had been upfront about it when it broke, he would have survived . . . "

Sport served as an icebreaker for him with the other Presidents as well, though Jimmy Carter, who was in The White House when Fianna Fáil returned to power in 1977, wasn't into it in any big way.

"I have always felt that our sportsmen have been our best ambassadors abroad," says Lynch.

"The goodwill that can be generated by sport is immeasurable. Sport knows no bounds."

Jack was as proud as the rest of the nation of the achievements of the other Jack and the Irish team in the 1990 World Cup in Italy.

"I always say that when it comes to sports my tastes are catholic with a small 'c'," he adds with a grin.

"Though I cede ground to no one in my conviction that hurling remains the greatest field game in the world."

Kennedy, Johnson, Nixon, Ford, Carter, Reagan *et al.*, might not agree.

But then they weren't at Croke Park in 1946 when Lynch, Ring, Young, Lotty, Kelly *et al.*, demolished Kilkenny.

Mind you, it wasn't just in the august surrounds of The White House that the mix of sport and politics surfaced in an unusual way in Lynch's life.

In the twilight of his inter-county career as a hurler, when he was a TD, he played corner forward for Cork against Tipperary on a day when Tony Reddan was having an inspired game in goal.

Reddan, widely regarded as the greatest goalkeeper of all time, suffered from a speech impediment. Half-way through the second half, with the Cork forwards frustrated, Willie John Daly, who was half-forward for Cork, ran into Lynch.

"Will you get into the square and do something about Reddan, he's breaking our hearts. Give him a dig or a box of the hurley, but knock some of the gizz out of him."

Lynch nodded. "Right. Here's what you'll do. Next time you get a ball out around the middle of the field, lob a high one into the square, and I'll take care of Reddan."

Sure enough, four or five minutes later Daly got possession and floated a high ball into the Tipperary square.

Reddan was standing under the dropping ball, waiting to grab it, when Lynch came charging in from the left.

The Tipperary keeper saw him coming from the corner of his eye, grabbed the ball, neatly side-stepped the charging Lynch, and cleared the ball out the field.

The latter missed the tackle and finished up in the back of the net.

As Lynch was picking himself up, Reddan, angry, turned to him.

"F-f-fuck you Lynch," he shouted. "The next f-f-fucking time you try that there'll be an early f-f-fucking by-election in Cork!"

12. The Poll-Topper

"Political prognostication is a hazardous business, in spite of the fact that Fianna Fáil, mainly through the popularity of Mr Lynch, seems to have consolidated its position in recent times..... "

I wrote these words in June 1969 as part of a team headed by political correspondent, Michael Mills, chosen to cover the General Election for the *Irish Press.*

That year I shared a "first" with Jack Lynch: the 1969 Election was his first since becoming Taoiseach in 1966, and my first as a reporter (I joined the *Press* in 1967).

As Leader of Fianna Fáil, Lynch contested three General Elections – 1969, 1973 and 1977 – winning two, and narrowly losing the 1973 one.

In those three electoral contests he established his reputation as the greatest vote-catcher, the most popular politician Ireland has seen since Independence.

That popularity was built on multiple bases, including what became known in 1969 as "the Reverend Mother circuit".

This passage from a report by Michael Mills in the *Irish Press* encapsulates an important facet of the 1969 campaign: "In Waterford yesterday the local Fianna Fáil organisers brought the Taoiseach and Mrs Lynch on a tour of the city to meet the people. They called at two convents and chatted with the nuns and the children . . . Mr Lynch later went to a supermarket to buy a packet of blades before leaving for Cashel . . . "

And later: "Scarcely a town is visited but the local convent is on the Taoiseach's schedule . . "

A few days afterwards Mills had this to say: "Mr Lynch is a different man when he gets away from his government functions. His manner becomes easier and he is more at home with people. They come up to shake his hand in the streets, lorry drivers wave to him as they pass, and mothers bring up their children to be introduced".

And here is Mills on 6 June 1969 on Jack's way with hecklers: "The Taoiseach is developing a nice technique in dealing with hecklers. He does not give a short answer; he treats their questions seriously. When the Gardai move in on a heckler, he says 'Leave him alone, sergeant. He is not offensive. I will answer any question he has to ask.'

"But the sergeant is not worried about the Taoiseach so much as the well-being of the heckler. There are a couple of local farmers moving in steadily on the man . . . "

In Longford, when a heckler made a derogatory remark about the President, Mills tells us the Taoiseach's fire was up.

"If it were not for Mr de Valera and people like him, neither himself nor the heckler might have the democratic right to speak," Lynch pointed out.

But the convent circuit was the thing. "If prayers could win an election, Fianna Fáil would be home in a canter," wrote Mills on 12 June 1969. "They must have nearly every convent in the country behind them . . . "

It worked. And how!

A close struggle had been forecast, but in the end Fianna Fáil took 74 seats (a gain of two since 1965), with 50 for Fine Gael, 18 for Labour and one Independent.

But if the convent circuit helped Fianna Fáil, so did the "Red Scare".

The Labour Party under Brendan Corish had come out in true socialist colours for the 1969 election, with the promise that the "seventies would be socialist".

This was blatantly exploited by Fianna Fáil, with allegations that the Labour leaders were admirers of Castro's Cuba, that they were crypto-Communists and such like.

Haughey and Blaney set the tone in this regard, though one must assume with the tacit approval of Lynch.

It was the most distasteful aspect of the campaign, and reflected no credit on those responsible.

For Lynch the 1969 result was very important, and consolidated his position as party leader.

"The scale of Lynch's victory in the 1969 election left his rivals restless," concluded Joe Lee. "He could no longer be dismissed as an interim party leader, a mere stop-gap while the heirs apparent, and semi-apparent, fought out the real battle between themselves. They could now anticipate long years of thwarted ambition."

Professor John A. Murphy had this to say: "The star of the 1969 election was Jack Lynch who conducted an American presidential type campaign. He had already four by-elections to his credit but the general election, against all the predictions, was a resounding personal victory, not only over the opponents of Fianna Fáil but over his own ambitious lieutenants, some of whom had condescendingly regarded him as a mere caretaker."

Some caretaker.

Lynch was now Taoiseach in his own right, with his own mandate.

Writing in February 1973, in an article to mark Lynch's 25 years as a TD, Liam O'Neill, now the political editor of the *Cork Examiner*, put the result into context.

"He had not been a unanimous choice as Taoiseach . . . But the 1969 general election changed all that. Thanks mainly to a strong personal campaign by Mr Lynch, Fianna Fáil were returned to office with an enhanced majority.

"He was now Taoiseach in his own right, with the support of the majority of the people, and free to put his own stamp on the office."

And within a year, any doubts that he wasn't his own man, or that he was weak, would be very firmly, indeed brutally, scotched.

Here is Lee again: "The Northern crisis provided his rivals with the ideal issue on which to mobilise the party rank and file against a leader who could be portrayed as reneging on the founding aims of the party. But Lynch skillfully mobilised the issues of party unity, and of loyalty to the leader, to outmanoeuvre not only the vociferous Blaney and Boland, but the craftier Haughey, who emerged as the most dangerous threat of all".

The 1969 election put Lynch beyond their reach, but as events unfolded, they showed the accuracy of the predictions made by some Opposition deputies back in 1966 on the day Lynch was elected Taoiseach in the Dáil in succession to Lemass.

Although Lynch and Fianna Fáil were to lose in 1973, their performance was impressive in the circumstances. And that election, as I will show later, should not have taken place at all.

It was originally planned for December 1972. The two bombs which exploded in the centre of Dublin on 1 December 1972 killing two men and injuring 127 other people – put paid to those plans.

A number of events of direct electoral significance had occurred in the 1969-73 period.

Ireland's application for membership of the EEC, originally made in 1961 and re-activated in 1967, was renewed again after the resignation of de Gaulle in June 1969, together with the UK, Denmark and Norway.

Negotiations were reopened late in 1969 and continued *pari pasu* until 1972, when Ireland signed the Treaty of Rome.

On 10 May 1972 a referendum to amend the Article in the Constitution (which vested legislative power solely in the Oireachtas) was held, with the people overwhelmingly supporting the move to join the EEC.

Meanwhile, in Northern Ireland there had been alarming developments, and in December 1969 a convention of Sinn Féin resulted in a schism in the movement, and the birth of the Provisional IRA.

What happened next has been pithily described by Cornelius O'Leary: "It was common knowledge, during the lull of early 1970, that arms for the Provisionals were coming into Ireland from American sympathisers. But the country was staggered by the sequence of events in the first two weeks of May.

"First, on 5 May, the Minister for Justice resigned for health reasons. Then, on 7 May, the Taoiseach announced that he had dismissed two of his most powerful Ministers, Charles Haughey, Minister for Finance, and Neil Blaney, Minister for Agriculture, for alleged involvement in the illegal importation of arms.

"A thunderstruck Dáil was informed by Lynch that the two ex-Ministers would stand trial for this alleged criminal offence. On the same day, Kevin Boland resigned as Minister for Local Government, out of sympathy for Blaney and Haughey, and on 8 May he was followed by his Parliamentary Secretary, Padge Brennan.

"After the 1971 Árd Fheis it was clear that the existing leadership had survived, but at a high price in internal party dissension," notes O'Leary.

These were difficult years for Lynch, and the 1972 Budget, introduced by George Colley – which has since come to be regarded as an exercise in irresponsible financial management – was designed to set the scene for victory in the election which Lynch eventually called, for 28 February 1973.

The North featured only in a marginal way in the campaign, and the performance of Dr Garret Fitzgerald in a television debate with George Colley on the economy was undoubtedly influential.

Fianna Fáil lost – but only just, despite all the difficulties and problems from 1969 to 1973, including the debilitating wrangles caused by the Arms Crisis.

"It says much for Lynch's skill as a party manager that Fianna Fáil would almost certainly have won, despite all the traumas of the previous four years, but for the electoral pact, based on a fourteen-point manifesto containing promises for virtually everyone," says Professor Lee.

In fact, Fianna Fáil actually increased its share of the popular vote, but the vagaries of PR meant a loss of six seats.

In Bruce Arnold's judgement, it was an honourable defeat.

"Lynch's electoral performance in 1973 was remarkable. He regarded it himself as his greatest electoral achievement, outclassing the twenty-seat majority achieved in 1977."

That 1977 result was astonishing. "There has been nothing like it in Irish electoral history," wrote Vincent Browne in the *Sunday Independent*. "Never has there been such a swing to a political party and never has a single party commanded so many seats in Dáil Éireann."

It marked the apogee of Lynch's career, both in party and in personal terms.

In Cork City (which was a five-seater in 1977) Lynch polled 20,077 first preference votes, two-and-a-half times the quota (8,577) and the largest personal vote ever in Irish politics.

None of his predecessors, not even Dev in his heyday, had ever matched this performance.

And his achievement is all the more remarkable when one considers that his successor, Charles J. Haughey, was unable, in five successive Elections to lead Fianna Fáil to an outright majority in the Dáil.

The 1977 landslide was all the more noteworthy because it happened at a time and in circumstances when the political pundits (without exception) were forecasting a "photo finish".

The result led one journalist to remark that "Lynch has again proved himself to be the most charismatic personality since De Valera".

The National Coalition (Fine Gael and Labour) had been in power for four years (1973-77), and it was generally agreed in the post-mortems afterwards that its emphasis on the North and law and order, had backfired badly.

The Fianna Fáil emphasis was on jobs, taxation, rates, youth and women.

The emphasis on the latter was well received.

In the *Irish Times*, Christina Murphy wrote: "Mary Harney and Síle de Valera, incidentally, are outstanding examples of the success of Jack Lynch's imposition of six un-nominated women on constituencies. Síle de Valera was elected (in Mid-County Dublin) with a whooping 6,000 first preferences on her first time out. Mary Harney was a total newcomer to Dublin South-East and literally, in less than two weeks of campaigning polled 1,500 votes . . . "

Lynch later rewarded her by including her in his nominees to Seanad Eireann.

"There is no doubt about it," said Hilary Pratt, chairwoman of the Women's Political Association. "Fianna Fáil paid more attention to the women's vote and gained from it. And we are sure that Fine Gael lost out badly because of Liam Cosgrave's ostrich-like attitude to women.

Fianna Fáil ran the most women candidates – ten – and ran advertisements in the papers accusing the Coalition of discrimination against women and treating them as second-class citizens.

It was a factor that tended to be overlooked in the aftermath, when the emphasis was on the "Manifesto of Promises", as one journalist termed it.

One factor which was not overlooked was the personality and popularity of Lynch himself.

"At one level it is easy to understand Lynch's personal popularity," wrote political scientist Maurice Manning afterwards, in an analysis of the result.

"His early prowess as a hurling star for his native Cork had made him a popular hero. Even more important were his personal qualities – great charm and courtesy, an easy and friendly manner, an ability to appear equally relaxed in a pub, at a football match, or in a shopping centre chatting with housewives.

"But these qualities do not explain how he arrived at the top of a most competitive and professional political party against a series of tough and able rivals – and how he stayed there through twelve extremely difficult years . . ."

Even today it is not easy to provide a solid explanation.

In June 1977 Lynch was back on top.

But how long would he remain there?

Given the size of his majority, not very many people would have given you a decent bet that he would be gone within two-and- a-half years.

Vincent Browne, not for the first time, showed prescience, when he wrote: "For Fianna Fáil, the riches of 84 seats is an embarrassment. How can the recalcitrant element in the party be contained with such a huge majority?"

The massive majority was to prove a millstone around the new Taoiseach's neck.

The day of reckoning lay ahead, closer than anyone could have realised in 1977.

Indeed, there had been predictions that, with another election unlikely until 1981, Fianna Fáil could be in power until the mid-1990s.

Looking back, it was a case of what might have been.

Despite the rumblings of discontent, rumblings which were quite loud by 1979, Jack Lynch could have held on.

"He had ten, twenty people at the most who would have come out openly against him," says Dick Walsh. "He could have handled that."

Raymond Smith's conjecture is interesting.

"I am convinced that if Jack Lynch had decided to go to the country, instead of allowing the two by-elections in Cork to go ahead, he could have retained power, thus confirming his control over the Parliamentary Party. He could have out-flanked those who had so carefully planned to accelerate his resignation. I believe also that he would have had a much better chance of seeing George Colley emerge as his successor.

"Jack Lynch needed only to have stayed a year, or six months if he so wished after winning the General Election."

Smith, in his 1986 book *The Quest for Power*, recalls that Peter Prendergast, Government Press Secretary in Garret Fitzgerald's Administrations, thought in 1977 that Fianna Fáil might be in power for two terms before Fine Gael could make the big breakthrough.

He was thinking in terms of 1985 – that is eight years from 1977.

"He never believed that victory would come as early as 1981," says Smith. "If Haughey came so close to victory in 1981, could it not be argued that Jack Lynch, with his far greater popularity in the country, must surely have won in November 1979?"

It could indeed.

Smith says it will remain one of the great imponderables of Irish political history whether Lynch would have gone at that point, if he had thought that Charles Haughey would emerge as leader in his place.

This has ceased to be an "imponderable": Lynch would not have moved if he could have foreseen the outcome.

There is not the slightest doubt about that now.

As Smith himself says, he was "convinced he was handing on the torch to the then Tanaiste, George Colley".

Dick Walsh concurs: "Colley and O'Donoghue advised him that a quick contest would suit them best and, on 5 December, a month earlier than he had planned, he announced his departure".

But for that advice, he would have stayed at the helm.

That is the simple truth.

And the greatest vote-getter in modern Irish electoral history had all the cards necessary to ensure victory.

Despite the discordant voices on the backbenches, Lynch held a handful of aces.

But he threw in his hand.

How he won that powerful hand in 1977 remains one of the most contentious episodes in Irish politics.

President Hillery and Taoiseach Jack Lynch with his Ministers – 1977

13. The SIS Connection

Thanks mainly to Hollywood and the James Bond novels, the world of espionage, of spies, secret agents and Intelligence Services such as the CIA, the KGB, M15, MI6, and Mossad, is perceived as glamourous, exciting and daring, and the ideal setting for the romantic hero.

The reality is a good deal more sordid and sinister. Those who engage in "cloak and dagger" activities in real life are the very antithesis of the romantic hero.

Since the outbreak of the Northern "troubles" in 1968, such types have been active in Ireland, both North and South.

Their nefarious activities may well have cost Jack Lynch an extra term in office as Taoiseach.

It happened in 1972.

The full story of the two bombs which exploded in the centre of Dublin on 1 December of that year may never be known.

There is no shortage of theories about the blasts – one outside Liberty Hall and one in Marlborough Street – which killed two people and injured 127 others.

What is clear is that these terrible events dramatically changed the course of a crisis in the Dáil – a crisis which would almost certainly have led to the toppling of Liam Cosgrave from the leadership of Fine Gael, disarray within the Party, and victory for Fianna Fáil in the resulting General Election.

The crisis had arisen over a move by Dessie O'Malley, Minister for Justice in the Lynch Government, to introduce an amendment to the Offences Against the State Act.

The debate was extremely contentious. Fine Gael and Labour, plus a number of Independent deputies, including Neil Blaney, were opposed to the Bill.

The Government was staring defeat in the face. And the prospect of an election before Christmas was looming large.

The problem on the Fine Gael side was that although the Parliamentary Party had decided to oppose the new Bill, Cosgrave was determined to support it.

James Downey summed up the situation: "The Fine Gael left assumed that he would then have to resign the leadership. Lynch, for his part, had made up his mind to call a snap general election and fight it on two gold-plated issues: law and order and a divided opposition."

If that scenario had gone ahead, the political pundits are in agreement that Fianna Fáil would have won, and probably with a handsome majority.

Lynch concurs: "This would have been a propitious time for us to go to the country . . . It was my intention to call a general election immediately after the debate . . ."

The two bombs changed everything.

When news of the explosions reached Leinster House, Fine Gael deputies rallied behind Cosgrave and abstained.

Tom O'Higgins was actually on his feet in the Dáil when the bombs exploded, and the crump of the second bomb could be heard quite clearly in the Chamber as he spoke against the Bill.

He was still on his feet minutes later as ambulances could be heard rushing to the scenes of the explosions.

The Bill became law by 69 votes to 22 at 4.00a.m. on 2 December.

The crisis had passed. The threat of a snap General Election had receded.

Lynch eventually called an election for the following February.

By then the situation had changed. And the suddenness of the dissolution, plus the fact that only three weeks were allowed for campaigning, acted as a spur to Fine Gael and Labour.

Differences were set aside, and the parties arranged a pact with each other.

They came together to formulate a "Statement of Intent", in effect, a joint electoral manifesto, which was to prove crucial.

Polling day was 28 February, and for the first time in 16 years Fianna Fáil found itself out of office.

But for the bombs, the story might have been very different.

Who planted them?

The theory persists to this day that the explosions were the work of elements within the British Secret Intelligence Services (SIS), though the finger had also been pointed at the UVF.

In late 1973 Lynch was reported in newspapers as having a "suspicion" that the bombings were the work of British intelligence agents.

When I asked him about this, he said he had merely become aware of these suspicions.

"I never had a scintilla of evidence, beyond the rumours which I heard," he told me.

Martin Dillon, in his 1988 book *The Dirty War*, points to a UDA/UVF involvement, and says:

"If the former Taoiseach, Jack Lynch, and other prominent Irish politicians had carefully examined the evidence . . I believe they would not have hinted at British Intelligence involvement."

Whatever about that – and Lynch would say he never claimed the bombs were the work of the SIS – he could claim that the incidents led to the postponement of an election which he would have certainly won.

Fianna Fáil would have been returned to power on a fifth consecutive occasion – and Jack Lynch might never have become Leader of the Opposition!

It was while in opposition that there occurred a second event in Lynch's career which had an SIS dimension to it.

It is remembered today as the "Littlejohn affair".

In terms of the Lynch story, the affair is of little consequence other than that it was the occasion prior to his definitive decision in 1977 when Lynch considered resignation."

And it was all due to a lapse of memory.

The two Littlejohn brothers – Keith and Kenneth – operated for the SIS from 1970 onwards, part of the time in Ireland where they were under instructions to infiltrate the IRA.

They were imprisoned in Dublin in August 1973 for a bank robbery, having been extradited as part of a secret deal between the British and Irish Governments.

The deal involved the transfer to Britain of a British agent in Dublin, John Wyman and Patrick Crinion of the Irish Special Branch, who was his operative. Both were in custody in Dublin at the time.

The Littlejohn case caused problems for Anglo-Irish relations, not least because the brothers claimed they had contacts with British Defence Minister, Lord Carrington, and a Junior Minister.

In the midst of it all, Lynch was embarrassed when he said he "forgot" that he had been informed of the British Government's involvement with the Littlejohns.

"When the Littlejohn affair arose in July 1973, I felt my position had been compromised to the extent that I should reconsider my position as leader of Fianna Fáil.

"It had quite escaped my mind that I had been informed that a Junior British Minister had had some contact with the Littlejohn brothers before they came to Ireland.

"The information was passed to me almost as I was boarding a plane for America, and I had simply directed that the papers be handed over to the relevant Minister to let him deal with the matter."

However, a groundswell of sentiment urging him to carry on convinced him that he should lead the party into the next election.

Nevertheless, as Garret Fitzgerald pointed out to me, the episode weakened Lynch, and focused certain minds within Fianna Fáil on the possibility of replacing him.

Indeed, it is not too fanciful to claim that the "campaign" to force Lynch to resign can be traced back to the murky activities of a couple of British agents in Ireland.

Henceforth, Lynch's enemies would be waiting in the long grass.

The snipers were in place.

Jack Lynch with Senator Edward Kennedy, Irish Ambassador John Molloy and Speaker "Tip" O'Neill

14. Into Europe

In David Hare's 1989 political thriller *Paris By Night* there is a scene in which Euro MP Clara Paige (played by that beautiful actress, Charlotte Rampling) seeks to assure a group of constituents about the relevance of the European Parliament.

"I know what you're thinking. 'What has this European Parliament which is miles away in Strasbourg got to do with me?'

"The Parliament embodies an ideal – peace and prosperity in Europe. And this is something in which we all believe," says Clara. If the history of Europe in the twentieth century teaches us anything it is surely that the realisation of this ideal is a most desirable objective.

It may, at first glance, seem a far-fetched and even preposterous claim, but the person responsible for the present movement towards a "United States of Europe" is none other than the Führer of Nazi Germany.

Adolf Hitler is the real architect of the European Community.

This is, of course, a tragic paradox - but true nevertheless.

The horrific destruction wrought across the European mainland in 1939-45 – for which he as Führer of the German people, bears the primary responsibility – created in the minds and hearts of men and women a longing for a political order in which this nightmare could never again recur.

Of course, the origins of the concept of European unity can be traced back, according to some scholars, to the First World War (1914-18).

Its totally new scale of senseless slaughter led to a determination on the part of some statesmen to find political structures which would prevent such bloodletting ever again in Europe.

It was Aristide Briand, French Foreign Minister in the 1920s, who first coined the phrase "Common Market".

In 1929 he put forward a scheme for European Union to the League of Nations. It was, however, deemed to be too vague, and it was overtaken by events, particularly, after the death of Briand himself in 1932, the rise of Nazism.

"It was the impact of the Second World War which really stimulated genuine moves towards European integration," writes Keith Perry in his *Modern World History.*

The devastation and dreadful horrors of World War II created the necessary political will for moves to be made towards greater co-operation in a rebuilt Europe.

Three of the key figures in the vanguard of the movement towards European integration in the post-1945 situation were devout Catholics who shared a deep loathing for the internecine in Europe since 1914.

They were Konrad Adenauer, who became Chancellor of West Germany; Alcide de Gasparri, who became Prime Minister of Italy after 1945, and Robert Schuman, who served as Prime Minister of France.

But, as Keith Perry has emphasised, special mention should be made of Jean Monnet, the French economist and public servant, who died in 1979.

"He was more responsible than any other man for bringing the nations of Europe together in the Common Market, and his ultimate aim was a truly united Europe," writes Perry.

A key stepping-stone in the process was the creation of a "club" of nation-states in which their interests and their prosperity and well-being would be interlinked.

Initially, that "well-being" was conceived very largely in economic terms.

And when Lemass and then Lynch undertook the task of negotiating entry to the EEC, the initial motivation was undoubtedly economic.

The wider vision and aims were never lost sight of however.

Not all statesmen thought in those terms.

But some-did. And from the very outset both Lemass and Lynch were prepared to think in terms of a fuller European integration, and what that might mean for Ireland.

In Britain too, for instance, the initial hesitancy was not shared by all leading political figures.

The desire to ensure peace in Europe was the predominant consideration for some.

This approach was best exemplified by a man who played an important role in Northern Ireland and in the preparations for the Sunningdale Agreement.

The first Secretary of State for Northern Ireland, William Whitelaw, outlined this approach in his *Memoirs.*

"Personally, my strong support for joining Europe was based more on broad foreign policy than on economic grounds. Having lived through the 1939-45 war, I was desperately keen to ensure that no further world wars would start through quarrels in Western Europe.

"European unity, embracing France and Germany in particular, provides a major insurance against such an eventuality . . . I only hope that the great gains of a united Europe will not be submerged in petty disagreements about economic details."

Here in Ireland, the first approaches for membership of the European "club" were couched overwhelmingly in economic terms.

The burden of negotiating our membership of the EEC (as it was then known) fell on the shoulders of Lynch.

And, as one civil servant has pointed out to me, it is worth making the point that while he was shouldering this responsibility, he was also contending with the problems of Northern Ireland – and with a Taoiseach's Department which, in terms of staffing levels and ready expertise, bears no relation to the greatly expanded units that were the creations of Dr Fitzgerald and, in particular, Charles Haughey.

Ireland's first application for membership was made in July 1961, and the formal presentation of our application was made by Sean Lemass in January 1962.

The British negotiations proceeded from about that time while the Irish negotiations and those of Denmark and Norway were held in abeyance pending progress with Britain.

"However, a year later, almost to the day," recalls Lynch, "de Gaulle effectively pronounced his veto on the British negotiations, and so negotiations with all four applicant countries were more or less suspended.

"They were not re-activated until mid-1967 and these led to the accession of three of the four applicant nations in 1973 – Norway having by popular referendum refused to accede."

As bells all over Ireland "rang in" the New Year of 1973, they were also heralding a new era for this country.

On 1 January 1973, along with Denmark and Britain, Ireland joined the European Economic Community.

The referendum to prepare the way for entry into Europe had been held on 10 May 1972.

The vote in favour was almost five to one, and as Taoiseach a delighted Lynch said that the extent of the victory had exceeded his expectations.

Equally importantly, he has always maintained that the Irish people knew exactly what they were voting for.

"The issue was never fudged," he would say later.

Speaking at a conference in Blarney, County Cork, in April 1985, Lynch left no doubt that the implications of membership were fully appreciated from day one.

"At the outset, the original six envisaged, in the very first article of the Rome Treaty, that the purpose of the exercise was ultimate European union – this is political union so as to ensure as far as possible that war between European countries would never happen again.

"Therefore it was inherent and explicit from the outset that the Community we were joining had, as its ultimate objective, the political union of the member countries which formed it."

Lynch emphasised that Lemass made it quite clear that he realised and accepted the political commitment and consequences of Ireland's membership.

"In July 1962 he stated unequivocally that a defence commitment would be an inevitable consequence of our joining the Common Market.

"When we re-activated our application in 1967, I stated equally unequivocally that, while the immediate purpose of our application was to be part of a Common Market, we recognised that by joining we were becoming part of a wider European Community, and that as part of that Community we recognised our obligations in the event of the Community having to defend itself."

Referring to the 1972 referendum, Lynch said he was satisfied that when the Irish people voted on that occasion there was "no ambiguity in their minds as to how membership affected our sovereignty or our attitude to neutrality".

He was to repeat this on several other occasions, most notably at a special one-day seminar on "Ireland – Europe in the 1990s" organised by the *Cork Examiner* and held at UCC on 2 January 1991.

"We went in with our eyes open," he said at that seminar. "We knew exactly what we were doing, and there was no hidden agenda."

It is a fair bet – though Jack Lynch is not a betting man – that one of the key issues of Irish political life between now and the year 2000 will be neutrality.

Ever since Ireland joined the Common Market (as it was then called) in 1972, the issue of neutrality and all that it implies has been moving more and more centre-stage in terms of political debate. One might also say in terms of political dynamite, though that would be considered an ill-chosen phrase in some quarters, or one that might be misconstrued.

To persist with the metaphor, it could be argued that neutrality has been lying like a ticking time-bomb at the heart of Irish politics over the last decade.

And because of the Gulf War, the ticking mechanism has speeded up.

Sooner or later the neutrality issue will explode in our faces – unless our political leaders act to defuse the whole matter.

Lynch has consistently tried to do that.

Even if there had never been a Gulf War, the trend of events in Europe since the Treaty of Rome was signed by the original six member-states on 28 March 1957, has been moving inexorably in a direction destined to collide head-on with our traditional policy of neutrality.

Jack Lynch saw that from the outset, just as his predecessor Sean Lemass did. Further back than most of his contemporaries, Lynch saw and understood the implications of what he was doing when, on 22 January 1972, he signed the Treaty of Accession (the referendum consequent on this followed in May, and our membership became effective on 1 January 1973) .

Others saw this as well.

Speaking in London in June 1991, one of our most committed Europeans, Dr Garret Fitzgerald, said he believed Ireland would not risk "secondary status" by opting out of a European Defence Pact.

"No Irish Government would risk being relegated to a second tier by opting out of defence arrangements."

He could have been reading from a Jack Lynch script.

The latter has repeatedly contended that for Ireland to stay out of the EC would have been a mistake of immense proportions and unforeseeable consequences.

We'd have been isolated on the edge of Europe – forever condemned to be outsiders.

Lynch also saw that involvement in Europe – as John Hume has again and again emphasised – would change the context of the Northern Ireland situation.

The "totality of relationships" binding the islands of Ireland and Britain together – and also at the same time, complicating and occasionally poisoning Anglo-Irish relations – would take on a new meaning in a new Europe.

The full fruits of that have yet to be seen. But the more Europe draws together, the more unreal and unsustainable will become the divisions, traditions, myths, cultures and politics which are causing communal disharmony, suspicion, fear, mistrust and conflict on this small island of five million souls.

Lynch was far-seeing enough to appreciate this.

In the judgement of Vincent Browne, now Editor of the *Sunday Tribune:* "His most significant achievement was to steer Ireland into the EEC".

That judgement will stand the test of time.

Taoiseach Jack Lynch and President de Gaulle at the Elysee Palace (1967)

15. Auction Politics

Did Jack Lynch introduce "auction politics" to Ireland? Did he try to buy his way back into power in 1977 with what one commentator has termed the "Manifesto of Promises"?

Did he tempt the electorate with what one of our most eminent historians has termed the "Crock of Gold", or what has been described by a leading political commentator as "an Aladdin's cave of bribes"?

Opinion, as one might expect, is sharply divided on this.

Lynch continues to defend the 1977 Manifesto.

But then, as Mandy Rice-Davies said in reference to a Tory politician on a famous occasion: "He would, wouldn't he?"

Was it a gimmick to win?

That's the conventional wisdom.

However, Dick Walsh of the *Irish Times* recalls an interesting meeting with George Colley, Tanaiste and Minister for Finance in the 1977-79 Government, who died in a London hospital on 17 September 1983.

"I remember meeting him on the eve of the 1977 Election on the lawn of Leinster House and, in a reference to the Manifesto, he said the whole thing was designed to ensure that Fianna Fáil didn't go down too badly. He didn't expect to win . . !"

And in Foxrock, as the polling stations were closing, Kevin Healy, then with the RTE "This Week" team, recalls meeting a gloomy Martin O'Donoghue, who thought Fianna Fáil were not going to make it.

Dr O'Donoghue disputes this, pointing out that the Party's own internal polls indicated they were going to win comfortably. However, he admits he may have been putting on a bit of an act in public so as not to appear over-confident.

Entitled "Strategy for National Construction", the Manifesto concentrated on three major issues – prices, unemployment and youth.

The document made very substantial promises, and included an ambitious job creation programme supported by a specific pre-judgement on Lynch's part that any Government in Ireland allowing unemployment to rise above 100,000 deserved to be rejected by the people.

In passing, one is left to wonder what might happen if that criterion were applicable today.

It also promised grants for new householders, the abolition of rates on all private dwellings from the beginning of 1978, the abolition of road tax on cars up to 16 horse power, and increased tax allowances.

More importantly, it made assumptions about trends and targets which, over the following two years, went badly wrong.

Lynch and his Cabinet colleagues gambled – and lost. By way of mitigation, he can argue that his intentions were laudable.

External factors in the post-1977 period, factors outside the control of any Dublin Government, played a part in derailing the Government's economic plans.

According to Lynch, the Manifesto was "a responsible and realistic programme".

But many today now accept Bruce Arnold's verdict: "It was anything but; from it stemmed a growing tide of problems".

The Manifesto, the first ever devised by Fianna Fáil, was not the only new feature of the 1977 Election.

Lynch had managed to persuade the 1976 Árd Fheis to allow the Leader to nominate one candidate in every constituency, thus giving the party a wider range of candidate potential than in the past.

According to Cornelius O'Leary, the publication of the Fianna Fáil Manifesto effectively stole the Coalition's thunder, a fact which might well be seized on by Lynch as justification enough in purely electoral effects.

Of course, matters didn't just end after the count. And it was the knock-on effect of the Fianna Fáil electoral strategy which brought the problems and the criticism.

O'Leary highlights one other important fact. "Fianna Fáil's traditional lack of academic personnel in its ranks was rectified by the presence on its team of Professor Martin O'Donoghue, an economist from Trinity College, Dublin, who for several years had been the party's chief economic adviser."

In fact, Lynch had recruited him in 1970, and he was to play a crucial role in 1977.

O'Donoghue was a soft-spoken, fastidious, methodical academic, cool and dogged in presenting or defending policy or pursuing objectives.

To this day Lynch's admiration for him has not diminished.

And, unlike others, he steadfastly refuses to make O'Donoghue the scapegoat for what others see as the "economic ills" which stemmed from the 1977 Election.

O'Donoghue himself was elected to the Dáil in 1977, as part of the Fianna Fáil tidal wave that swept aside the Cosgrave-led Coalition.

Lynch appointed him head of a new Department of Economic Planning and Development, a Department abolished by Haughey when he succeeded as party leader and Taoiseach.

As Deaglán de Breadún has said: "Future historians will probably see him as an important social engineer in the Ireland of the 1960s and 1970s, whether as a backroom boy or an upfront Minister. They may also decide that he wasn't 'cute' enough to survive and thrive in the jungle of party politics".

The methodical mind of Martin O'Donoghue had its date with history in 1977, when he was a principal architect of the party's election Manifesto, a document which, as de Breadún has correctly observed, has since become part of the demonology of Irish politics.

O'Donoghue, no more than Lynch, does not need to be reminded that many people are under the impression that the Manifesto caused many of our ills, including the generation of a huge national debt.

He still insists today that such an impression is erroneous.

He argues that the 14-point programme hastily put together by Fine Gael and Labour in February 1973 was "the most shameful piece of auctioneering".

It is unfair, in his view, to describe the 1977 Manifesto as "the great giveaway".

"It was designed to stop the appalling mismanagement of the economy which had occurred from 1973 to 1977, and some people forget now that the highest borrowings in terms of a percentage of GNP occurred not in the post-1977 situation, but in 1975."

He pointed out that Fianna Fáil published a version of the Manifesto in the autumn of 1976, under the title "The Real Emergency".

This was when the Cosgrave-led Government had declared "a national emergency" in the aftermath of several events, including the assassination in July 1976 of the British Ambassador, Christopher Ewart-Biggs.

"We believed the real emergency was the economy, and we set out to show what we proposed to do about it."

And he says that far from criticising the early version of the Manifesto, the Opposition actually "cogged" bits of it!

"We knew we had to take action on a number of fronts, and Jack was anxious to do something about the rates, because he remembered a remark Sean Lemass once made to him: 'People pay their other taxes in sorrow, but they pay their rates in anger'."

Dr Garret Fitzgerald takes a very different view.

"In any assessment of Lynch, one must conclude that 1977 was the big negative. That election led to a mess which cost us dearly."

His successor as Leader of Fine Gael, Alan Dukes, is equally forthright. "Lynch was responsible for the economic disaster of 1977. He reduced politics to the level of a Dutch auction, and that should never be forgotten."

Fitzgerald delivered this verdict to me: "Martin went 'political'. I thought at first he would be an ideal economist, a good quantifying economist, but the party got in the way".

Garret believes that up to 1973 Lynch had been fortunate in the economic sphere – "by accident".

"When we came into power in 1973 we found the Civil Service very resistant to policy initiatives. Jack didn't push them at all."

Even though Lynch served as Minister for Finance in 1965-66 under Lemass, Fitzgerald says economics was not his scene.

"I remember Mairin when Jack became Minister for Finance, saying to me – 'Now, don't be teasing him, Garret, he knows nothing about finance'.

"And on another occasion she approached Ken Whitaker, Secretary of the Department of Finance, and pleaded with him. 'Ken, you must help Jack'."

I know Lynch still feels deeply hurt by much of the criticism levelled at him for his handling of the 1977 election.

I spoke to him in Cork in 1990 shortly after an article by Brian O'Mahony had appeared in the business pages of the *Cork Examiner*, and he was angry over it.

He quizzed me about it, and then referred me to an article entitled "Irish Economic Policy 1977-1979" which Martin O'Donoghue had written for the autumn 1990 issue of *Studies*.

O'Mahony's article contained this passage: "The cancer that has been undermining the health of this nation goes back to 1977 when one of our more revered politicians won the biggest mandate ever from the Irish people . . .

"... in truth, the real rot set in in 1972 when the Government o the day failed to balance its books for the first time in the history of the State ... "

That still rankles with the former Taoiseach.

Dr O'Donoghue, who is currently Professor of Economics at Trinity, can still contend that the 1977 Manifesto has been the subject of "wild and ill-informed comment".

Jack Lynch can point to the fact that we all tend to be wise in hindsight.

The knowledge that he might have done a disservice to the plain people of Ireland is very difficult for him to stomach.

"It is convenient now for Garret Fitzgerald to blame me for subsequent economic problems."

Somebody once said there are lies, damned lies and statistics. And economists like Fitzgerald and O'Donoghue can go on tossing sheafs of figures and statistics at each other.

O'Donoghue rejects the late John Kelly's conclusion that by 1980 "Fianna Fáil's two-and-a-half years in office were recognised as a disaster."

He would surely reject James Downey's contention that the 1977 Government "merrily presided over an uncontrolled – and soon, uncontrollable boom", and that within two years the state of the public finances had got "totally out of control".

The former Minister has, in his 1990 article in *Studies* highlighted short-term outcomes which did match targets.

"Economic growth did accelerate through 1977-78; employment did increase .. the numbers at work in April 1980 had risen by 80,000 on the April 1977 level ... inflation did fall from the 18 per cent of 1976, and the 15 per cent of the first half of 1977 to 7.5 per cent in 1978 ... "

By 1979 the situation had deteriorated. Strikes, wage hikes, a rise in inflation due to the oil crisis that year, the breaking of the link with sterling (the European Monetary System – EMS – came into operation on 13 March 1979: Ireland joined, Britain did not), PAYE protest marches, angry farmers – all contributed to a rapidly worsening economic situation.

The overall outcome provided a basis for Alan Dukes's condemnation of "the politics of boom and bloom" at the 1990 Fine Gael Árd Fheis.

The then Leader of Fine Gael told the delegates that in the 1970s Fianna Fáil "let the debt problem get out of hand, and it took ten years to get it back under control".

This is the downside of the Lynch story, the blackest chapter, economically speaking.

And it won't go away no matter how much he protests. Indeed, at this stage he can be assumed of falling into the Shakespearean trap of protesting too much!

Dr O'Donoghue, on the other hand, would say the protests are justified.

He told me in his office in Trinity that the situation has now been reached where it can best be summed up by a line used by John Wayne in the 1962 film *The Man Who Shot Liberty Valance:*

"When the legend becomes established, you print the legend and not the fact".

Lynch himself still claims he is a victim of the gap between intention and perception.

We are surely in the land of Alice and her Looking Glass.

Yet there is no escaping the fact that it is still widely believed that he made a botch of things in 1977 – even if the blame, by and large, tends to be laid at the doorstep of the "Trinity egghead".

Garret would say that's just another example of Jack's good fortune.

The comment of one of Lynch's admirers remains the common perception: "We have been picking up the tab ever since!"

And there is little doubt that, in spite of Lynch's protestations, this is how history will view the effects of the 1977 election and its controversial FF Manifesto.

"That election gave FF the greatest overall majority in the history of the State, and put the country into hock!" is Dick Walsh's verdict.

It will, no doubt, remain the conventional verdict.

Taoiseach Jack Lynch addressing "his own" people in Cork after the 1977 victory in the general election.

An Taoiseach Charles J. Haughey makes a presentation to Jack Lynch who was chosen on the Team of the Century. In the centre is Maureen Haughey

Jack Lynch greeting Liam Cosgrave outside Dáil Éireann

*Jack Lynch with the then Taoiseach Dr Garret Fitzgerald at the launch of Bruce Arnold's book –
What Kind of Country*

An Taoiseach Jack Lynch with the Chinese Foreign Minister Mr Li Quang

"Happy Man" Jack Lynch holding both the Sam Maguire and McCarthy Cups in 1990 – Cork Double

Taoiseach Jack Lynch signing Ireland into the EEC

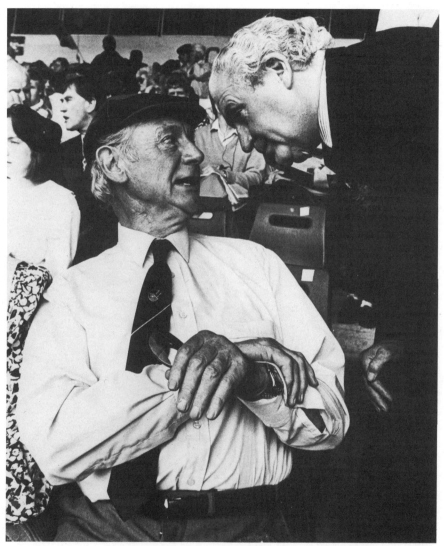

Jack Lynch at the 1991 Munster Hurling Final talking to An Tanaiste John Wilson T.D.

Amongst his own in Cork

Welcome Home – Jack in Cork 1977

Jack Lynch talking to Christy Ring's widow

Jack Lynch's old home – Church Street, Cork

An Taoiseach Jack Lynch talking to Christy Ring

16. Jack The Man

"Did you hear the story about the first time Christine Keeler came to Ireland . . . ?"

The setting is the sumptuous multi-million pound Convention Centre at the Fitzpatrick Silver Springs Hotel in Cork.

The date is 20 November 1990.

The occasion: a corporate luncheon organised by the Fitzpatrick family.

And Jack Lynch is the guest speaker.

He's in very good form, relaxed and expansive. The theme suggested to him is, 'the future of Irish tourism', but he's too experienced a public performer to labour over that.

He knows that lunchtime speeches shouldn't be too heavy. Short and light is his recipe.

After a few perfunctory observations, he decides a little bit of entertainment wouldn't go astray. People always appreciate a few laughs.

But wait a minute – Jack Lynch telling a story about a notorious call girl?

I kid you not. Trust me. It happened. As somebody said to Brian Boru after the Battle of Clontarf, I was there.

This, for the record, is the Lynch version:

"Christine Keeler was being driven through County Kerry one beautiful spring day, and she spotted a man ploughing a field. He was stripped to the waist and was a magnificent specimen.

"Naturally, being Christine Keeler, she was interested. She instructed the driver to stop the car, and went to meet this hunk.

"He was just finishing the field as she approached, so he untackled the horse, picked up the plough, and threw it over the ditch into the next field.

"Then he picked up the horse, and threw him into the next field.

"This was almost too much for Christine, who was very impressed indeed by this performance. This was some man.

"'Hello,' she said, 'I'm Christine Keeler . . . '

"'Christine who . . . ?'

"'I'm Christine Keeler. I'm the greatest whore in all of England.'

"The man, looking puzzled, scratched his head. 'And I must be the greatest whoor in all of Kerry, for I've just ploughed the wrong field! ......'"

Things must have changed. It used be said that the one way to offend Jack Lynch was to tell a dirty story in his presence.

But the Keeler story wasn't really dirty.

That's not Lynch's style.

His sense of humour though is well-known.

On that same occasion he was introduced (formality demanded it) by John Gately, the hotel manager. Jack got to his feet.

"I'm reminded of something the great black athlete Jesse Owens once said at a function in Dublin at which I did the introduction.

"Jesse turned to me and smiled and said: 'That was a very short introduction – you didn't read out half as much as I gave you!'"

John Gately enjoyed that.

Lynch's humour and his ordinariness were, and are two of his most endearing qualities.

He was the epitome of the "nice guy" next door, so much so that one sceptic once asked: "If nice guys finish last, how come Jack Lynch is always first?"

After he had been made a Minister, he was found in the Glen clubhouse helping Donie O'Brien (the man who looked after the hurleys and famous jerseys – the national colours plus black in honour of the leaders of 1916, the year the club was founded) to lay out the jerseys on chairs in front of an open fire to "air" them.

On another occasion, as Minister he delivered the jerseys for St Nicholas (the sister team of the Glen) to Church Road in Blackrock in the back of the State car.

And Seamus Brennan, who was party secretary from 1973 to 1977, said that even in the midst of the most pressing party or Oireachtas business, Lynch always found time to take a call from a widow somewhere worried about her pension, or a mother looking for a job for her son.

His own background wasn't exactly humble, not by the standards of Blackpool in the 1920s, but he was (and remains) throughout his public life a genuinely humble man.

One memorable scene occurred in May 1985 in Blarney, County Cork, when Lynch and Mary Hegarty, the Cork-born operatic singer, won a standing ovation when they sang "The Banks of My Own Lovely Lee" together at an Association of European Journalists' dinner in the presence of the Ambassadors of Britain, Spain and Portugal.

At the end, as the applause died away, Jack turned to the lovely Mary and remarked: "When you sing with Pavarotti some day in the Metropolitan Opera House, tell him about the night you sang 'The Banks' with Jack Lynch!"

Kevin Healy, now Head of Radio Programming at RTE, remembers another incident at The White House in 1979. Kevin was a member of the group of Irish journalists covering the Taoiseach's US visit.

"Jack was introducing us to the Vice-President Walter Mondale, and as I was shaking hands, Mondale said: 'Is he the Walter Cronkite of Irish radio?'

"Jack replied: 'No – but he's trying to be. He keeps asking me if I'm going to resign.'"

Prior to one of his American trips, the Irish Embassy in Washington sent a telex asking for confirmation of his blood type. When I mentioned this to him one day, it triggered off the following story.

"The Blood Transfusion Service decided to visit Leinster House one day, and a lot of TDs, including myself, gave blood. There was one particular TD who liked his pint, but couldn't really handle it.

"He was drinking in the bar when another TD approached him and enquired if he was a blood donor. The answer he got, in a rather slurred voice, was: 'Blood donor? I'm not even a blood owner.'"

At the reception following the conferring of the Freedom of the City of Cork on President Mary Robinson on 23 February 1991, Lynch was slightly disconcerted when he found that only wine was being served.

He summoned the barman and, eyes twinkling, asked: "Any chance of a native drink?"

Apart from the common touch, and the ability to swap stories with anyone, Michael D. Higgins believes that the fact that Lynch was not "ostentatiously wealthy" made it easier for people to relate to him.

In that sense, he was always a simple man with simple tastes, and neither he nor Mairin ever displayed a tendency to vulgar affluence. On the contrary, they treated with a certain degree of scorn the "get rich-quick" attitude of many others in the era of new Irish prosperity.

"As a politician, he had the warm, homely qualities that people associate with being Irish, and people like the fact that Mairin travelled around with him," said Michael D.

His trust and confidence in his own Irish people was also impressive. And there was never even so much as a hint of scandal, financial or sexual, where he was concerned.

Lynch himself maintains that one of his objectives in office was to establish the integrity of Government.

He believes politicians should serve the country, and he says: "I never subscribed to the theory that people were in politics for what they got out of it. To my knowledge, then and still, very few people got much out of politics in the sense of making money easily."

Lynch himself never accumulated wealth, and is not a rich man today, though with no dependants he would no doubt be regarded as very comfortable.

As a former Taoiseach he has a State car for life. And while his house in Rathgar is modest, he did reputedly get close to the asking price of £65,000 in April 1990 for the picturesque farmhouse at Ardagh, Church Cross, Skibbereen, which overlooks Roaringwater Bay, and which he and his wife used as a summer retreat for over 20 years.

In addition to a number of directorships, which would only involve token fees, he also has a pension of £40,122 (along with Liam Cosgrave), according to figures given to the Dáil – on 30 April 1991.

Michael Conlon, now chairman of Bord Gais and former chief executive of the Cork Trustee Savings Bank, recalled for me the time when he was approached by Fianna Fáil to run for the Dáil.

Conlon had just resigned as Cork County Manager and joined the Bank. He turned down the offer to run for the Dáil – it was in 1979 with a by-election pending in Cork City. As it happened, John Dennehy was the FF candidate – and lost.

"Before any of that happened I was summoned to the Taoiseach's room in the Metropole Hotel. I found Jack in his underpants - he was changing for a dinner. And it was in that condition, half undressed, that he asked me to stand for Fianna Fáil in the by election."

On another occasion, according to Conlon, Lynch was on board a yacht owned by Cork businessman Archie O'Leary. "Jack was steering under instructions, when someone shouted that the boat was heading for some rocks.

"'Don't blame me,' said the Taoiseach, 'I'm just doing what I'm told – as usual!'"

Some would see that as symbolic, because there was certainly a belief that in his days as Minister, Lynch did what his civil servants told him.

It was only later, as Taoiseach, that he really took charge.

He had a natural empathy with the underdog.

He could always relate to people in difficulty, and feel sympathy for them.

As former Fine Gael TD Paddy Lindsay once observed: "Lynch was a decent man, and was always willing to help a lame dog over a stile".

Senator Des Hanafin, who admits that he came close to ruin because of his drinking, says Lynch was very supportive and very helpful in assisting his recovery.

"He stuck his neck out for me, and I'll never forget that."

And it was very much in that spirit in November 1990 that he told a group of journalists in the midst of the Presidential Election and the furore over the Duffy tapes – that he sympathised with ex-Tanaiste Brian Lenihan's forgetfulness of exact details of contacts with Áras an Uachtaráin in 1982.

Writing the story, which was told at a luncheon of the Association of European Journalists in Dublin, Val Dorgan of the *Cork Examiner* said:

"Mr Lynch recalled a similar experience he had when in office. He said he had forgotten about the British Littlejohn brothers who were sent by British Intelligence to try and infiltrate the IRA, even though he had been given details.

"He was told about the Littlejohns just as he was getting on to a plane for an official visit to the US. He had asked for the then Minister for Justice, Desmond O'Malley, to be informed and had forgotten about the affair immediately."

In January 1986 Jack went on stage at the Opera House in Cork and regaled the audience with the story of his last stage performance – as a Roman soldier.

He played the role as a schoolboy in a passion play in the North Monastery, guarding the good thief on Calvary, complete with wooden spear.

"Before the lights went up, I tickled the fellow who was playing the good thief. He accidentally kicked away the box he was standing on, and when the curtain went back he really was hanging on his cross!"

In May 1985 he told students at Mount Merrion in Dublin of his embarrassment when he attended EEC meetings and was unable to converse with other politicians and diplomats in their own language.

"When we attended working dinners, I might have a Frenchman on one side, and a German on the other. While they were able to converse, I was like a dummy right in the middle."

He told the students it was always a regret he did not have a modern foreign language. "I left school with Irish, a working knowledge of Latin, and I could make myself understood in English."

The students liked the last bit.

On another occasion on a golf course in Cork, he was spotted by the late Tom Crosbie, a member of the family which owns and runs the *Cork Examiner*, swinging a left-handed golf club.

"Aren't you right-handed?" asked Crosbie.

Lynch smiled. "I find it very convenient as a politician to be able to swing either to the Right or the Left!"

Asked once about a player who had an exaggerated sense of his own abilities, Lynch, dead-pan, replied: "You'd want a great pair of legs to keep up a big head – and he hasn't those either".

When it came to sport, which he loved, he always said that records or medals didn't matter. "Playing the game is what counts."

And he had a fondness for sporting metaphors and references, even when dealing with the important business of Government.

One story which illustrates this was told to me in 1991 by the man who was still Secretary to the Taoiseach's Department – Padraig Ó hUiginn, a good Corkman.

It concerns a time when our former President, Dr Patrick Hillery, was Minister for Labour, and had been subjected to particularly harsh criticism by a member of ICTU.

"Hillery was hurt and was determined to respond, and instructed Tadgh Carroll, Secretary of the Department (and a former classmate of Lynch's) to draft a response.

"Tadgh did so reluctantly, having tried to dissuade the Minister, because he didn't think it was wise to respond to this particular attack.

"When he showed Hillery the draft, the latter felt it was not strong enough, and proceeded to rewrite it.

"Carroll again intervened, and finally prevailed upon the Minister to go and discuss the matter with the Taoiseach before doing anything.

"A week passed and nothing happened, so Tadgh finally asked his Minister what advice the Taoiseach had given.

"Hillery replied: 'Jack said to do nothing but to always remember that the ball will come down into our half of the field again.'"

His fondness for the sporting metaphor is well known. Less well known was his willingness to find time, even as Taoiseach, to deal with the most mundane enquiries from constituents.

The present Minister for Tourism (also Communications), Seamus Brennan, who was brought in by Lynch as General Secretary of the Party (Frank Dunlop came in to organise media relations) during the period in Opposition in 1973-77, was often amazed at this trait.

"Even with urgent Government business to be dealt with, he would always find time to take a call from Mrs Murphy about her son, or to organise a letter to someone in Cork."

Yet the easy familiarity masked a core of privacy which few, if any, penetrated.

In sport and in politics it remained. Few people got close to Lynch. He kept people at a distance – his Ministers, even his family.

Even today, with the pressures gone, there is an impenetrable quality to him, a point beyond which few are permitted to venture.

Perhaps no one. Not even Mairin.

Jack Lynch has many admirers but few close friends; far, far fewer than one might expect for one so much in the public eye.

His late brother, Theo, acknowledged this.

He also offered this interesting insight in 1978: "I've seen people over the years acting as if they believe Jack Lynch can mean one thing and say another. If they had asked me I would have told them that Jack Lynch means what he says. He won't blast you out of it, but he's tough underneath, tougher than many seemed to believe . . . "

That toughness was displayed in unmistakable fashion one time in the Barleycove Hotel in West Cork where a study group Lynch had set up, was holding a weekend seminar.

Businessman Paddy McCarthy of Cork was a member of the group, and they were meeting at a time in the early 1970s when feelings were still running very high in Fianna Fáil, in the aftermath of the Arms Trials.

"We were given a tip-off that a group of Haughey supporters were going to gatecrash the seminar, and were going to attempt to interrupt a session which the Taoiseach was scheduled to address," says McCarthy.

"The organisers were unsure how to handle matters, so a few of them went to see Jack. They found him sitting in his chalet, smoking his pipe, gazing out over the beach. He was totally relaxed.

"Anyway, they told him what they had found out, and asked his advice.

"Without even turning around, he said: 'What would you do if you heard that a bunch of bums were planning to break into the hotel and disrupt a meeting?'

"'We'd give them the bum's rush,' replied one of the organisers.

"'Then proceed,' drawled the Taoiseach . . ."

17. Mairin

She was the picture of elegance. And very much the centre of attraction, especially for the women, as she arrived for lunch at Cork's Imperial Hotel.

Jack walked two steps behind her as they made their way to the table reserved for them, with the *maitre d'hôtel* hovering in the background.

Though long out of public life, the Lynches are still celebrities in Cork.

As I watched them, I pondered.

"There's no doubt she's the boss domestically – but does it end there?"

The statement and the question came from Mary Kenny.

We must judge for ourselves.

"He has paid me not to talk," Mairin told me when I mentioned an interview for this book. "He'd get rid of me if I do," she smiled, her eyes dancing with mischief.

She was wearing a tourqoise suit, and her silver hair, shimmering under the lights, had a mild blue tint.

As she moved through the restaurant heads turned.

Behind her Jack rummaged through his pockets, looking for his pipe tobacco.

"She wouldn't eulogise me, anyway," he commented as people at a nearby table called out a greeting.

Mairin tried to keep a straight face, but behind the spectacles, also slightly tinted, her eyes sparkled.

One's initial impression of her is one of shyness. Yet she possesses great charm, and as one gets to know her better there is evidence of an underlying strength of character and purpose.

Was she, in the years of power, merely a decorative addition to Jack? Or was she more than that?

Was Sean Lemass right? Was it a case of "petticoat power"?

I recalled a comment made by a colleague some years before. He said Lynch showed all the signs of being a "hen-pecked" husband.

Is it true? Is she the boss?

There is no doubt she is a strong-willed woman; some would call her domineering.

If she is, she does it with subtlety.

Those who know him well say Lynch is not hen-pecked. But Mairin could occasionally boss him around.

I recall an incident in Jury's Hotel in Cork during his second period as Taoiseach (1977-79), when she wouldn't let him stay for one more drink.

"Come now, Jack," she said taking him by the arm. 'We have to leave . . . "

An interesting aside to a reporter with the *Sunday Times* in July 1972 may have been more revealing than she intended. It happened at their West Cork holiday home (since sold): "I decide what we do."

One mustn't make too much of that, but she was no retiring wallflower in his political heyday.

Both Síle de Valera and Mary Harney have stressed how supportive she was to him, especially at the most critical junctures of his career.

"He was always supported by Mrs Lynch," says Ms de Valera.

"That's something I've always admired about her. She was always a tremendous support to Jack Lynch and his career. I think, really, she lived to promote him and his career. That's what came across.

"They were, and are, a very devoted couple, and certainly set a tremendous example. They were a couple that were looked up to by people of all political persuasions and views."

Whatever about promoting his career, Mary Harney believes Mairin was influential in getting him to end it.

"She wanted him to get out . . . "

As far back as 1970 Mairin Lynch told a reporter: "When we retire from this job there will be no tears."

Mairin Lynch (nee O'Connor), formerly a Dublin civil servant and an only child, was a reluctant entrant into national politics. But once in the footlights, she displayed a natural talent for the role.

She was the leader's right arm. And when he was attacked she was quick to leap to his defence, drawing the anger and often the admiration of political enemies and women's activists.

"Oh heavens, I should never have been in public life! I'm exactly the wrong sort of person for it."

The comment was made by Mairin Lynch in March, 1970, in an interview with the *Sunday Press*.

It simply wasn't true.

Mairin Lynch is a deceptive woman. Unlike the wives of other prominent politicians, then and now, she was never "pushy", never overtly ambitious for her husband.

We know she counselled against his entering the contest for Taoiseach in 1966.

But once in, she became fiercely protective and supportive of him.

She wrote to RTE and the newspapers to set matters straight when she felt he was not getting a fair shake.

In November 1971 she spoke out at a Fianna Fáil dinner in Monaghan against the tarring and feathering of young girls in Derry, describing these as "despicable acts carried out by women".

And in February 1978 she made a spirited defence of her husband against Nobel Peace Prize winner, Mrs Betty Williams, when the latter seemed to suggest that Jack Lynch could or would encourage murderous violence.

She wrote to newspapers advising Mrs Williams to "pause and think a while", after the latter had alleged that Lynch had given the Provisional IRA the "go ahead" to continue their campaign.

Further testimony to the fact that she was no "token woman" comes from old pros in the political game, who will tell you how expertly Mairin could "work a crowd" for Jack.

While he was often content to sit with friends or people in whose company he felt at ease, Mairin always saw the need for him to mix.

And with this in mind, she would act as a "crowd taster" for him, moving to tables ahead of him, sussing out the people and the conversation, and then going back to insist, gently but firmly of course, that it was time for him to move from Table A to Table B.

"Jack, there are people over here who want to talk to you. Will you excuse us while I take Jack over here . . . "

With Jack safely situated at Table B, Mairin would then leave him and move on to Table C, her antennae on full power.

Time and again she did this with unforced finesse and no small degree of grace. And only those who appreciated that side of politics could marvel at her always polished performance.

In what she did, she was a consummate operator.

Where her married life to the quiet-spoken Taoiseach was concerned, she never hid the unpalatable realities, especially the loneliness. She never attempted to camoflauge the fact that being the wife of a Minister, and particularly a Taoiseach, called for considerable adjustments.

It demanded, above all, that she wear a public face. But behind the persona which went on public display, there was considerable pain – which is not to say that she didn't enjoy the travel and the VIP treatment when abroad.

She also enjoyed the opportunity to dress up, for she is a lover of good clothes, treasuring to this day a number of ball gowns specially made for her by Sybil Connolly, once described by Jack as "one of Ireland's national treasures".

But public life exacted a heavy price.

"When my husband became a Parliamentary Secretary I was thrilled. I could hardly believe it, it seemed so wonderful. Then when I became used to the life, it made me feel very sad because I could see what our life was going to be like in the future.

"Not that it ever occurred to me that my husband might become Taoiseach. I never looked further than the possibility of the next Ministry. In one way, I suppose I was lucky; the breaking-in was a gradual process."

She also admitted she was lucky in another way, in that she did not miss having a settled life, never missed knowing in advance what she could do, things like buying a house and putting down roots.

"Oh no, that has never bothered me. I don't mind moving around. In fact, Jack would tell you, even if it's not necessary, after a couple of years I'm inclined to look around and ask: 'Well, aren't we moving?' That's it exactly . . . my roots are emotional . . . "

Despite the glamour and the glitz, the years when Jack was at the pinnacle of power were undoubtedly lonely for her.

There are hints of this in several interviews (she never liked being interviewed) she gave over the years.

"Mrs Haughey has children, and I had not that great advantage," she said on 9 December 1979 – just days after her husband had resigned as Taoiseach. "And there are times that I have been very lonely in the 32 years of Jack's political life."

She told Sheila Walsh of the *Sunday Press* that everyone in public life needed the support of their family.

"I think people are lucky to have children, and the older I get the more I realise this.

"After my hysterectomy seven or eight years after my marriage, we thought of adopting two children. But then Jack was appointed a Minister, and I decided to devote all my time to him so that I could travel around with him everywhere."

She said then that she never wanted to be in public life. "I would have much preferred if Jack had stuck with Law, but when he opted for public life, I went into it with enthusiasm and did my best to come to terms with my innate dread of having to make speeches or public appearances on my own."

During the 1979 General Election campaign she told Mary Kenny: "Those two years when he was a barrister were the happiest years of our lives. I don't like public life. I hate to be alone at the head table, in the spotlight. But I love meeting people, talking with people, so I suppose that what I had to give up in private life balances out with what I gain by meeting people.

"You give up an awful lot of yourself in politics. Your private life, your family – they're all public. Everyone values his privacy, and that has to go; a politician's door is always open. It takes a tremendous lot of dedication."

For her, political life did not turn out the way she had hoped when it all started.

"You go in thinking you're going to solve every problem, help everybody in distress, do so much good for the country, the environment, the social services.

"And then you come up against the hard realities of life, and find that you can't do one quarter of all that you wanted to do.

"You dream so many dreams, and you have to settle for so very much less.... "

Mairin Lynch's advice to any politician's wife is "cover the hurts and keep smiling".

She recalled how in November 1979, "Jack and I had to do this at The White House, for we had just heard the disappointing results of the Cork by-elections. Meanwhile, President Carter had the gigantic problem of Iran on his mind ... "

Nine years earlier, in March 1970, she again told the *Sunday Press* how much she missed children of her own.

"Do you know, I'd have loved to have had a huge family. Just think of the opportunity for conversation. And everybody in a large family always help out during a crisis, I've noticed. It would be lovely to have lots of grown-up children to argue with."

Religion remains very important to her – and to her husband. On Sundays, they often go to an Irish language liturgy in Church Street, or to Mount Argus.

Mrs Lynch has what she once described as a "fantastically deep" faith. "Probably, I'm not half as good a Catholic as I should be, but I do feel terribly deeply about God and about Christianity. I think it's terribly important to use your faith in the world around you."

On another occasion, in the context of saying that a New Ireland, embracing all traditions and beliefs, must eventually emerge, she said:

"We are all God's creatures, created by Him to live together in equality and harmony, and with respect and understanding for each other's convictions and beliefs."

She also feels strongly about the role of women in modern society, and she says she would like to see more women in public life.

"They bring an understanding to certain spheres of public life, particularly to social problems."

Mairin and Jack met for the first time in Glengarriff in 1943, when they were both on holiday, and both were working in the Civil Service at the time.

Lynch had gone there with his great friend, Paddy O'Donovan. It was the evening of a Munster Final in which they had just played.

At the old Golf Links Hotel, they came across a group of girls who were staying there.

Mairin O'Connor and her close friend, Beryl Fagan (who afterwards married Brendan Smith of Dublin Theatre Festival fame) were two of the girls.

Jack and Mairin didn't hit it off right away.

"We put on very heavy Cork accents, just for fun," recalls Jack. The girls were not impressed.

"We thought they were a bit hoighty–toighty!"

The girls, for their part, initially regarded Lynch and O'Donovan as a couple of uncouth Cork men.

"Who are those awful fellows?" was Mairin's reaction.

Jack was 26 at the time, the same age as Mairin.

"Later on we teamed up with them, going for hikes, swimming, and in the evenings to dances," says Jack. "Many a time we rolled back the carpet for an eight-hand reel and then settled down for a sing-song."

Shortly after that holiday, Lynch transferred to Dublin to continue his studies for the Bar. "So I was able to keep up contact with Mairin, who was living there."

The romance blossomed.

Jack Lynch was the love of her life, her first man.

Other women had shown a keen interest in Lynch, and he had dated some of them. But this was his first serious relationship. And his last.

They were married in Dublin on 10 August 1946.

As John A. Murphy has observed, "Like all childless couples, they are very close".

That closeness endures. Theirs is a remarkable relationship.

In a world of politics notorious for liaisons, not a whiff of sexual scandal has ever touched the Lynches.

That, too, would be considered remarkable by many.

18. Armsgate

"Charlie Haughey was in tears". The description comes from Jack Lynch.

He was the only one to witness the distressful scene. It happened in a ward of the Mater Hospital in Dublin. And it almost unnerved the Taoiseach.

Confronted with just one option – a brutal one – Haughey broke down and cried.

"It was a deeply distressing and very trying occasion," Lynch recalls.

For Charles J. Haughey it was all over. Or so he must have thought at the time.

His career – and few careers in Irish public life had been as carefully plotted and planned – was in ruins.

As he struggled to regain control of himself, an embarrassed Jack Lynch thought: "My God, he's going to collapse!"

He didn't.

But he seemed like a man in shock.

Lynch had just told him he wanted his resignation.

Charlie's world was suddenly in tatters.

He must have been expecting it of course.

Neil Blaney says that while the Taoiseach was being driven from Government Buildings to the Mater Hospital, he 'phoned ahead to alert Charlie.

But when the dreadful moment arrived, Haughey couldn't believe it was happening.

He was out. Finished. Kaput.

For any politician who had reached Ministerial rank, that would be quite a blow anyway.

But for Haughey – a man "obsessed with power, status and position" in Blaney's own description – this must have seemed like endsville.

Disgrace and disaster were staring him in the face. Whether he felt any shame is another matter.

For a brief moment, Lynch actually felt sorry for him.

As Mairin Lynch remarked afterwards, "Jack is a compassionate man".

None of this was easy for him.

On the contrary, he was finding it very difficult. He had come through an excruciating fortnight.

For the first time in his life, sleep wouldn't come. The nights were terrible.

"Neither of us slept very much during the Arms Crisis," recalled Mrs Lynch afterwards.

Jack had confided in her – but only the outline of what he had learned.

He kept the frightening details to himself.

"He is a very calm person during big traumas," according to his wife.

But this was by far the biggest trauma of his career. This was the stuff of which *coup d'états* are made.

Lynch was facing his biggest test. A wrong move and he would go down for keeps. So would his Government. And perhaps the Republic as well.

The very thought transfixed him. The scenario unfolding in his mind was numbing in its scale and implications.

This is how the *Sunday Times* described his situation.

"Although Lynch was quick to state that he was not Prime Minister 'in a caretaker capacity', his show of reluctance, together with his style of leadership and even his personal demeanour, left doubts that were not to be finally resolved until the extraordinary melodrama of the Dublin Arms Crisis of 1970.

"Most politicians who achieve power have a moment of truth when all – or nothing – lies before them. This was Lynch's."

His decision to face the crisis head on had brought him face-to face first with Blaney, and now Haughey.

Lynch would have preferred to get things over with quickly, once he had determined on a course of action.

But Haughey was in hospital.

The day before Budget Day – 22 April – he had had an accident.

His story was that he had fallen from a horse.

Not everyone was disposed to believe that, though Lynch apparently was.

At least three versions of what actually happened were soon circulating.

The version most widely believed by those in the know was that Haughey had been injured in an incident in a licensed premises.

According to one newspaper, the Secretary of the Department of Justice, Peter Berry, noted down this account and several others after meeting Garda chiefs.

"Within a matter of days there were all sorts of rumours in golf clubs, in political circles and in Leinster House as to how the accident occurred.

The rumours ranged from the bizarre to the lurid.

Lynch had to get the doctor's permission to go and see Haughey, which he did, finally, on 29 April.

Now it was done.

First Blaney. Now Charlie. They had to go.

Within days a third Minister – Kevin Boland – resigned.

Lynch emerged the undisputed victor. His mere survival was triumph enough. But he was also able to rid himself of three of the most troublesome members of his Cabinet.

The repercussions of that political crisis which shocked the nation over two decades ago, are still being felt today at various levels of Irish life.

When the Taoiseach set in train events which were to culminate in the Arms Trial, few in May 1970 could have foreseen the ultimate consequences.

Two of the most powerful men in Irish politics – Blaney and Boland – were to be permanently sidelined, never again to occupy central positions on the political stage.

A third – Haughey – would survive, and his day would come. But only after he had demonstrated enormous, some would say uncanny, powers of tenacity, determination and ambition to claw his way back from the oblivion to which events consigned him in 1970 to the pinnacle of power.

It was a time of high drama, frightening in its intensity and, above all else, in its explosive potential.

A single sheet of paper with three names typewritten on it precipitated the greatest and, in some ways, the most bizarre crisis in Ireland since the bitter and bloody Civil War of 1922-23.

Known ever since as "The Arms Crisis", it broke with all the explosive and shocking force of an Exocet on an unsuspecting public in May 1970.

Today sections of the acrimonious Dáil debate which followed read like background notes for the scenario for a James Bond movie or a John Le Carré novel.

All that's missing are busty blondes – and who knows what the secret archives may yet turn up?

The crisis of 1970 – hinging around a conspiracy to import arms into this country which led to the dismissal, on grounds of suspicion, of two Cabinet Ministers – marks a watershed in Irish political life.

It is the single most fascinating and traumatic event in post-Civil War Ireland – and the irony, edged with tragedy, is that the full story may never be known.

Former Taoiseach, Dr Garret Fitzgerald, TD, who has written an account of his own years in office, asserts that "much of what happened in and around the Arms Crisis remains puzzling, and may never be sorted out".

One journalist, who was better placed than most at the time, maintains today that only six people know the full story. Jack Lynch, who demanded the resignations of Haughey and Blaney, and to whom fell the difficult task of cauterizing the wounds caused by the crisis, of holding Fianna Fáil and the nation together, is not one of them.

It is impossible now to recreate the atmosphere which existed at the time, an atmosphere in which speculation about a possible *coup d'etat* flourished.

Fears for the security of the State motivated people at the very centre of power, including Lynch himself. But for a time things were so confused, so filled with suspicion, mistrust, rumours of conspiracy and subversion, that even the Secretary of the Department of Justice, the late Peter Berry, was alarmed at one stage, that even the Taoiseach himself might be implicated.

So nervous and uncertain was he that he did a most unusual thing for a civil servant – he asked for, and got a private meeting at Áras an Uachtaráin with the President.

There he laid out the facts as he knew them – he was the effective head of the security service for Eamon de Valera, and made known his fears. And then sought the President's advice.

The answer from Dev is as great a tribute to Lynch's integrity and loyalty to the State as he is ever likely to be paid.

"You must tell the Taoiseach," the President told Berry. "You must trust Jack Lynch."

Which is what Berry did, though to this day there is a dispute about exactly when Lynch came into possession of the frightening information which prompted him to act against two of his most senior Ministers.

Lynch has consistently maintained that April 20 1970, was the date on which he first learned of what was afoot. The dismissals of Haughey and Blaney occurred on May 5 1970.

Hours before, on the evening of May 4, the Fine Gael leader, Liam Cosgrave, met with Lynch in secret and showed him the piece of paper with the three names.

Some Special Branch sources said the information passed on by Cosgrave had come originally from British Intelligence.

In a review of the highly dramatic events of 1970 Lynch has said there was nothing on the paper which he did not already know, and his mind was made up to act anyway.

He has acknowledged, though, that a combination of the meeting with Cosgrave and a tip-off that the *Sunday Independent* was on to the story forced him to act sooner than might otherwise have been the case – because he wanted to give Blaney, and particularly Haughey, time to respond.

In other words, any perusal of Lynch's own accounts in the Dáil records, and accounts from other contemporary sources, suggest that while his mind was made up to act, the Cosgrave intervention influenced the timing of his action. He was forced to move sooner than he had planned because of his knowledge that the story was about to break.

Lynch's account (especially on the crucial matter of precisely when he learned of the plot to import arms) has been challenged by others, notably by Vincent Browne in *Magill* in three extensive articles in May-June-July 1980.

Browne's main contention – that Lynch knew of promises of money for the IRA, and plans to purchase guns, at least six months earlier – has always been categorically denied by the former Taoiseach. To this day Lynch is adamant that the first he heard about it was on April 20 1970. The broad outlines of the "Arms Crisis" – the trials, the acquittals, and the subsequent revelations to the Dáil Committee of Public Accounts, that most of the £100,000 set aside by the Government in 1969 for the relief of distress in Northern Ireland was unaccounted for – are now part of the public record.

That said, there are still aspects of the crisis which remain shrouded in mystery, and we are never likely to learn the full, unvarnished story.

What is not in any doubt is the crucial role played by Lynch in calming and steadying the nation in the aftermath, and in forcing a major rethink within Fianna Fáil about the nature of "republicanism" and its commitment to the objective of national unity.

Any doubts about this resolve as a leader vanished after 1970. "He kept his head, and by so doing enabled all of us to keep ours as well," says Professor John Murphy, in a comment on the events of that highly charged period when Northern Ireland was on the boil.

"In any assessment of Jack Lynch, I think 1970 is the period people will look at with the greatest interest," according to Dr Garret Fitzgerald, TD.

"It does raise the question of how much he knew about The Arms Crisis, and when he got to know it, and whether the fact that he didn't act until May 1970, was because he was unsure he could act successfully."

But when he did deal with it, he did so very successfully, adds Dr Fitzgerald, "in halting something which could have been disastrous for the State". He goes on: "Jack Lynch could have been displaced, and the damage could have been very great".

What Lynch was faced with was a party at odds with itself, a Party which, up until then, had never had to face the question of how its primary aim – national unity – was to be attained, or whether in fact it was attainable in reality.

Lurking behind this question were ghosts from the War of Independence and the Civil War, ghosts whose presence was always powerful within Fianna Fáil up to the time of Lynch, and who appeared to validate, for some, the option of violence.

The legitimacy of violence as a means of attaining political objectives was the real issue at the heart of The Arms Crisis. Lynch confronted this in 1970 and in its aftermath, and forced a major rethink within the Party.

"He did undertake in the process after 1970 and up to 1977 a gradual weaning of Fianna Fáil away from the traditional but less constructive aspects of their extreme nationalism, and the irredentist thesis that Northern Ireland didn't have the right to exist," acknowledges Dr Fitzgerald.

"By 1973/74 he had brought the party around to an acceptance of the Sunningdale Agreement – all within 3 or 4 years of the Arms Crisis. So his achievement in that regard was considerable, and deserves to be remembered."

Dessie O'Malley, the leader of the PDs, and Lynch's one time Cabinet colleague, goes further: "His greatest contribution was that he held the Irish nation together in 1969-70, when it might have been divided with horrendous consequences. He calmed people at a time when we could have had thousands and thousands of deaths in a tragedy certain to have been more serious than the Civil War had been."

In effect, Lynch brought about a fundamental change within Fianna Fáil, and, as Bruce Arnold stressed in his 1984 book *What Kind of Country?*, "successfully protected the country from the escalation of Northern Ireland violence".

According to former *Irish Press* editor, Tim Pat Coogan, author of *The IRA*, "the Arms Crisis was a watershed in Irish life, especially in relation to attitudes to Northern Ireland".

Vincent Browne says Lynch effectively changed policy on Northern Ireland at a time of high emotion on the issue within Fianna Fáil.

"He managed to restore unity within his party and to give coherence and leadership to his Government to the extent of being able to increase his party's share of the vote in the 1973 General Election, even in spite of the most serious crisis the State had witnessed since the Civil War ..."

Others who followed – notably Dr Fitzgerald – developed what Arnold has described as the "careful and conscientious work of Jack Lynch in eviscerating the mindless republicanism" which found its most lethal flowering in the Provisional IRA.

The work achieved by Lynch in the post-1970 situation laid the groundwork which later made possible developments such as the Sunningdale Agreement, the setting up of the New Ireland Forum, and ultimately the Anglo-Irish Agreement and the Brooke talks.

By way of a postscript, it should be noted that one aspect of the Arms Crisis which annoyed Lynch was the widely held belief that he was responsible for the decision to prosecute Haughey.

"There have been suggestions that I orchestrated the prosecutions throughout the affair, but the fact of the matter is that I had no involvement whatsoever in anything to do with the prosecution or with the conduct of the case once I handed the papers over to the Attorney General."

This is a common misbelief and one which, amazingly, was not corrected until 1991.

The Attorney General at the time was Colm Condon, and in a revealing two-part interview given to 'County Sound' (the Mallow based local radio station) in January 1991, he had this to say:

"It was my function to decide the matter on the material furnished to me by the investigation. It was not the function of the Taoiseach.

"I have heard people says Jack Lynch prosecuted Charlie Haughey. That is not true. I decided that Charlie Haughey would be prosecuted.

"Jack Lynch had nothing whatsoever to do with it. He wouldn't dream of interfering in the function that the Attorney General carried out during that period, and he did not in any way interfere.

"That was a decision reached on the papers, as they were at that time, in the investigation..."

19. A Very Irish Coup?

In a movie called *Red King, White Knight* there is a scene set in Washington in which a CIA man ruminates about the exercise of power at the highest levels in the USA.

"You know, it's an interesting thing, Doug, every four years in this country we have an election. We get a new President, a new Administration and a new Congress.

"But the Government boys go on and on, feeding 'em the same information. Now if you want to get anything done, you see the Government boys. It don't matter a damn who's President. . ."

Allowing for some exaggeration (but not much), that can be applied *mutatis mutandis* to any Western democracy in modern times.

The best-selling novelist John le Carré, who has specialised in writing about the closed world of espionage and the activities of intelligence services, had much the same thing in mind when he said: "Within the British Establishment there is a fondness for secrecy which goes beyond anything you will find in any other democratic system."

By extension, and with appropriate adjustments, that applies to Ireland as well.

Some people may be shocked by this, or deeply sceptical. We like to believe in honour and decency and probity – and it is comforting to do so.

But the world of White Knights – as Jack Lynch found out in 1970 – is a fantasy world.

It is the creation of incurable romantics who believe the good guys always win in the end; that the cowboys are always right, and that they will always triumph over the Apaches.

In the Ireland of 1970 there was one White Knight, and quite a few Red Kings and more than a few Black Knights.

And in the struggle for control, for power, for the right to shape policy and determine the future, the latter almost won.

In looking back, that's one of the scary things about the whole episode which came to be known as the Arms Crisis.

After the sacking of two Ministers, and the resignations of two others (Justice Minister Michael Moran resigned at Lynch's request just before the crisis erupted into the public forum), approaches were made to the President.

Rumours of a *coup d'etat* were widespread.

It was a time of great uncertainty, and of great fear. One senior RTE man said after the startling news of 6 May 1970 (the sacking of Haughey and Blaney) that he expected to see tanks on the streets of Dublin.

It was, as Andrew Hamilton of the *Irish Times* stressed, an unreal time in which, suddenly, all the certainties of the State seemed that much less certain.

"It was the nearest we have ever come to listening for the rumble of tanks in the streets," says Hamilton, who covered the Arms Trials.

"Rumours flew and, as they flew, took on new dimensions. The Army would not hold. The guards would walk out. Jack Lynch was going. British Intelligence had taken the reins again in Dublin Castle. The judges would refuse to try the case. Charlie Haughey was gone to South America."

By one reckoning, the Arms Crisis lasted 20 weeks. By another, it has never ended. For the bizarre events of 1970 have shaped, and still bear upon the political realities of Ireland, North and South, today.

In the dramaturgy of Irish politics, the events of 1970 hold a Kafkaesque place.

Over two decades later, those in the know are still reluctant to talk about the possibility of a *coup d'etat*.

"The only thing that one can say for certain," wrote Martin Dillon in his 1988 book *The Dirty War*, "is that there was a hidden agenda, a conspiracy of a kind which was dangerous for the Irish State."

Conspiracy is difficult to prove, particularly when it reaches into the shadowy world of intelligence services.

The question was (and remains): how widespread was the conspiracy?

One journalist, with very special contacts in the world of politics, believes we shall never know.

But there is little doubt now that it was wider than was generally realised then – or since.

In an interview in 1990, I asked Lynch if he was fearful, at any stage, that he might be ousted from power, that there might be a take-over.

He smiled and replied: "The chain was on the door all the time, so I don't know how they were going to get in."

Was there an inner clique within the Cabinet plotting to take over the country?

"There was no real danger of that."

Were attempts made from within to destablise him?

"It wouldn't have worked."

Why?

"They knew bloody well they'd be knocked out of the ring."

But for weeks in April-May 1970, Lynch had to cope with frightening uncertainty.

The truth, as one senior civil servant has admitted, is that the Taoiseach didn't know which members of his Cabinet he could trust.

"It was the worst time of my entire life, the only time in my political career when I couldn't sleep," reveals Lynch today.

"For a fortnight I couldn't tell anyone, I couldn't confide in anyone. . ."

For once, even Mrs Lynch was kept in the dark, though he had discussed the sackings with her.

"I couldn't talk to a soul . . . "

At a time when some Ministers were assuming that armed intervention in the North was part of Government policy, Lynch was in the dark about what was going on in some departments and within some sections of the security forces.

"He wasn't sure, when the crunch came, that he could fully trust sections of the Army or the Gardai," said the same civil servant. Today Lynch blames himself for this.

"I was too trusting. I always worked with a team. And I always felt that if some member of that team couldn't accept and play with the strategy of the team, that he would come to the captain and say so."

Admitting that the then Minister for Justice, Michael Moran, had failed to keep him informed about allegations of arms importations – "he couldn't accept what he was being told about the goings-on in other Departments" – Lynch says he should have intervened more.

"That was one of my ultimate – I wouldn't say weaknesses - one of my ultimate mistakes: that I didn't have a finger in more pies than I had."

Does he regret that he didn't keep a tighter rein on his Ministers?

"To an extent, yes. But then you must remember that I succeeded two men – De Valera and Lemass – who were monumental figures in their own era.

"There was no question whatsoever when Dev retired that Lemass wouldn't succeed him. In fact, there was no vote whatsoever in the Fianna Fáil Party. It was automatic.

"When Lemass resigned he found he had a lot of fellows around, more or less of the same age. And each felt himself entitled to be the Boss.

"But having followed the democratic process, I was elected, and I picked my team. I said you do this, you do that. And I said let us play as a team from here on in.

"Unfortunately, my confidence wasn't justified in the end ... "

The implications of what happened during the Arms Crisis reached out beyond the personalities involved, and touched the very foundations of the Republic.

Dáil deputies brought guns into the precincts of Leinster House. Rumours mushroomed. The whiff of conspiracy was in the air.

Matters appeared to have slipped out of Lynch's control. And to an extent they had.

From the beginning of 1969 the "hawks" within the Cabinet had been distasting policy on Northern Ireland.

In an interview with Brian Farrell for RTE television, the day after he resigned in 1979, Lynch admitted that the eruption of the Northern crisis had taken him by surprise, but he felt he had "learned fast".

He agreed that "perhaps he had not been tough enough" on Neil Blaney after the latter's speech at Letterkenny on 8 December 1969, when the latter said that force was not ruled out in relation to Northern Ireland.

Throughout this period Lynch's own laid-back style, his quiet, diffident demeanour did not help.

He had strong, ambitious Ministers to contend with, and he may not have fully appreciated that some of them had already written him off as a "caretaker" Taoiseach.

Around the Cabinet table he was not calling the shots.

Garret Fitzgerald's account is accurate: "Cabinet meetings went on interminably. Lynch found it very hard to bring things to a head, to take decisions. And that indecisiveness may well account for a lot of his problems at that time."

A clue to Lynch's apparent impotency for much of the 1966-70 period may be found in the following observation made by the former British Chancellor of the Exchequer, Nigel Lawson: "To govern is to choose. To appear to be unable to choose is to appear to be unable to govern."

Such a power vacuum is bound to attract ambitious men. And they made the running for a time.

Typical of what was happening was the claim made by Neil Blaney in a *Hot Press* interview in June 1990 that the now famous "we will not stand (idly) by " speech of 13 August 1969 was not Lynch's.

"That speech was composed word for word, every comma, every iota, as a collective Cabinet speech. It was not Jack Lynch's speech ..."

Lynch admits there was a lot of "blood and thunder" around the Cabinet table during these crucial months, but he insists that at all times he was in control.

That seems to have been the case – but only just.

And a clue to the tenuous nature of his hold on power may be found in a comment made by Blaney in his *Hot Press* interview. Having claimed that he initially refused to resign in 1970 when Lynch asked him to, he said if he had to do it all over again that's not all he would do.

Hot Press: "What else would you do?"

Blaney: "Without doubt we'd have brought him and his Government down. Full stop. And not a bother."

There would, of course, have been enormous bother, for, as Lynch maintains, the "chain was always on the door".

At no stage, according to one civil servant, was the situation out of his control.

Not totally.

But for a while uncertainty ruled.

That uncertainty is graphically mirrored in the conflicting claims about the Government's intentions *vis-à-vis* a possible invasion of the North in 1969.

Neil Blaney claims such an invasion was on.

Jack Lynch says it was never on.

In his 1990 *Hot Press* interview Blaney says that during the siege of the Bogside in 1969 the Army Command were put on the alert to invade the North.

Lynch denies this, though he admits he was under pressure from within the Cabinet to send troops over the border into Derry and Newry.

"There would have been a massive bloodbath if I had given way to pressure to send the Irish Army across the border," he said in 1990.

He told a meeting of the Association of European Journalists in Dublin that up to a quarter of a million people would most likely have been killed in 1969 if he had ordered Irish troops to cross the border to aid Catholics under attack.

It didn't happen. Jack Lynch was the Taoiseach. The conclusion is obvious. Even Blaney admits that Lynch blocked all discussion of an invasion.

He did.

Eventually.

The Arms Crisis revealed several things about Lynch. It revealed the ineptitude with which he had run his Cabinet up to then.

Some of the Cabinet – Blaney, in particular – should have been fired in 1969. Another leader, more ambitious and ruthless, anxious to guard his back and secure his position, would have wielded the axe.

Instead of scattering his enemies, Lynch helped them to consolidate their positions, especially the Blaney-Haughey-Boland triumvirate.

It was something he would live to rue.

But live he did, and the scattering came later.

In the end, the Arms Crisis revealed how decisive and even ruthless he could be – if compelled.

It also demonstrated the extent to which his rivals underestimated him.

He was drawn into the crisis almost like a victim; he emerged from it as a victor.

Up to then, all his own people saw was a man with a velvet glove. Henceforth, they would know that the glove concealed an iron fist.

Lynch told Brian Farrell in 1979 that although he had been surprised by the upheaval in the North in 1968-69, he felt he had "learned fast".

In retrospect, it has to be said that he almost didn't learn fast enough.

For a time, his own safety – and that of the Republic – was up for grabs.

A batch of posters which went up on buildings in Dublin in 1970-71 were ominous indicators of what was being thought and said in some quarters.

Their message was as stark as it was simple: **"LYNCH JACK"**.

An Taoiseach Lynch and the British Prime Minister Harold Wilson

20. Republicanism Revisited

In 1922, when Jack Lynch was four years old, he was standing at the door of his home under the shadow of Shandon Steeple when a shot rang out.

It struck the wall of the house, a moment after the boy had been pulled inside.

"I have a hazy recollection, as a young fellow, of being shot at by a soldier during the Civil War. I was just pulled back out of the way in time."

Later, the Lynch house, which was suspected of being Republican, was raided by Free State troops.

"I think our house was probably identified as having some sort of contact with the 'Irregulars'. We had friends and relations in West Cork, where my father came from. They used to come to visit while they were still on the run, so to speak.

"Even though my parents never talked about it, there was some sort of succour by way of food, clothing, shelter or concealment of arms for IRA fellows at the time.

"That's the first recollection I might have . . ."

If this was Lynch's introduction to "Republicanism", it left no lasting impression – other than an abhorrence of violence.

In 1975 he told the *Irish Times* "Yes, I am a Republican, with a small 'r' and a big 'R'."

Either way, his Republicanism was inclusive rather than exclusive; much closer to Wolfe Tone's than to the "Brits Out" variety.

Which is not to say it didn't evolve. It did.

In 1975, for instance, he could still say that the "soul of Fianna Fáil is still anti-partition".

After 1970 even that apparently core value was being rethought.

At that time strong anti-partition feeling was still prevalent in Fianna Fáil, by history and tradition the "greener" of the two main parties.

After 1968 Lynch was coming under pressure, not only to aid the beleaguered Catholics in Derry, Belfast and elsewhere in the North, but also to avail of the extraordinary events to advance the party's stated ambition to dismantle the Northern State.

Contending with that pressure proved to be his greatest test.

"In all discussion of this," he said in 1975, "you must remember that to be in Government in 1969-70 was a very traumatic experience. And following the scenes in Derry in 1969 there was a very strong feeling that there should be something greater than diplomatic activity. I can understand the feeling of a lot of people in this regard. I knew plenty of good, decent people who were saying: 'Why don't we do something more positive?'

"But in those days to have done 'anything more' would have led to annihilation. I don't mind telling you that I had a hard job maintaining the balance at the time."

That balance was threatened by a controversial speech made by Neil Blaney in Letterkenny on 8 December 1969, in which he said "the Fianna Fáil Party has never taken a decision to rule out the use of force if the circumstances in the Six Counties so demand."

Lynch, in responding, alluded to his statement in the Dáil on 22 October 1969, in which he said: "The Government in this part of Ireland has no intention of mounting an armed invasion of the North".

He went on to reiterate the "peaceful means" by which unity would eventually be achieved.

The balance between confrontation and reconciliation had been safeguarded, and would henceforth be maintained through the stormy times which lay ahead.

At all times in his political life, there was a dissociation in his mind between Republicanism and physical force.

And this would be the key to his policy of protecting the country from the escalation of Northern Ireland violence.

"I have never considered it necessary to carry a gun in order to be a Republican."

But circumstances would compel him to play a double-game at times, trying to face, Janus-like, two ways at once.

This led to a memorable headline in *Magill* magazine in October 1977 – "The Artful Ambiguities of Jack Lynch".

In it Vincent Browne attempted to analyse what became known in some quarters as "Lynch speak", his appearing to say something and not say it.

Browne came, *inter alia*, to this conclusion: "The truth of the matter, of course, is that while it is Fianna Fáil's policy to press the British to declare Britain's commitment to implement an ordered withdrawal, it is not Mr Lynch's policy.

"He was pushed into accepting the policy at one of the lowest points in his leadership of Fianna Fáil . . . "

What was his policy? The answer came from an unlikely source. In an RTE interview in June 1979, the former British Ambassador to the USA, Peter Jay, said Britain should align its policy with that of Jack Lynch, declaring that the long-term future of the 32 counties was to come together, by agreement, and not at the point of a gun."

Given the history and provenance of the party he joined and eventually led, this was seen as a marked departure; indeed, in some quarters it was seen as treachery.

Lynch knows full well the futility of trying to wish history out of existence.

He does not have to be reminded that but for a specific historical process, a specific chain of historical happenings, he would never have followed in the footsteps of Dev and Lemass.

Perhaps he might even modify the maxim of Karl Marx: "Men make their own history, but they do not make it in conditions of their own choosing".

At the same time, he never saw himself as a prisoner of history, and he certainly didn't feel its constraining hand on his shoulder in a way that his two predecessors did.

That was partly an accident of birth and of timing. But it was also a matter of resolution, part of a conscious understanding that, by drawing on the past, we can re-shape the present and set a new agenda for the future.

Dev and Lemass spent much of their formative years with guns in their pockets.

Lemass was born in 1900 – making him 17 years older than Lynch.

Dev was a child of the year 1882, making him Lynch's senior by 25 years.

They were men of an earlier, more violent and bloodier time in Ireland, and it inevitably coloured their thinking and their outlook.

When Lemass made his famous remark in 1928 that Fianna Fáil was a "slightly constitutional" party, he was doing so in an atmosphere of uncertainty, at a time when there were real fears that if the defeated side in the Civil War came to power through the electoral process a *colpo di stato* might be staged.

The party wished, added Lemass, to achieve its aims by constitutional means, but "if not, then we would not confine ourselves to them".

In digesting this, one must allow for the fact that it was uttered just six years after a very bitter Civil War.

Some of Fianna Fáil's founder members had so little trust in the process of parliamentary politics that on their first entry to Parliament in 1927, they brought with them the guns with which they had fought the Civil War – just in case.

They lingered long enough to become model democrats and, in the years which followed, the party itself became, with the Unionist Party of Northern Ireland, the longest reigning party in Europe.

It was this later tradition which influenced Lynch. He was incapable of making the kind of comment Lemass had made.

For him, in his time, Fianna Fáil was a totally constitutional party.

And that was the essential difference between between Lynch, Lemass and Dev.

That's what set him apart within the Fianna Fáil context.

The other tradition lingered, of course, fed and sustained by what has been appropriately termed "verbal republicanism".

The twin national aims of abolishing Partition and restoring the Irish language, Fianna Fáil's basic policy, had served the party well for decades – at least in electoral terms.

Until 1968-69.

Then all was changed, changed utterly.

The ghosts of 1916 had finally to be faced.

Even before then, the twin aims were a bit frayed around the edges.

Lynch could also point back beyond Lemass, particularly to 1955. In that year Eamon de Valera told the Árd Fheis that Irish unity could not be achieved by the exercise of force.

"Even if it were militarily successful," he added, "we would not have the harmony essential for real unity."

He could even point further back to the minutes of the proceedings of the private session of the Second Dáil for 22 August 1921 – during the Truce period – which recorded the following from Eamon de Valera:

"They (i.e. Dáil Éireann) had not the power and some of them had not the inclination to use force with Ulster. He did not think that policy would be successful. They would be making the same mistake with that section, as England had made with Ireland.

"He would not be responsible for such a policy . . . For his part, if the Republic were recognised, he would be in favour of giving each county power to vote itself out of the Republic if it so wishes."

Incidentally, as Dr Conor Cruise O'Brlen noted in a long article entitled "Shades of Republicans" for the *Irish Times* in March, 1975, this statement, though made in 1921, was not officially published until 1972.

By then, after the trauma of the Arms Crisis, the voices indulging in verbal republicanism or dreamy rhetoric and ambiguous sentiments about Partition and the North, were all but stilled within the party.

In the immediate post-1968 period, even Jack Lynch seemed to fall victim to aspects of this.

To many it looked as though the party had reverted to verbal republicanism in its policy statement on Northern Ireland with its calls on Britain to declare its intent to withdraw from Northern Ireland.

On 13 August 1969, after the "Battle of the Bogside", Lynch made his famous speech on RTE stressing that the Irish Government "will no longer stand (idly) by".

The following day the first British troops arrived in Northern Ireland.

"I was unhappy from the outset about the introduction of British troops on to the streets of Northern Ireland. But their presence there soon became a political reality, and there were obvious dangers in their precipitous withdrawal."

By mid-1970 the harsh realities had effected change.

Colm Toibin has summed it up: "The evasions and shadow language of the previous generation still held sway, however, except now the difference between what was being said and what was actually meant was getting greater."

By the time of the 1971 Árd Fheis the harsh realities had taken a firm hold on the mind and soul of the party.

Toibin, writing on the party and its culture in the *Sunday Independent* in November 1990 is again pertinent: "The Arms Trial was the drama in which traditional values and beliefs met head-on with modernity. The voice of traditional nationalism sounded hoarse after 1970 . . . "

By 1971 modernity, in the shape of Jack Lynch, had won.

The "hawks" were in disarray. "When it erupted in the Dáil and later in the courts, and later still in the party's annual Árd Fheis, the action taken by Jack Lynch, as leader, was to test each man and woman in a commitment to law and order republicanism," wrote the late John Healy in May 1976, in an article in *The Word* magazine marking the 50th anniversary of the founding of Fianna Fáil.

"This 'slightly constitutional' party still contained hawks but Lynch, an advocate of peaceful means, faced down the hawks in the Árd Fheis, in the Oireachtas party, and in the country ..."

That was in 1971. Thereafter, the evolution of Lynch's thinking on Republicanism and the North was clearly evident.

Domination of the North by the Republic was never part of his credo, as he was to tell the Cambridge Union in 1980.

Since the 1960s he had been, along with Sean Lemass, in the forefront of the tentative rapprochement between Dublin and Stormont.

He accompanied Lemass to Belfast on 14 January 1965 for the historic meeting with Northern Prime Minister, Terence O'Neill. That visit did much to break the sterile years of cross-border acrimony.

And after taking over from Lemass, he himself continued the "thawing" process by travelling to Stormont to meet O'Neill on 11 December 1967.

It was a case of too little, too late – with history, rather than the personalities involved, to blame.

And after the North exploded, after the initial crisis of 1968-69, Lynch's instinct was to avoid confrontation with Stormont and, beyond that, Britain.

In declarations aimed *urbi et orbi* he disseminated his brand of "gunless" republicanism.

Typical of these was the way he dealt, in February 1974, with a question about a conflict of opinion within Fianna Fáil over the definition of "Republicanism" in the following way:

"In the past Republicanism connoted militancy to some people. But there is now no support, nor has there been for a long time, for that concept of Republicanism within the Fianna Fáil ranks.

"Certainly, there has been no support for that concept since the 1970 Ard Fheis when there was a strong upsurge from the floor against permitting the Party to have a militant tinge."

Hand-in-hand with this, over the next decade, went a series of proclamations (harking back to his famous speech in Tralee, County Kerry, on 20 September 1969), emphasising his commitment to "unity by consent".

In June 1984, after the visit to Ireland of President Ronald Reagan, Lynch told a powerful lobby of Irish-American opinion that the "vast majority of people in this country want to achieve unity in a non-violent way".

Within a matter of months (October 1984), there occurred the most dramatic illustration of his aversion to the "republicanism" of the Provisional IRA. It also showed that Lynch was no longer locked into a "unified Ireland" solution.

The scene was Kilfeacle, County Tipperary, where the annual commemoration service for old IRA campaigner Sean Treacy (shot dead in Dublin in 1920) turned into a major debate on the national question when the former Taoiseach and the Sinn Féin President, Gerry Adams, made conflicting statements.

Both speakers mentioned the Brighton bombing the previous week, with Lynch describing it as an "atrocity" and Adams claiming it was "an inevitable result of British interference in Irish affairs".

In his address Lynch referred to the Report of the New Ireland Forum (issued in May 1984).

"I understand that, from a nationalist point of view, the unitary state is the preferred option. But if our preferred option is not available we must, in accordance with the Forum Report, look at the other alternatives, be they the federal/confederal model, the joint authority model or other views which might lead towards peace and stability."

And he criticised the Provisional IRA. "If their aim is genuinely to re-unite the Irish people, let them turn away from violence and follow the constitutional path and peaceful methods."

A year earlier (November 1983) there was another Lynch-Adams clash when the former Taoiseach entered a controversy over the Kilmichael Commemoration by speaking out strongly against the proposed attendance of the Sinn Féin President.

He said the stated policy of the Adams' party was to destabilise this country that "McSwiney and MacCurtain sought to make free".

And he went on: "They would have abhorred the brutal and sacrilegious activities of those who, while calling themselves freedom fighters, would blow young husbands to pieces in the sight of their wives and families, or would shoot down people while worshipping our common God".

If his belief in a peaceful settlement of the Northern Ireland problem never wavered, his willingness to initiate changes to speed that process along was another matter.

After all, Wolfe Tone's concept of Republicanism embraced "Catholic, Protestant and Dissenter".

By 1979, his last year in power, his timorousness in this regard had even begun to annoy the SDLP.

On 23 September 1979, a week before the Pope's visit, John Hume, who was to become leader of the SDLP in November, spoke at a conference on Anglo-European Relations in Waterville, County

Kerry, and said the Irish and British Governments should act together and take a decisive initiative on Northern Ireland.

Hume criticised the South for failing to make its intentions clear.

"Do they accept that the goal is a pluralist Ireland, one that is dominated by no section or tradition?" he asked. "I believe that they do, but it is long past the time when the meaning of unity should be spelt out. Agreement, yes; coercion, no!"

His remarks were directed at Lynch, and reflected a general impatience with the Fianna Fáil regime.

A paragraph by Barry White in his 1984 biography of *Hume, Statesman of the Troubles,* is revealing.

"In visits to Dublin, another leading SDLP member said it was impossible to tell what Jack Lynch's Northern policy was. He seemed to have lost interest, prior to resigning in December."

The Taoiseach (he had only a couple of months left in office) had other preoccupations at the time.

But Hume's impatience was understandable.

Lynch may not, at that stage, have regarded the political unification of this island as an unrealistic national objective (though Kevin Boland and Neil Blaney had asserted that Fianna Fáil's first national aim – Abolish Partition – had been abandoned by him long ago) .

He may not have yet come to accept that, in Con Houlihan's trenchant description, "the concept of Irish unity is a stultifying myth".

Movement in that direction would come down the road.

Either way, his concept of Republicanism did not appear to extend to a New Republic that would be pluralist and non-sectarian.

Much later, free of the responsibility, the demands and the constraints of office, with time to reflect, he would work towards a broader, more all-embracing definition of Republicanism.

By then all the power had gone – except the power of argument, of reason, and of conviction.

But conviction in this area, as with much else for Lynch, came by a process of gradualism.

There were no mighty leaps, no conceptual breakthroughs. That just wasn't the Lynch way.

There is a ring of truth about Bruce Arnold's belief that Lynch, certainly in this area, was "the reluctant man of power", doing the minimum and delaying it for as long as possible.

"He was the classic Irish leader, passive, seeking consensus, pushed towards firmness and action by others . . ."

Yet his achievements remain impressive.

If his brand of Republicanism was not flexible enough for John Hume at times, we mustn't forget where Lynch was coming from, nor must we overlook the cultural and socio-political baggage he was burdened with.

He changed the fundamental thinking of Fianna Fáil ("The Republican Party") on the "national question".

And there was no going back – not even, as some expected and hoped, after Lynch's departure.

I remember speaking to Fine Gael's Paddy Cooney, who served as Minister for Justice in the Cosgrave-led Coalition of 1973-77, about Lynch, in Luxembourg in July 1990. This was his summary of what Lynch managed to achieve:

"He changed the thinking within Fianna Fáil. He weaned them away from the notion that the future of Northern Ireland could only be determined by the consent of the majority of the people of Ireland, to the notion that it must be determined by the consent of the majority of Northern Ireland.

"That was a great achievement, and he'll hope to get credit for that..."

In his 1988 book *Under Contract to the Enemy*, Kevin Boland said Lynch, as Taoiseach at the time, "can be said to have founded the new post-Republican Fianna Fáil".

That is both extreme and inaccurate, and also based on a misconceived and narrow notion of "Republicanism".

It was a notion Lynch had long since eschewed.

But, that Boland should even acknowledge this is the best indication of what Lynch achieved.

Although intended as a scathing criticism, it is in fact a tribute to the Corkman.

Boland, in saying this, is in fact granting Lynch something which the latter never claimed: a major overhaul and reformation of Fianna Fáil's original concept of Republicanism.

Oddly enough, it was Mrs Mairin Lynch who was explicit about that.

"I feel my husband has done much in the evolution of the overall policies and philosophies of the Fianna Fáil Party today, to face up to the realities of Ireland's increasing international status and obligations, and to seek an understanding between all its peoples."

Raymond Smith is wrong when he says that when Haughey succeeded Lynch in 1979 the wheel had turned a full circle in less than a decade, particularly in regard to the re-definition of "Republicanism" and Northern policy generally.

It had perhaps in personal terms for Haughey; but not in party or policy terms.

Whatever Haughey's own proclivities, he had to face the reality that by 1979 Fianna Fáil had abandoned the possibility of any crude, simple or quick solution to the problem of Northern Ireland.

The "post-Republican Fianna Fáil" was a reality Haughey had to accommodate himself to and live with.

On the national question, the party has not changed under Haughey. He has changed with it.

The changes initiated by Lynch have determined the context within which Haughey has to operate.

And we have seen this most demonstrably in relation to the Anglo-Irish Agreement of 1985 and its aftermath.

That is a true measure of what Lynch brought about.

Bruce Arnold's assessment of him is germane.

"He referred to Northern Ireland as his major preoccupation as Taoiseach. His essential policy approach was established in Sean Lemass's footsteps, well before the troubles began in 1968, and was based on reconciliation rather than confrontation.

"It was at least a two-way reconciliation: North-South, as well as Nationalist-Unionist within Northern Ireland. It embraced also, a calmer and more positive approach to Anglo-Irish relations.

"Lynch achieved a genuine change of attitude in the South on what is euphemistically called the 'national question', and he did so without losing broad support ... "

"In my estimation, Lynch has been the bravest leader of the party. History may say he was also the ablest political leader, for de Valera or Lemass never had to cope with the crises, both in the Party, the Cabinet and the North, with which Lynch has had to cope."

An Taoiseach Jack Lynch and Captain Terence O'Neill

21. Lynch and the GAA

He was one of the brightest stars in the constellation of the GAA, a god in its pantheon, the first dual star of hurling and football at a time when the term was hardly in use.

His record of six consecutive Senior All-Ireland medals stands as a unique achievement, unlikely now ever to be matched.

Yet it isn't generally known that Jack Lynch was once suspended by the GAA for three months – for attending a rugby match.

What's more, Lynch had just captained the Cork senior hurling team in a victorious All-Ireland final, one of the famous four-in-a-row.

The year was 1943.

And the circumstances, to say the least, were somewhat strange.

"I was attending law courses at UCC at the time, and I knew a lot of rugby people. On the day in question – a Saturday – I had lunch with some of them, and they invited me to the match that afternoon at The Mardyke.

"I saw the match from the Pavilion, and afterwards I walked down The Mardyke towards the centre of the city.

"The following Sunday week, Cork were playing a game in the National Hurling League. I had captained the 1942 team. Tom O'Reilly was the Glen delegate to the Cork County Board at the time, and at a meeting of the Board, the Cork team for the League game was called out.

"Jack Lynch's name wasn't mentioned, which was a bit unusual. Tom O'Reilly asked why I hadn't been picked. He was told by an official that I had suspended myself.

"What that meant was that I was seen either going into, or coming from the Final Irish Trial, and someone had reported me.

"However, knowing a bit about the law, I decided that a man had a right to be heard in his own defence, so I wrote an appeal to the Munster Council.

"I sent it off, and a couple of days later I got a call from a member of the Council who knew me. 'If I were you I'd withdraw that appeal'," he advised me.

"'Why should I?' I replied."

The answer Lynch got – which clearly astonished him – was that it wouldn't be accepted because he had not signed his name in Irish. The three months suspension was upheld.

Two years earlier, Lynch was involved in another controversy with the GAA authorities over an "incident" which concerned his friend and team-mate Dr Jim Young.

They had played together for the Munster hurling team which won the 1940 Railway Cup, and sometime later the players were invited to a ceremony in Clancy's Bar in Cork for the presentation of the medals.

Lynch arrived at the door of the bar, and was waiting outside to meet Young as part of a pre-arranged appointment, when he was told that the latter had not been invited to the function.

When Jack enquired as to the reason for this, he was informed that Young had "suspended himself" because, on the eve of a match against Kilkenny in the old Cork Athletic Grounds, he attended a rugby club dance in the Metropole Hotel.

On hearing this, Lynch decided that he too would not attend the function, and made this known.

"I refused to go to the dinner because of the suspension of Jim Young."

But he was to pay a price for his boycott.

"I was regarded as being very *persona non grata*, and for the next three or four years I was only a sub on the Munster team. In fact, I think I have the record for being a sub with Munster!"

Even then there was a clue to the way Lynch's mind was working on the "national question".

The Gaelic Athletic Association's pronounced and narrow nationalism always made him feel a bit uneasy. And of the GAA's "politics", he took a somewhat jaundiced view, even before his own career in politics began.

There was clear evidence of this later on, when he espoused a more ecumenical approach to what, for decades, had been known as "foreign games".

Long after his own playing career was over, he still got embroiled – unwittingly – in controversy.

Paddy Downey, GAA correspondent for the *Irish Times*, recalled the occasion while attending the 1991 Texaco Awards dinner in Dublin.

"The Texaco Awards have not been immune to controversy, a condition which, from time to time, befalls all selections of this kind.

"Although it never flamed into a major row, the strangest and saddest episode in more than three decades of these awards occurred in 1980 when Jack Lynch, who had resigned as leader of Fianna Fáil and Taoiseach the year before, was chosen by the sports editors for the Hall of Fame Award.

"The legendary Cork hurler was informed of that decision but then, the management of the sponsors or the sports editors – or both – changed their minds.

"But why? Because they thought, foolishly, that a crisis (what crisis?) might arise if Jack Lynch walked onto the stage to receive the trophy from his successor, Charles Haughey, who had agreed to present the awards.

"Always the sportsman, Jack Lynch accepted without demur what, to another, might have seemed to be a grievous slight. Amends were made a few years later, however, and he duly entered the Texaco Hall of Fame."

That episode apart, it is fair to assume that the GAA authorities were less than happy with his independent approach, though there was precious little that they could do about it.

That didn't deter one President of the Association from obliquely lecturing Lynch, when the latter was Taoiseach, about the need to take a "tougher line" with the British at a delicate juncture in Anglo-Irish relations.

And it wasn't done in private either. No – it was done at Croke Park while Lynch sat in the Hogan Stand.

Lynch doesn't need to be reminded of the overlap between the GAA and Fianna Fáil, or of the tendency of both to see themselves as more Irish, and better Irish, than the rest of the people.

Some might even say that he himself was a beneficiary of that overlap, given the practice within Fianna Fáil of wooing leading GAA figures to its ranks.

He wouldn't deny that. He wouldn't deny that it was through Blackpool, Glen Rovers and the GAA that he made his way into active politics.

In fact, in discussing his entry into politics in 1948, he admits that Glen Rovers decided they would conduct a campaign for him.

"The Fianna Fáil organisation was not happy when the Glen put out special polling cards and did a personalised canvass for me.

"I asked Glen Rovers not to do it, but they argued that it was a purely private matter for them and didn't involve the Fianna Fáil party. I went so far as to impound the personal canvass cards but they got out another supply.

"There was some tension for a while as the other Fianna Fáil candidates, quite rightly, didn't approve of what was happening."

It did Lynch no harm, however; in a sign of things to come, he topped the Fianna Fáil poll with 5,594 first preference votes.

For him the link between the GAA and Fianna Fáil, at least at local level, was very real.

And nor would he deny, in the broader context, that in the early years of the Party, and indeed for many decades after 1926, there was almost a symbiotic relationship between Fianna Fáil and the GAA.

The Association had been founded in Thurles in 1884 with avowedly nationalist aims and objectives.

It was anti-British in outlook and imposed a ban (Rule 27 rescinded in 1971 at the Congress in Belfast) upon its members which prevented them from participating in or observing certain specified non-Gaelic games.

Its rules also excluded those serving in the British Army and the RUC from membership – a situation which still pertains today and which is still a matter of contention.

In an interview with Paddy Downey of the *Irish Times* on 16 February 1991, for instance, the then new President of the Association, Peter Quinn, had this to say:

"If that ban wasn't there we would not feel it necessary to introduce it. But there are two things which make it very difficult to change.

"One is the continuing occupation of the Crossmaglen grounds and the harassment of the Association's members. The other is that the RUC are not acceptable to a large proportion of the population of the Six Counties.

"And the main reason for that is that they are seen to have a political as opposed to a policing role. There is some evidence that that perception is justified.

"In fact, Chris Ryder confirms it in his book *The RUC – A Force Under Fire.* That is obviously unacceptable to the nationalist community.

"My own view is that the ban will go when we have a normal society in the area, but that is some way off yet."

Jack Lynch's view is that removing the ban now would help to "normalise" society.

This was implicit in what he had to say in an address which he gave on 22 March 1985.

Throughout his political life he had spoken from many platforms – but never until then from a pulpit.

That was remedied when he delivered an address at an

ecumenical thanksgiving service for the "gift of sport" in the Church of the Sacred Heart, Donnybrook, Dublin.

His debut parable was distinctly non-ecclesiastical. Before a large congregation which included dozens of sports people, he extolled the virtue of sport as a means of breaking down barriers, and of inculcating discipline and respect in young people.

And, more significantly, he promoted the idea of an All-Ireland soccer team.

Of sport in general he declared: "It is a tremendous antidote to crime, a great chastener, a builder of character."

He might have added that when motivated by a narrow philosophy, sport can also be a builder of barriers, and a creator of divides.

Like many others, he believes the burden of history hangs heavily on the GAA.

And he would surely have endorsed the trenchantly expressed views of Tom Woulfe of the Dublin County Board on RTE's "Liveline" programme on 26 February 1991.

He argued that there was still a pronounced "nationalist ideology" at the Association's core.

"The notion still prevails that it is unfitting for the true Gael to play soccer or rugby because of their foreign or British connection."

Like Lynch, Woulfe is critical of the "politics" of the GAA, and they share common ground in objecting to a concept of republicanism based on hatred of Britain.

That particular programme set out to explore why the GAA authorities still refused to allow soccer or rugby to be played at Croke Park or other GAA venues.

Given the huge impact made by the Irish soccer team under Jack Charlton – "Jack's Army" is perhaps an ill-chosen label – over the past few years, this debate has taken on a new relevance, and involves a bigger audience than ever before.

As Jack Lynch has acknowledged, the outpourings of national sentiment, the enormous and genuine pride in the achievements of the team in the European championships and the 1990 World Cup in Italy, lend added cogency to the "ecumenical" nature of sport.

When Tom Woulfe says that "a lot of people would like to see soccer in Croke Park" , he is undoubtedly giving voice to a widely held feeling.

It is a feeling shared by Jack Lynch, and articulated by him even before Jack Charlton became Irish team manager.

On 24 September 1986 on *The Late Late Show*, and again on 17 February 1987 at the final of the *Irish Times* student debate in Dublin, Lynch called for the opening up of GAA facilities to other sports.

He suggested on *The Late Late* that Pairc Uí Chaoimh in Cork might be opened up to rugby football and other sports in the interests of fostering good relations between all sports.

"I had in mind, for example, rugby matches where Munster teams played big visiting teams from, say, Australia or New Zealand. I thought this would be good all round, but the GAA turned it down since, as the GAA was competing with other games for players, Gaelic games might suffer as a result, they said."

And in 1987 he told the students that he had always been opposed to the ban on foreign games, acknowledging that he was once suspended from the Association for attending a "foreign" game.

"I always regarded the ban as divisive, and therefore a negative factor in the development of Irish society."

Responding to student criticism of the GAA, he also said he regretted the GAA's decision to alter the rule which said it was a "non-political" organisation and substitute it with "non-party political".

He stressed that he felt it should be a sporting and not a political organisation.

In a strictly sporting context he has not been slow to speak out against what he once called the "hidden professionalism" in the GAA, or the need to reform the rules.

In the course of an address to the Philosophical Society at UCC in November 1986, the former Taoiseach – referring both to the GAA and the IRFU – said they were two great amateur sports bodies, which had to resort to some degree of professionalism in recent years in order to meet financial demands.

There was nothing wrong with this, indeed it had become necessary, and amateur players were entitled to the same standard of facilities as those in the professional area.

He acknowledged that collective team training was a necessary facet of these games today. And it was only right and fair that players be paid some travelling expenses and compensation for loss of wages.

At the same time, he did not approve of the practice of players going to America at weekends to take part in games there. That was not fair to club or to county, and the players could not give of their best. It was a practice which should be discouraged – and has been since.

He made it clear he had nothing against professional sports. It was a valid means of earning a living. But he could not help feeling that those who played the game they loved for money were lacking in the dignity and independence associated with amateur sports.

"It is degrading to see soccer players bought and sold by clubs," he told the students. "It is a great shame that a person, because he loves his game, can be bought and sold like a chattel. It takes from the spirit of the game."

There was bound to be a degree of commercialism in the GAA and the IRFU in modern times, and he sees nothing wrong with that.

"But I hope that truly amateur sport in this country will never be professionalised."

More recently, in November 1990, he called for a change in the rules (a theme he has addressed before), and warned the GAA that unless the reforms were introduced, both hurling and football would continue to suffer as spectator sports.

"The games are in a mess because of their rules," he told the bosses of the GAA. "And if their grandeur is to be restored, then you must review and reform the rules."

The former Taoiseach also poured scorn on the current practice of selecting a 'Man of the Match' on big game occasions at club and county level.

"Hurling and football are team games, and you can't win medals unless you are playing with great teams.

"More often than not, the 'Man of the Match' award goes to someone who scores goals, but what about the players who set up the goals?

"And when did we last see such an award going to a goalkeeper? Yet how many times have winning teams been kept in the game by a great keeper?

"I am not old-fashioned, but I must confess I am not at all keen on this 'Man of the Match' concept. I object to it."

Emphasising that he would yield ground to no one in his admiration for Gaelic games, Lynch warned on that occasion that unless there was a major overhaul of the rules, the quality of the games would continue to deteriorate.

Describing hurling as the greatest field game in the world, he is adamant that it is being ruined by over-use of the hand-pass.

He also stressed that the tackling rules, especially in relation to Gaelic football, were not working.

"To say they are inappropriately set out would be an understatement. They are turning football into a scrambling game. Here also I would only allow perhaps two hand-passes . . . "

Over the years, of course, the former Taoiseach, apart from reiterating his love of hurling and football, has had many very positive comments to make about the GAA. He believes it was a very positive factor, for instance, in healing the wounds of the Civil War.

"I need only point to the fact that the people who opposed each other vehemently in the Civil War, played in the immediate aftermath in the same teams at club and county level, and on the same GAA councils and committees," he commented in 1987.

In the context of the 1990s a new kind of "civil war" exists on this island, and new departures are called for.

Mr Lynch believes the GAA has a new role to play here.

As far back as October 1981 he had put on record his views about a "political" GAA.

Addressing a Bord na nÓg meeting of the Cork County Board, he warned that many dedicated GAA people might become disenchanted by ambiguous statements from prominent GAA members on paramilitaries in the North of Ireland.

"A debate has been going on for some years about the alleged involvement of the GAA in Irish politics in the light of the continuing troubles in the North over the last decade. . ."

He acknowledged that, in addition to promoting its own games, the GAA also had the role of promoting Irish culture generally, and that it aspired to – "and justifiably so" – the reunification of Ireland.

"The vast majority of its members seek this reunification through peaceful, political and democratic means, in harmony and reconciliation with our Northern brethren.

"A small minority must not be permitted to use the organisation in pursuit of that aspiration or otherwise, under the umbrella of the Gaelic Athletic Association."

In a much broader context, wherein one might consider or attempt to redefine the concept of "Irishness", Lynch also has sympathy for those who argue that the sentiments aroused by the success (relative though it be) of the Irish soccer team, or the success of any Irish sportsmen or sportswomen on the international scene, are part of a new emerging nationalism.

This is a nationalism which no longer relies for its core definition on being "anti" something or someone, or some ideology or creed or "ism" or race.

It is a nationalism which is making new demands not just on the GAA, but on all of us.

And Lynch recognises that the problem facing the GAA is a microcosm of the problem facing the Oireachtas and political leaders.

Do they wait for public opinion and society to change perceptibly before responding with changes of their own?

Or do they help to promote change by changing themselves and making changes for the specific purpose of giving a lead.

Everything that Jack Lynch has said on this over the past four decades suggests, either implicitly or explicitly, the latter course.

Jack Lynch in Croke Park on All-Ireland day with Cardinal Tomás O'Fiaich and Máirín

22. The Presidential "Affaire"

The streets of Dublin were relatively quiet when the black Ford Granada carrying the Taoiseach, Jack Lynch, left the Government Buildings and headed through the darkness for Cabra.

It was the evening of Saturday, 29 September 1979.

In the back seat, wearing a dark suit and tie, an unusually sombre Mr Lynch fiddled with an unlit pipe, his thoughts still on a file he had left on his desk as the car picked up speed.

The file, from Garda Headquarters in the Phoenix Park, was an update on the investigation into the murder of Earl Mountbatten off the Sligo coast.

The death of Mountbatten, who came for annual stays at Classiebawn Castle near Sligo, had caused widespread shock, anger and revulsion, and had focussed world attention onto Ireland and its "troubles".

On the morning of Monday, 27 August 1979, he had been killed (along with three others, including the 15-year old boatboy from Enniskillen) when the boat he was sailing in – a 28 foot cruiser called the Shadow V – was blown to smithereens by a bomb placed on board by the Provisional IRA while the vessel was berthed in Mullaghmore Harbour in Sligo.

The assassination of Mountbatten and the murder the same day of 18 British soldiers at Warranpoint in Co. Down, had placed new strains on Anglo-Irish relations.

Mountbatten, who was 79, was related to Queen Elizabeth II, and there was understandable outrage in the British media at the cold-blooded murder of such a prominent member of the British Establishment.

Earlier that year Margaret Hilda Thatcher had taken over from James Callaghan as Prime Minister, though in September of 1979 few could have guessed at the impact she would make over the next eleven years, not least on Anglo-Irish relations.

Lynch had already met her in a formal context, and they had spoken briefly when he flew to Britain to attend Mountbatten's funeral. ·

He had not yet formulated an opinion on her, though her steely self-assurance and her implacability towards the IRA had already impressed him during their earlier meetings.

The killing of Mounbatten and the 18 soldiers had saddened Lynch, and had added to his feelings of gloom about the whole Northern Ireland situation.

He regarded the IRA's campaign of violence as mindless and pointless. Although the IRA apologists in Sinn Féin mouthed platitudes about "unity" and "freedom" and "justice", Lynch was convinced that the so-called "armed struggle" was creating new divisions and exacerbating old ones.

He also knew that the killings had forced the Vatican to make a significant alteration to the Pope's programme. Plans for a visit to Armagh had been scrapped, much to the disappointment of the Irish Bishops.

The Taoiseach himself was also disappointed, because he believed the presence of John Paul II in the North could only be a force for good, and might conceivably help to end violence and heal divisions.

Like most Irish people who are old enough to remember 1979, Jack Lynch will never forget the historic visit to Ireland of Pope John Paul II, the 283rd successor to St Peter as Vicar of Christ.

For three days, at the very end of September and the beginning of October, there was a very special spirit abroad in the land, a spirit characterised by goodwill, generosity, unselfishness and magnanimity.

Church leaders talked, hoped and prayed for some kind of permanent transformation. Editorial writers made much of phrases like "spiritual renaissance" and the "dawning of a new era for Catholicism in Ireland".

The visit of Karol Wojtyla – who a year before had made history when he became the first non-Italian Pope in 450 years – touched Christians of all denominations, though it had special significance for Ireland's 3.7 million Catholics.

The arrangements for the visit were elaborate and costly. They were also complicated and touched by controversy. And all because of Northern Ireland.

Behind the scenes in Rome, as high Vatican officials sat down with key members of the Irish Hierarchy, such as the Archbishop of Armagh, Cardinal Tomas Ó Fiaich, difficulties over the Papal itinerary emerged.

The key question was – would the Pontiff visit Northern Ireland?

We know now that he wanted to go there, and that the initial itinerary provided for that. In mid-August the Vatican had told the Irish Primate, Cardinal Ó Fiaich, that the Pope would visit Armagh.

The Cardinal was delighted. There were several reasons why the North should have been included in Pope John Paul II's programme.

There was first of all its Catholic population, and the desire on the Pope's part to show that he was mindful of the situation.

In addition, Armagh, as the See of St Patrick, is the ecclesiastical capital of Ireland, the home, not just of the Catholic Primate, but of the Church of Ireland Primate as well. And a Papal visit in 1979 could have had profound symbolic and ecumenical ramifications.

On the 27 August the Cardinal travelled to Rome to finalise the details of the itinerary. Very soon after he arrived, the news of the deaths of Mountbatten and the soldiers came through.

Ó Fiaich knew the IRA outrages would change the entire situation, even though it took the Vatican Secretary of State, Cardinal

Agostino Casaroli, to convince the Pope that a visit to the North was now out of the question.

It was to be. The IRA had seen to that. And instead of crossing the Border, the Pope went to Drogheda on 29 September and, at a vast open air Mass, made the most dramatic address of his Irish visit, appealing "in language of passionate pleading", to the IRA.

"On my knees I beg you," he said, "to turn away from the paths of violence and return to the paths of peace."

Those words, spoken just hours earlier (a copy of the Pope's speech had been sent in advance to Lynch), were recalled by the Taoiseach as his Granada crossed through Dublin. Momentarily, his spirits lifted as he dwelt on the possibility – remote though it seemed – that they might actually have an effect on the godfathers of the IRA.

The meeting with the Pope in the Nunciature in Cabra had been delayed for two hours because John Paul II, who had been greeted by tumultous crowds on the first day of his Irish visit, was behind schedule.

Lynch was looking forward to meeting the Polish Pontiff who had already, a year into his pontificate, shown himself to be a strong and charismatic leader, a man determined to restore stability to a Church shaken to its very foundations by the reforms of Vatican II (1962-65).

Never hesitant about describing himself as a traditional Catholic, Lynch had mixed feelings about aspects of the post-conciliar Church.

In addition, like his idol Eamon de Valera, he did not possess a well-developed sense of the need for the separation of Church and State.

He was not a conceptual thinker, least of all in this area.

As he shut out all thoughts of the file from Garda HQ, the Taoiseach little realised that, very soon – within a matter of minutes, in fact– he would be confronted with a situation which had enormous potential for upsetting Church-State relations.

Moments later his car was flagged down by a senior Garda officer, and the message passed to the Taoiseach took him completely by surprise, and filled him with alarm and foreboding.

In essence, Lynch was informed that information had reached the Gardai indicating that an English tabloid newspaper was about to break a story implying that the President of Ireland had a mistress.

The disturbing news could hardly come at a more sensitive time in Church-State relations.

And Lynch knew straight away that if what he had been told had any basis in truth, it would erupt into a scandal of international proportions and would cause enormous embarrassment for Ireland, its Government and people, for the Irish Church, and for its most distinguished visitor, Pope John Paul II.

Could it possibly be true? Was his old friend, President Patrick J. Hillery, involved in an extra-marital affair?

The thought shocked Lynch. In matters of sex, as one colleague put it, he was "very straight-laced". He had no time for hanky-panky.

If Lynch was taken aback by the news passed to him while on his way to a papal audience in Cabra, others in Dublin were not.

During the previous 24 hours, word of a possible Presidential scandal had filtered through to media circles.

The night before, top editorial staff in the *Irish Press* certainly thought a major story was about to break.

Not that anything other than rumours had surfaced from London. If the Taoiseach was unsure of what the true situation was, so were the newspapers in Dublin.

I was in the Burgh Quay editorial offices of the *Press* Group as part of the team covering the papal visit on the day before Lynch got the tip-off. The Chief News Editor called me over, told me what was happening, and said, as religious affairs correspondent, I was to begin work immediately on a background piece dealing with the possible implications for Church-State relations of a Presidential scandal.

At this stage the newsroom was feverish with activity, with the decks being cleared for what was being regarded as a major news story.

This is how I began my article:

"A number of very delicate problems in the area of Church-State relations will have to be faced as a result of today's announcement from Áras an Uachtaráin.

"Although there is no Irish precedent for the situation now facing Church and State, it is not, in a world context, a novel set of circumstances.

"Under existing Church legislation all matrimonial matters concerning Heads of State are reserved to the Pope. He alone would deal with a request for a decree of nullity from Áras an Uachtaráin..."

Later, it must have been some hours afterwards, I was told the overall situation was "unclear".

Nothing relating to Áras an Uachtaráin or its occupant appeared in print in any of the Irish papers the next morning.

By this stage, on what was a glorious day in the capital, a day of bright sunshine and blue skies, the thoughts and attentions were firmly fixed on another man.

The President wasn't in the news; but the Pope most certainly was. In fact, he was the in news that day, and would monopolise it for days to come, to a degree not seen in Ireland since the visit of President John F. Kennedy in 1963.

It might have been very different.

And for a while Jack Lynch thought it would be.

The last thing he needed in the presence of the Pope was a major sex scandal.

To clarify the situation, he arranged with the Gardai to make a private telephone call to the Áras before going on to the Nunciature.

He had to know the true situation. And the only way to find out for sure was to speak directly to the man concerned – President Hillery.

Nobody knows the thoughts that flashed through his mind as he made that call. But it would come as no surprise to learn that in his concern for his friend and the reputation of the Presidency, he was mindful for a moment of the Profumo scandal of 1963 or the tales of an affair between another President – John F. Kennedy – and the Hollywood sex goddess, Marilyn Monroe.

Lynch has no recollection of what his thoughts were, except his deep concern, and his growing sense of trepidation.

But he will never forget the words spoken to him by President Hillery in reply to his direct question: "If I had another woman, Taoiseach, I could put her away from me. But I do not."

For Jack Lynch that might have seemed the end of the Presidential "affaire".

He went on to Cabra to meet the Pope, a much relieved man, no doubt in his mind that Paddy Hillery had told him the truth.

They had known each other a long time.

But there was still cause for worry over the next few days as rumours persisted that an English paper – the *Daily Mail* was mentioned – was going to run a story about the President.

The Pope left Shannon on Monday, 1 October, for the United States, and I was part of the team of journalists who accompanied him.

We were now concerned with Church-State relations of another kind.

Meanwhile, at home, the worrying situation continued for the Taoiseach.

The news media had still to be dealt with.

What if the allegation of an affair – although unfounded – was published by one of the English tabloids?

The President was also troubled.

"What should I do?" he asked the Taoiseach.

Jack Lynch gave his advice without hesitation. "Call in the Editors from the newspapers and RTE," he told Dr Hillery. "They are responsible people, and you can trust them."

And that is exactly what happened.

But the Editors, having listened to the President, in effect passed the buck.

"Call in the political correspondents," they advised him. "Let them handle it."

Sean Duignan of RTE, who went to the Áras with the other correspondents, remembers how embarrassing it was for all concerned.

"We weren't sure what we were faced with, and when we did find out we weren't sure how to handle it."

Dr Hillery didn't seem to know either.

"This is not easy for me," said the President.

"It is very difficult for us also," replied Michael Mills of the *Irish Press.*

Matters were not helped by a telephone call in the middle of the briefing. It was from Mrs Hillery, who was out of the country at the time. The President spoke to her for a few moments.

"We sat there wondering how to deal with this," recalls Duignan. "The President didn't say much for a while, and I was getting very anxious about the time factor because I had a news bulletin coming up that evening.

"Eventually I had to say this to Dr Hillery."

With the minutes ticking away, Duignan had no choice.

Glancing at his watch, he said: "I gotta go soon, Uachtaráin . . . "

It was then that the President read a short statement.

Back at the RTE studios, Duignan ("Diggy" as he is known far and wide) agonised about how he would treat the story.

How was he going to break it to an unsuspecting nation that President Hillery's marriage was not in trouble?

"Nobody knew, you see," he emphasised, recalling the 1979 visit to the Áras for me.

"Was I just going to go on the air cold and tell the nation the President was not going to resign, and that he had denied he had an involvement with any woman other than his wife?"

Which is exactly what he did.

"It was 8.55pm as I was writing my story. I had less than five minutes before the newscast."

A colleague came over.

"What did the President say?"

"He says he has no mistress; he's not involved with any other woman."

"Jaysus!"

The following morning, Thursday, 4 October, the headline over Chris Glennon's lead story in the *Irish Independent* said "HILLERY SCOTCHES THE RUMOURS".

And Glennon wrote:

"President Hillery last night flatly denied reports of difficulties in his marriage that would lead to his resignation from office.

"He declared: 'Thank God we have a happy family life.'

"And in a formal statement he said: 'I am not resigning'.

"The President took the unprecedented step of calling in the political correspondents of the national daily newspapers and RTE to deal with a spate of rumours that had gained momentum since the weekend.

"Earlier, he had advised the Taoiseach of the situation and sought advice on what he should do. That led to urgent consultations between Mr Lynch and some Ministers.

"Fine Gael Leader, Dr Fitzgerald, and Labour Leader, Mr Cluskey, also were advised by the President of his intention to make a statement.

"He read, to seven newsmen a short formal statement.

"He said: 'In recent days it has come to my attention that there are rumours circulating as to the possibility of my resigning as President.

'There is absolutely no foundation for such rumours. I am not resigning.'

"Dr Hillery, whose wife Maeve left for a holiday in Spain immediately after the Papal visit, went on to answer questions.

"He was asked if there were difficulties in his marriage. He replied: 'No. There is not a problem there.'

"And he repeated, at a later stage of the interview, at Áras an Uachtaráin, that there was not a problem in his marriage.

"President Hillery was asked about rumours that a court action for legal separation was pending. He said that there was no legal action, that the rumour was totally without foundation.

"Dr Hillery, who will be three years President in December, referred to reports that he had made trips outside the country without the authorisation of the Government, which was required under the Constitution.

"He replied that he had bought a boat and had made one trip outside territorial waters – that was authorised by the Government. He went to the Isle of Man but, while some members of the crew went ashore, he did not ...."

Readers were also told that the President had first heard the rumours about a month before.

The following day, Glennon ran another story in the *Independent* under the heading: HILLERY: LYNCH GAVE SUPPORT.

The story quoted a spokesman for the Taoiseach who said: "The President has the Taoiseach's full support in the action he took".

The other Irish papers also carried the stories, and that was, to all intents and purposes, the end of the matter.

Today, it is remembered as "the affair that never was".

Various theories have surfaced during the interim, purporting to be the background to that strange episode in 1979.

Gordon Thomas suggested in an article in the *Sunday Independent* in 1981 that the KGB tried to topple President Hillery in order to wreck the visit of the Pope to Ireland.

Since the Pope was the KGB's real target, it is not clear what gain there was for the KGB in this supposed Irish venture, other than embarrassing John Paul II and the Irish Government.

In his 1985 book, *Garret – The Enigma*, journalist Raymond Smith came up with the more interesting theory that the attempt to "smear" the President was orchestrated by (unnamed) people in Ireland (presumably from within Fianna Fáil) who were determined that Dr Hillery would not become leader of Fianna Fáil".

The problem with that is that there is no evidence at all throughout 1979 pointing towards Dr Hillery as a possible successor to Lynch.

Furthermore, if the intention was to do as Smith suggests, then the perpetrators of the smear were leaving matters far too late. Either that, or else they were very badly informed. Or perhaps a combination of both.

The reality is that by September 1979, those who wanted Lynch out were well organised, and they were not looking to the Áras for his replacement. They were looking in one direction and one direction only – that of Charles J. Haughey.

An alternative interpretation is possible, and credible.

The intention could have been to smear Hillery, to force him to resign and, in so doing, create a convenient vacancy in Áras an Uachtaráin into which to slot Lynch.

The pressure would then build up, with the conspirators pulling out all the stops to oust Lynch, thus paving the way for a successor.

And we all know who that was.

It's as plausible an explanation for what went on in semi-secrecy over the weekend and in the immediate aftermath of the visit to Ireland of John Paul II as any other.

It is also very distasteful, but then the quest for power often is.

In an interview with Joe Carroll of the *Irish Times* on 5 August 1991, the former President talked publicly for the first time about the nightmare episode in the autumn of 1979, for him and his family over the rumours that he was about to separate from his wife, and the innuendo about "another woman" from Brussels.

As Carroll pointed out, Dr Hillery these days cannot help being ruefully tickled at the idea that a mistress could be kept secretly in the Áras with all its staff and security.

"As you know, this was a staged rumour," said the ex-President. "A lot of money was spent on spreading it. I thought it was quite normal to speak to journalists and say, 'this is your Presidency and you are Irish people'."

Pressed by Carroll on the reference of a "staged rumour", Dr Hillery indicated that while Gordon Thomas had claimed that the KGB were behind the rumour, he himself believes it was part of the moves then underway concerning the succession to the then Taoiseach.

There had been unfounded rumours that Dr Hillery was considering resigning as President to succeed Lynch. If these rumours were believed, then he would undoubtedly be seen by some factions within Fianna Fáil as an unwelcome rival.

It is more likely, however, that the attempt to smear him was part of a strategy aimed at forcing him to resign in order to create a convenient opening in the Park into which to slot Lynch.

Dr Hillery believes that if the KGB were involved, it was a KGB with a domestic political flavour.

One other theory remains.

Oddly enough, it first came to light in the Irish language weekly paper *Anois* on Sunday 11 February 1990.

The following day, under the heading "Hillery 'a victim of dirty tricks", the *Cork Examiner* carried the following story:

"A report in yesterday's Irish language newspaper *Anois* suggests President Hillery may have been the subject of a dirty tricks campaign carried out by the British Secret Services in 1979.

"The newspaper said an effort was made to destabilise the Presidency by a series of innuendos and allegations about Dr Hillery's private life.

"At the time Dr Hillery made it clear he had no intention of resigning, and there was speculation in political circles that the President might have been the victim of a dirty tricks campaign.... "

Anois went on to imply a link between the allegations against Dr Hillery and the revelations which followed the Colin Wallace dirty tricks operations in the North.

Former Taoiseach, Dr Garret Fitzgerald, shook his head when I questioned him about the stories of an "affaire" in the Áras.

Was it black propaganda? Was it MI6 up to "dirty tricks"?

"That's what I make of it," replied Dr Fitzgerald, when I asked him in the course of a 1991 interview.

His view is shared by Jack Lynch.

The belief now in some quarters is that some sections of MI5 or MI6, angered at the assassination of Earl Mountbatten, and blaming the Dublin Government for poor security arrangements, decided to get their own back by creating a major embarrassment during the Pope's visit.

They didn't succeed. But they came close.

Nobody is sure where the clearance came from for the operation.

The official view here is that it did not come from 10 Downing Street. The belief is that it was an operation mounted by a "cowboy" element within the Secret Services.

Of course, this entire theory is a much easier one to sell and to stomach. We would much rather believe that the conspirators were foreign rather than native.

It is clear now that Dr Hillery believes the attempt to smear him was of native rather than foreign origin.

Either way it was an extremely nasty and potentially very embarrassing episode.

For a while, a President, a Pope and a Prime Minister were involved, albeit indirectly in the case of the latter two.

And, but for good judgement, speedy action and sound advice on the part of Jack Lynch, the abiding memories of the autumn of 1979 for millions of Irish people might well be of a major sex scandal rather than a joyous visit from the Vicar of Christ.

As a news story, the Presidential "affaire" died a death there and then.

But some of the correspondents still feel the President legitimised the rumours by calling in the news media.

And, as one of them said afterwards, it lingers on in the Irish imagination.

Former President Hillery with Jack Lynch in Croke Park

23. The Washington Debacle

Did the bomb which destroyed Earl Mountbatten also destroy Jack Lynch's political career?

The BBC certainly thought so. On the night of 5 December 1979, the day Lynch announced his resignation as Taoiseach, the main BBC news carried the story.

And their correspondent in Dublin concluded that Lynch was "a political casualty of the Mountbatten murder".

While that was not wholly true, there was nonetheless a good deal of substance to it.

And it was most definitely true in the sense that the pressure put on Lynch by the British Government in the aftermath of the Sligo tragedy, wrung concessions from him which hurt him politically at home.

Indeed, it is not improper to speculate that, were his mind not already made up to go, the damage done to him in the immediate post-Sligo situation might well have proved fatal.

He could have hung on, as he himself still insists today, perhaps up to the Árd Fheis of 1980. But after that would his position have become unsustainable?

Opinion is divided here, as in other areas.

Even allowing for the fact that there may have been an understandable tendency for the BBC's Dublin correspondent to look for a British "angle" to the Lynch resignation story, it is possible to argue that the bomb which killed Mountbatten would also have terminated Lynch's career.

Professor Joe Lee gives us part of the basis for this supposition in the following passage from his highly-acclaimed book: "Síle deValera, a young Fianna Fáil TD, grand-daughter of Eamon de Valera, chose the Liam Lynch annual commemoration ceremony in September to portray Lynch's increasing co-operation with the British Government on cross-border surveillance, since the assassination of Lord Mountbatten by the IRA in August, as collaboration, thus revealing the depths of the smouldering resentments in the party."

There can be no doubting the damaging impact of Ms de Valera's role, even though she would today dispute the claim that she ever accused Lynch of "collaboration" (any reading of her text would have to conclude that it was implied). ·

But the real background, and the real damage, can be traced to events in London before Ms de Valera's Kilcrumper speech and in the United States after it.

Mountbatten had been killed on 27 August. On 5 September Lynch was in London to attend the funeral service in Westminster Abbey.

He was also scheduled to meet Mrs Thatcher. It was their second meeting since Mrs Thatcher's election as Prime Minister in May, and the circumstances could hardly have been worse.

Since the tragedy in Sligo, the British news media had become increasingly hostile, and the atmosphere was charged with emotion as the two leaders prepared to hold a formal Anglo-Irish summit.

The scene had already been set by Mrs Thatcher's letter of invitation to the summit in which she referred to a meeting to discuss "this tragic affair and its implications".

From the point of view of the British media, matters had not been helped by Lynch's failure to return to Ireland from Portugal (where he had been holidaying).

Answering this criticism, the Taoiseach said he had been in constant touch with his office, and said there was nothing his return could have achieved that had not already been done.

When he flew into Casement Aerodrome at Baldonnel from his holiday resort in Portugal on 30 August, Lynch was met by Lord Romsey, Earl Mountbatten's heir, who told him the Earl would have wished that if anything came of his death, it would be that Britain and Ireland should get together for a lasting solution to the North.

On 31 August Lynch, accompanied by his wife, travelled by helicopter to Sligo General Hospital where he spent over an hour chatting to the three survivors of the Mullaghmore boating explosion.

Describing his feelings when the news of the blast reached him in Portugal, he said he felt "horror, disgust and great sadness – and, being abroad at the time shame, as well".

During an informal news conference on the steps of the hospital, the Taoiseach was asked whether he and Mrs Thatcher would be discussing improved cross-border security.

He replied that co-operation had been of the very highest, and successive British Prime Ministers had expressed their total satisfaction with it.

Significantly, he added that if any suggestions were made for improvements they would be immediately accepted and implemented.

This "promise" was to haunt him in the days and weeks ahead.

The next day, Sunday, 2 September, Lynch was interviewed on the RTE news programme *This Week*, where he said he would be requesting a political initiative on the North from the British Government at his meeting with Mrs Thatcher three days hence.

He denied that he was being summoned by Mrs Thatcher to the meeting to receive a "carpeting" on security in the Republic, in the light of the previous week's killing of Earl Mountbatten and 18 British soldiers.

The subject-matter of Wednesday's meeting – requested by Mrs Thatcher – was completely at variance with a newspaper report which suggested 'carpeting' .

"There will be discussion on the horrible murder of Lord Mountbatten and its implications in the broad context of the Northern situation," the Taoiseach said.

On Monday, 3 September, Lynch appeared on the BBC television programme 'Panorama', and the grilling he received prompted the *Irish Independent* to describe it as "Trial by Television".

The introduction to Raymond Smith's front-page story the next day read as follows:

"A week of anti-Irish hysteria in the British media reached its climax last night when the BBC 'Panorama' programme, with a viewing public of millions, put the Taoiseach in the dock over his security policies.

"Since the murder of Lord Mountbatten, the attacks on Mr Lynch in the British media have continued unabated – almost as if they were being orchestrated from Whitehall . . . "

Lynch fought his corner well, flatly rejecting suggestions that he was inhibited from taking firm action against the IRA.

And, expanding on what he had said on the RTE 'This Week' programme 24 hours earlier, the Taoiseach said he would take the initiative at the meeting with the British Prime Minister by pressing for a modified Sunningdale-type of political institution in the North. A solution could not be based on simply tackling the security problem alone, he stressed. It would have to go right to the heart of the bigger problem, especially in the aftermath of the murders at Mullaghmore and Warrenpoint by setting up political structures acceptable to the two communities.

On Lynch's own admission, the meeting with Mrs Thatcher, which lasted five hours at 10 Downing Street, was not an easy one.

He did raise the need for a political initiative but, inevitably perhaps in the circumstances, the emphasis was elsewhere.

In a story carrying the bylines of Maurice Hickey and Mary Punch, the *Independent* said:

"Security co-operation dominated the meeting, and a new British initiative on the Northern problem is not now likely for some time. However, Mrs Thatcher did make the vague commitment to take action 'at the appropriate time'.

"She believes that any major move now would be seen to be giving in to the Provos.

"While details of the increased security co-operation were not revealed, it is understood that Mr Lynch has ruled out any question of British forces crossing the Border in hot pursuit of suspected terrorists."

This was the phrase which Ms de Valera latched onto for her Kilcrumper speech four days later.

The British Government, she said at Fermoy, had "the affrontery to seek our co-operation in 'hot pursuit' as it has now become known."

In a passage which provides part of the justification for Professor Lee's claim, that she regarded Lynch's policy on security as "collaboration", she went on: "They have the affrontery to ask our permission for their Army to operate a mile or so over the Border".

That wasn't quite the case, though given the difference between the reports of the London summit in the *Independent* and *Press*, Ms de Valera might be forgiven for thinking so.

In contradistinction to the *Independent*, the *Press* report, written by its political correspondent Michael Mills, said that Lynch, in a briefing afterwards, referred to the question of "hot pursuit" by security forces in Northern Ireland of suspects fleeing across the Border.

The Taoiseach said there was no such concept in regard to "land boundaries" in use in Western Europe.

So nothing on land – okay. But what about the air?

That didn't come up. But it would. Very soon.

Where Ms de Valera was right was in her assumption that some new concession had been made – or if not made, sought.

Or both.

But what?

Two events in October – Pope John Paul II had come and gone in the meantime – added fuel to the fire, so to speak.

During parliamentary question-time in Dáil Éireann on 17 October 1979, Deputy Ruairi Quinn (Labour) asked the Taoiseach if the British Prime Minister and her advisers officially sought 'hot pursuit' facilities from Northern Ireland into the Republic.

Lynch, having acknowledged that a number of suggestions had been made aimed at improving security arrangements, replied as follows: "It was decided by both Governments, that it was in the public interest that details of these security measures would not be made public.

"For that reason it is not possible for me to give any information in this regard, additional to that conveyed in the communiques.

"I can say, however, that the question of so-called 'hot pursuit' was not raised at these meetings . . . "

If not 'hot pursuit', then perhaps something? The belief that some concession had been made persisted.

On 24 October, a meeting of the Fianna Fáil Parliamentary Party took place. And the following day Michael Mills told readers of the *Press* that the Taoiseach had given an assurance that Irish sovereignty would not in any way be affected by security arrangements made with the British Government.

"The Taoiseach's assurance, a spokesman said, was unanimously accepted by the 65 Deputies and 18 Senators at the meeting.

"And a motion in the name of Kerry's Tom McEllistrim, that the Government should not concede in any shape or form, a right to British forces in Northern Ireland to cross the Border by land, sea or air for the purpose of surveillance was withdrawn."

Despite the assurance, a right had in fact been conceded.

And its confirmation was to damage Lynch.

That didn't occur until nearly a fortnight later, in the setting of the National Press Club in Washington, when the real story of what had gone on behind closed doors in 10 Downing Street emerged.

In the meantime, it should be said, the ever busy Michael Mills had got a whisper, and had run a story alleging that the Government had agreed to an "air corridor" covering a distance of five kilometres on either side of the Border.

Mills's story claimed that aircraft could only cross in very special circumstances. The arrangement was supposed to operate for both the Irish and British forces, and there was no question of the aircraft landing.

That sparked off a controversy which followed Lynch all the way to Washington, and then grew into an even bigger one.

And it was in Washington itself, on the day before St Patrick's Day 1990 – 16 March – that I heard a first hand account of that now famous press conference from the man who asked the all-important question, Sean Cronin.

Then he was US Correspondent based in the American Capital for the *Irish Times*. And it was while we were standing in a cordoned off area of the Rose Garden on The Ellipse side of The White House that he told me the story.

Even after President George Bush had appeared to accept the traditional bowl of shamrock (the presentation was made by the man who was Tánaiste and Minister for Defence at the time, Brian Lenihan), I continued to listen to Cronin.

"My 'contribution' to Jack Lynch's fall was accidental. He was invited to speak at the National Press Club of which I am a member.

"The guest of honour makes a speech, and members send up written questions to the dais, where the president of the Club reads them out.

"The tradition is that the guest must answer. My question was about a then secret border security pact permitting the RAF to sweep areas of the Republic for the IRA.

"The Dáil was told there was no pact. Lynch admitted there was a pact."

In his 1987 book *Washington's Irish Policy 1916-1986*, Cronin has more to say about this key episode:

"That Press Club luncheon was a disaster for Lynch. The author asked a question about the border security pact since it was clear that there was one. Lynch agreed that there was a pact, but its terms were secret because 'there is no point in telling your enemy what you are going to do to offset him or overcome him'.

"British military aircraft overflew the Republic, but British troops did not have the right of 'hot pursuit'. Mrs Thatcher's had asked Lynch for the latter at Mountbatten's funeral and he had refused."

Cronin maintains that at Question Time in the Dáil on 17 October, after the Anglo-Irish summit in London but before his State visit to the US, Lynch had refused to discuss Anglo-Irish security arrangements since both Governments had agreed to keep them private.

I checked the official record of the Dáil Debates for October, and that is substantially correct.

I have also listened to a tape recording of the entire proceedings at the National Press Club (made by one of the reporters present), and while Lynch gave a semi-confused and confusing answer, it was one which amounted to an admission, however inadvertently given.

Dick Walsh of the *Irish Times*, who was present, told me that Lynch was very tired, and in replying to Cronin's question he unwittingly stumbled into the "confidential" sector of the briefing book he was using, thus letting the cat out of the bag.

Sean Donlon, who was Irish Ambassador in Washington at the time, confirmed that Lynch was tired and upset.

"He was given the bad results from the two Cork by-elections just before the National Press Club lunch. And it's amazing that he didn't perform worse than he did.

"He was rattled by the Sean Cronin question. But the reason, in my view, for his mishandling of that question wasn't any lack of comfort with the issue. It was that he had just been given very bad news. It was like a man getting a blow in the solar plexus. That knocked the heart out of him . . ."

Lynch was angry the next day, but the truth was the press conference in Washington had been a disaster.

It was of course a major story, and one which caused a furore when it broke in Ireland.

Here is how Michael Mills, in his report for the *Irish Press* from Washington on 10 November 1979, told the Irish public of Lynch's revelations:

"The Taoiseach, Mr Lynch, yesterday confirmed here that a new arrangement had been made by the British and Irish Governments in regard to flying across the Border for limited distances by military aircraft.

"He admitted that a very slight improvement had been made in the situation which had existed under the military aircraft overfly agreement of 1952, which allowed the military aircraft of another country to overfly our territory to a limited extent, but only on application and with our consent.

"He was asked by journalists at the National Press Club why the details had not been disclosed earlier. Mr Lynch said reports of the so-called air corridor were without foundation. It was an assumption made by certain people, he stated, that had no basis in fact.

"He then corrected himself and said: 'It had very little basis'."

Five days later in New York, before leaving for Dublin, the Taoiseach expressed strong criticism of the Irish newspapers for their comments on his statement in Washington in relation to the arrangements for limited overflying of the Border.

In his story for the *Press* on 16 November, Mills said that Lynch told reporters he was surprised and disappointed that it should have been claimed that he revealed details in Washington that he had not revealed to the Dáil.

Further down the report there was this paragraph: "Mr Lynch said he could not comment on things that were agreed on security, because if you said something, then people would draw their own conclusions from that."

Which is precisely what happened. He said something. And the journalists in Washington did indeed draw their own conclusions.

What actually happened is less important than the consequences.

By the time Lynch and his entourage got to New York, he was badly rattled.

And like other politicians in similar circumstances, he turned on the pressmen.

Lynch slipped up and did himself enormous damage in the process.

Cronin is right when in his book he concludes: "The combination of party criticism and British pressure on border security was Lynch's undoing".

What needs to be remembered, however, is that the party criticism stemmed not just from concern over security policy and the broader question of Northern Ireland: it was also fuelled by the two by-election losses.

These were mighty body-blows to Lynch.

But, in boxing terminology, one could say that they merely shortened the duration of a bout whose outcome was predetermined anyway.

Back in Ireland, the fall-out was considerable.

The County Clare Fianna Fáil backbencher Bill Loughnane said Lynch had lied and had misled the Parliamentary Party and the Dáil.

Lynch, furious, told George Colley, from New York, that he wanted Loughnane dealt with.

Colley called a meeting of the Parliamentary Party, but the attempted expulsion of Loughnane backfired.

One party official, who was very close to Lynch at the time, said Colley made a botch of it.

That inept performance did Colley himself no good, as he discovered within less than a month when he was beaten by Haughey in the contest for the succession to Lynch.

But it was the loss of the two Cork by-elections more than anything else that left Lynch exposed.

Despite his own disclaimers, he had suffered a serious setback, though he could undoubtedly have survived beyond the 1980 Árd Fheis.

He intended going anyway, as we now know, on 7 January.

But from the moment that bomb exploded on board the *Shadow V*, it is possible to argue Lynch's fate was sealed.

Mountbatten was killed in the blast, but Lynch's career perished in the aftermath.

The BBC correspondent was right.

Or, at the very least, one can build a very strong case along those lines – given the fact that Lynch's heart was no longer in it.

Debating on Television with Michael O'Leary and Garret Fitzgerald

24. Lèse-Majesté

Slimmer, more assured and more attractive than ever before, Síle de Valera shrugs and smiles when the possibility of her being the first female Taoiseach is mentioned.

But behind the huge scarlet-framed spectacles, there is no mistaking the significance of the gleam in her eye, or the understated ambition.

Ms de Valera certainly has the right pedigree, coming from one of the most famous political families in the country, the grand-daughter of the man eventually succeeded by Jack Lynch as the Leader of Fianna Fáil.

She also has the intelligence, and is accumulating the necessary experience.

King-making is part of that experience, given the role she played in helping Charlie Haughey to oust Lynch and take over as Leader.

Sitting in her book-lined living room in a small but elegant house on the outskirts of Ennis, she doesn't flinch from the question: "Would you like to be the first woman Taoiseach?"

A broad smile prefaces her reply: "I certainly don't ever see that happening, in my lifetime anyway. I don't see the day ever dawning when I'll be Taoiseach."

The prospects for that kind of radical breakthrough are no better now, she believes, than when she first came into Dáil Éireann back in 1977.

"All you have to do is look at the representation of women in the Oireachtas at the present time. It hasn't really increased, and I think that's significant."

Elsewhere, as she acknowledges, the breakthrough has been made, most notably in Britain in the formidable person of Margaret Hilda Thatcher.

"I'm not sure about the relevance of that. There are some women who would say Mrs Thatcher has done more damage to the cause of women than helping them on their way in politics.

"It really is an interesting psychological study as to whether women, in order to succeed, must be seen to be, as Mrs Thatcher herself said, the 'best man in the Cabinet'; or whether you would approach things in a more feminine as opposed to feminist way.

"I've never met her. I've been in contact with her, especially at the time of the hunger strikes, through letters and telegrams. But I've never met her face-to-face.

"Naturally, I wouldn't agree with very many of her policies, and certainly not on Ireland. But the one thing I would admire is that she came across as a very strong, determined person.

"That is something I admire in any person, male or female, because if you are going to be a leader you have to take a firm stance, and to be unequivocal in that regard . . ."

This is Síle de Valera in 1990. But what of 1979?

Was it the perceived lack of that in Jack Lynch, his failure to be unequivocal on Northern Ireland, which led to what became known as the "Kilcrumper controversy"?

"There is much that I admire about Jack Lynch, and there was much at that time. But I felt that, to me, what I wanted to see was a Leader of Fianna Fáil, whether it be Jack Lynch or anyone else, who was prepared to express what I believed the republican ideals and attitudes of the party to be.

"Remember, at no stage did I say that Jack Lynch was not a republican. I called on Jack Lynch to demonstrate his republicanism, because I believed there wasn't an overt expression of it within the party. The republican views weren't overt at that time, and I felt they should have been . . . "

On Sunday, 9 September 1979, Ms de Valera stood on the back of a truck at Kilcrumper, just outside Fermoy, and delivered a speech which contributed to the downfall of Jack Lynch.

To what extent it contributed is a matter of contention today, but there is no doubt that the manner in which that entire episode was handled was intended to inflict additional damage on a Taoiseach already showing signs of being punch-drunk.

The story of how that speech came to be written, and its effects, are central to an understanding of the circumstances which ultimately led to the resignation of Lynch on 5 December 1979 some three months later.

With other reporters, I stood in the cold that day, at the annual Liam Lynch commemoration and listened to that speech, and afterwards I climbed on to the truck to talk to Ms de Valera.

It has since been said that Ms de Valera was chosen by a cabal of backbenchers who had become disenchanted with Lynch's leadership because they knew she could be relied on to take issue with him on the "national question".

And if Lynch's nationalism was to be challenged, then who better to do it than the grand-daughter of Eamon de Valera, the founder of Fianna Fáil and the leading opponent of the 1921 Anglo-Irish Treaty which, in his view, copperfastened Partition.

And where better to do it than the graveside of General Liam Lynch, the most determined of the anti-Treaty leaders who was shot in the Knockmealdown Mountains in April 1923, the final month of the Civil War.

For those interested in symbolism, the location, the occasion, the timing, and the identity and pedigree of the person chosen to deliver the commemoration address that day, were all highly meaningful.

At the time, Ms de Valera was still three months short of her 25th birthday. Yet by virtue of her name and her own personality, she had a presence and an authority which guaranteed media attention.

This too, was a factor in the choice of her as speaker. First elected to the Dáil in the Dublin Mid-County constituency at the age of 22 in 1977 (making her the youngest deputy in the 21st Dáil), Ms de Valera had already shown the kind of spirit, independence of mind, and commitment to her grandfather's dream of a United Ireland which made her, despite her youthfulness, a formidable backbencher.

In Ennis (like her grandfather before her, she is now a Dáil Deputy for Clare), she talked about the background to that famous speech, and the controversy it sparked off.

"I was asked some time in advance if I would give the speech that year, so I said yes, I would be delighted to. And I accepted the invitation.

"It wasn't until about two weeks before that I decided to sit down and write the speech.

"Now, contrary to what people believe and what has been said, I wrote that speech totally on my own. There was no reference to anybody else – Charlie Haughey or indeed anyone as to (1) whether I would give the speech, and (2) if I wanted to give the speech, what I would say."

She remains adamant about not seeking anyone's approval. "Absolutely not. The speech was my own. I was expressing totally my own views in Kilcrumper that day. I put it as honestly as I could. I know some people didn't agree.

"I said what I had to say on that occasion because I felt it was the time to say it.

"I would have wanted the Taoiseach of the day – no matter whether it was Jack Lynch or anyone else – to express what I believe were the republican views within the Fianna Fáil party, and what we as members of Fianna Fáil stood for."

Interestingly, Síle revealed that when the Parliamentary Party met to specifically discuss the speech ("why I had given the speech and what was said in it"), she was approached beforehand and informed that the supporters of Charlie Haughey would have to keep their distance from her.

"I think it was the night before the meeting. One person came to me, who is now deceased – Deputy Joe Fox from Dublin. He said that the next day there would be a discussion on the speech, and the supporters of Charlie Haughey could not be seen, and would not be seen to be supporting me in what I had to say.

"I said, well, that is obviously their decision, and I was quite capable of explaining why I had said what I had said, and my feeling as to why it should be said at that time. And I had no problem with that whatsoever.

"I often wonder – and I'm no woman's 'liber' – was it just because I happened to be a woman, and a young woman at that.

"People felt – 'Ah, she's just a woman, and she wouldn't have the political cop-on to be able to prepare such a speech herself, or to be able to word the speech itself.

"It was always someone else – from my father to some other relative to Charlie Haughey – who wrote the speech. It was never myself. I still find that amusing. It was really put down to my gender and my age."

Did she realise she would run into flak from the top, and that she would come to be regarded as a "stalking horse" for Haughey?

"I knew there would be repercussions, but I felt that was the time to stand up and say what I had to say."

But did she appreciate the repercussions would come from Lynch himself?

"I was prepared for some kind of backlash, if you want to put it that way, because Mr Lynch had asked me not to give the speech."

In fact, one of the copies which had been sent to the news media beforehand had ended up on the Taoiseach's desk.

"He was given an advance copy. I don't know by whom. I suspect it was a press source that gave him a copy of the speech before I delivered it. I said no to his request, and I explained my reasons."

Ms de Valera agrees that others saw the speech as part of an anti-Lynch conspiracy. And she also agrees that it suited some people in the pro-Haughey faction of the party to allow that to be believed.

But she insists it was principles and ideals more than personalities that interested her.

Yet she wasn't blind to the implicit suggestion in her speech – its "coded message" as one civil servant put it afterwards – that Jack Lynch was not living up to the ideals, aims and objectives of the party as she understood them, and that the republican ideals of her grandfather were being abandoned.

"The speech expressed my own views, and whatever the consequences were, either for me personally or for other individuals, was something that would follow on logically anyway."

She knew also that his position as party leader was weakening; it was, in fact, being deliberately undermined.

"No, I wasn't helping him. That was part of the reason for the timing. In fact, it was the reason for the timing."

The clear message is that she believed a change of leader was desirable.

There may have been qualities that she admired about Jack Lynch. But it was also the case that she saw herself as a standard bearer for her grandfather, as a guardian of the party's "soul", and of its republican traditions.

And Lynch's revisionism, as she saw it, was threatening those traditions.

What was needed was a new Leader, someone who would uphold those traditions.

In 1979 she was very clear as to who that "someone" should be – Charles J. Haughey.

Although she maintains she wasn't "used" in 1979, her wish to see Charles J. Haughey as Leader was no secret.

Her comment on the day he defeated George Colley for the leadership is revealing: "I am absolutely delighted. We got what we needed, a strong man, able to handle the political and economic challenges now facing the country. The whole party will be behind Mr Haughey . . . "

She was off target on that one. Way off.

Over a decade later, this is her comment: "At the time, the reason why I supported Charlie Haughey was because I believed that, given the opportunity as Taoiseach, he would be expressive of those views.

"Now whether or not I feel that that has happened is the makings of another book!"

Jack Lynch with Erskine Childers, Joe Brennan and Gerry Collins

25. The Plot

The 1979 conspiracy to topple Jack Lynch as leader of Fianna Fáil and replace him with Charles J. Haughey was born of fear.

After the historic 20-seat majority in the 1977 General Election, backbenchers watched with growing trepidation as the fortunes of the party dipped lower and lower, following a series of problems and setbacks.

The glow of that unprecedented electoral victory was beginning to wane as the months of 1979 slipped past.

But what the conspirators didn't know was that all their backstairs scheming and all their secret plotting in Jury's Hotel was virtually an unnecessary exercise.

The result they so ardently desired – aimed, in the final analysis, at saving their own skins – was about to be brought to pass anyway.

And by no less a person than Jack Lynch himself.

One political correspondent almost stumbled on the truth. Liam O'Neill of the *Cork Examiner* was with Lynch in the United States in October 1979 when the news of the two by-election losses in Cork came through.

The effect on Lynch was devastating. In the words of another correspondent who was present – Kevin Healy of RTE – the Taoiseach, who was then 52, looked "shell-shocked".

Healy recalls a scene in The White House later where Lynch stood with President Jimmy Carter, both bored and preoccupied, and both wishing to be rid of each other.

The reason was not due to any personal antipathy, though there was very little warmth between the President and the Taoiseach (curiously, Richard Nixon was The White House occupant Lynch got on best with).

No – the reason the two leaders were finding the ceremonial in The White House so trying was because both were wrestling with personal crises.

Afterwards, Mrs Lynch would advise any politician's wife to cover the hurts and keep smiling.

"Jack and I had to do this the night we dined in The White House, for we had just heard the disappointing results of the Cork by-elections. Meanwhile, President Carter had the gigantic problem of Iran on his mind . . . "

Given the nature of the crises, neither could help the other.

For Carter it was the frustration of the hostage crisis in Iran. In Lynch's case, it was the damaging implications of the two electoral rebuffs in Cork – one in the city, virtually in his own backyard.

He knew that he, too, had a crisis on his hands.

And in both cases the crises would prove terminal.

Earlier, in the privacy of his hotel room, Lynch had sat on the side of the bed and, after a long silence, uttered three words in a strained voice: "It's all over".

Carter, meanwhile, had been telling aides in the Oval Office that his inability to end the captivity of the hostages, taken from the US Embassy in Tehran, would hinder his chances of re-election.

Little wonder that the two leaders were behaving like automatons in the grounds of The White House.

"How Lynch went through that ordeal at The White House I'll never know," said Healy, looking back on that fateful US visit.

But what neither Healy nor the other correspondents who were accompanying Lynch on his US visit knew was that he had already pencilled in his resignation date in his diary months previously.

And in uttering the words "It's all over", he was merely signalling his recognition that the timing of his departure might have to be brought forward.

Among the jumble of thoughts rushing through his mind, one was uppermost – prevent the leadership going to Charlie Haughey.

That and that alone, he has always claimed, would affect the timing of his departure, or rather, a bringing forward of the date of that departure.

George Colley was the man he favoured as his successor. But Colley would have to organise things for himself. And he, Lynch, would move when circumstances appeared most propitious for Colley.

Nothing else would shift him. On that he was resolute.

But none of the correspondents was privy to any of this, though they would have known that the bad results from Cork constituted a serious personal setback for Lynch.

Liam O'Neill came the closest to stumbling on the truth – and the real story.

Lynch recalls the encounter.

"He asked me if my plans for my own future had changed, and I said 'no'. But what he didn't realise was that my mind had been made up to go early in January 1980 anyway."

How much Lynch knew of what was actually happening at home is unclear.

The plotting against him had started, of course, long before he left for his American tour.

He claims he knew some of the details before his departure for the States. He certainly knew disaffection was spreading among the backbenchers.

Whether he knew it was widespread is a moot point. To say that he didn't know would be tantamount to admitting that he was out of touch with his own Parliamentary Party. Yet to admit that he was aware, and did nothing, would make him appear impotent.

It was a case of being caught between a rock and a hard place.

Perhaps at that stage he didn't care all that much.

Both he and Mrs Lynch knew that a decision had been taken, and that a date had been pencilled into his diary.

That date was 7 January 1980.

And it was their secret. And in that secret was considerable solace for both of them.

Did he know that there were messages from Dublin to members of his entourage in the United States? And if he knew, did he care?

There is reason to believe that he didn't know, because the tone and content of some of those messages – especially the messages from Charlie Haughey – would have aroused his anger.

That would have changed his general mien, bringing to the surface some of the old fighting spirit. And the correspondents would have noticed that.

There is no sign that they did.

Simply, there was no change in Lynch's personality or attitude for them to notice.

Conclusion: he didn't know what Haughey was up to.

Indeed, in his response to questions from the correspondents, and particularly in a taped RTE interview with Kevin Healy, there were unmistakable signs of a man suffused with weariness.

It is not going too far to say that he was past caring. His mind had long since been made up.

All of which rendered rather redundant the frenetic scheming and elaborate plotting that was intensifying back home.

The rebel backbenchers wanted to take Jack Lynch out.

But what they didn't know, what they couldn't know, was that he had taken himself out.

He was doing the work for them. Unbeknown to them, he was going to transform their scenario into reality.

That scenario was conceived in fear and brought forth in selfishness and ambition.

The story of "the plot" and of the "gang of five" has been told many times. The most comprehensive account is that given by Vincent Browne in *Magill* in the January 1980 edition.

The key players – the so-called "gang of five" – were Jackie Fahey of Waterford; Tom McEllistrim of North Kerry; Sean Doherty of Roscommon-Leitrim; Albert Reynolds of Longford-Westmeath, and Mark Killilea of Galway East.

But the real puppet-master was Charles J. Haughey.

Browne is unsure about how much Haughey knew of the backbench revolt.

"It is not clear exactly how much Charlie Haughey knew of these happenings."

But Dick Walsh, who was political correspondent of the *Irish Times* throughout much of Lynch's period as leader of Fianna Fáil, laboured under no such uncertainty.

"The belief at the time was that Charlie Haughey was orchestrating everything. He was pulling the strings," says Walsh.

The messages to the States – in one of them Haughey told a member of the Taoiseach's entourage to "Get back here, that man is finished"; in another he said "What the fuck are you doing over there? Don't you know Lynch is on the way out?" – suggest that he knew an awful lot.

Yet, but for bad information on George Colley's chances of beating Haughey in the succession stake in December 1979, the so-called "palace revolt" would have failed.

And Lynch, if he had so desired, might still be leader of Fianna Fáil and Taoiseach today.

Far-fetched? Not at all. He had the support, he had the necessary numbers if he wanted a show-down. Parliamentary and constituency arithmetic was on his side. Unmistakably.

Despite all that has been written and said since 1979 about a plot to bring Lynch down, that fact remains.

Despite the claims of "back-stabbing" (and Lynch was stabbed in the back – no doubt about that); despite the assertions that he was pushed out, the man who resigned on 5 December 1979 did so of his own volition.

"I wasn't forced out," says Jack today, puffing contentedly on his pipe. "I could have held on, and nobody could have forced me out if I didn't want to go . . ."

This view is corroborated by four men – a party official and three journalists – who were well placed at the time.

They are Seamus Brennan, secretary of the party then (now Minister for Transport, Tourism and Communications); Michael Mills, political correspondent of the *Irish Press* (now the Ombudsman); Dick Walsh (now political editor of the *Irish Times*), and Sean Duignan, political correspondent of RTE (now the station's anchorman for the Six One News).

All are adamant that Lynch could still be there today – if he had wanted to stay.

"He had the support," says Brennan. "There were some opposed to his leadership, and a push was on. But if push came to shove he could have resisted, and done so successfully."

Vincent Browne himself, who did extensive research in 1980 into the background of the "plot" against Lynch, conceded at the time that the absolute maximum number of deputies who would have supported a motion for a change of leader would have been 30.

"It seemed unlikely that an absolute majority could have been obtained to get rid of Jack Lynch come January," wrote Brown.

"However, with a minority of 30 supporting such a resolution, it is more than likely that Jack Lynch would have believed his position to be untenable and would have resigned."

Jack Lynch believed neither the figure of 30 nor the conclusions drawn by Browne from that figure.

Three factors influenced Lynch's decision to go – (1) his wife wanted him to quit; (2) he was tired of politics, suffering from "battle fatigue"; and (3) he believed George Colley had the support necessary to ensure that he would be the next Taoiseach.

"I was told everything was okay, that George would win any contest for the succession."

And while Lynch has never said so himself, the widely held belief is that Martin O'Donoghue, who was Minister for Economic Planning and Development then, was the one who assured Jack that everything was all right, that Colley would beat Haughey.

It was true that O'Donoghue was convinced Colley was going to win – but it was George himself who gave the assurance to Jack.

"Jack didn't interfere at all in the Colley-Haughey contest," recalls O'Donoghue. "He was very conscious of the manner in which Lemass stood aside in 1966, and he did the same."

O'Donoghue was present when Lynch met Colley in the Ministers' Dining Room in Leinster House just before the crucial ballot.

"All Jack said was 'How are things?', and George replied 'It's in the bag'..."

Bobby Molloy and Padraig Faulkner had been handling Colley's campaign, and they, along with O'Donoghue, believed they had the numbers to clinch the succession.

They were wrong.

Today Lynch brushes aside the assertions (they were boasts in certain quarters) that he was pushed.

The former Taoiseach is emphatic that he was not pushed, although he concedes he retired a month earlier than planned, with the timing determined by the assurances given him, that Colley would be the next leader of the Party.

"I could have held on for tactical purposes for that month by requesting a vote of confidence in my leadership, which I would have got. But it would have been cynical to do that, and then retire a month later."

He knew about the caucus meetings of TDs plotting his downfall, though there is reason to believe that knowledge came late to him.

But he says it wouldn't have mattered anyway if he didn't want to go.

"I had planned to retire on 7 January 1980, and my wife and I marked the date in our diaries.

"I was in my early sixties and had been in active politics for over 30 years, and leader of the Party for 13 years. And I had decided back in 1977 that I would give my successor at least two years to stamp his style on the party before the next election."

He was aware as 1979 wore on of growing unrest in the party, though he probably underestimated the extent of it. It grew in the summer, added to by the defeats in the Euro and local elections.

The situation was also aggravated by a long and bitter post office workers' strike.

And then in November Fianna Fáil lost two by-elections in Cork.

"These mid-term by-election defeats put pressure on the newly-elected deputies, many of whom didn't realise that they would have to go through times of adversity as well as triumphs like the 1977 General Election.

"I knew even before going to the States there was a bit of unrest, and I heard about the famous caucus meetings."

After returning from his official visit to the USA, he invited deputies to come and see him and discuss the situation if they wished.

"Some fellows came to me and said there was some unrest, but that if I told the Parliamentary Party that I was going to lead Fianna Fáil into the next election it would be killed off.

"I decided, in view of my promise to Mairin and for other reasons, it would be cynical of me to say I was going to lead the party into the next election, and to ask for a vote of confidence on that basis when I intended to resign a month later.

"So I decided to step down in December 1979."

James Downey, in his 1983 book *Them & Us*, touches on an important point.

"He was obviously tired and despondent, and his wife was pressing him to lay down the burden of office."

What happened afterwards is history.

George Colley was convinced he could win the subsequent leadership contest.

He was wrong.

Haughey's supporters were better organised, and Colley's camp made the mistake of thinking that because their man had the support of the majority of the Cabinet members, he would also have the support of the majority of the backbenchers.

In the event, it was the backbenchers who carried the day for Haughey.

Colley, perhaps a bit like Lynch himself, had been out of touch with what was going on among the backbenchers.

That Lynch wished Colley to succeed him is beyond dispute. In a report in the *Guardian*, which appeared on the very morning of the day Lynch announced his resignation as Taoiseach, Joe Joyce captured the flavour of his thinking.

"The conventional political wisdom in Dublin suggests that Mr Lynch would be happy to retire if his succession a candidate acceptable to him were assured. Mr Haughey, the front runner, does not meet that criterion."

That's beautifully understated and accurate – except that the Colley camp (including Lynch) did not at that stage believe Haughey was in front.

Outwardly, Lynch has no regrets about the Haughey triumph. "I am a democrat, and I've always been a democrat."

And, anyway, it was up to Colley and his supporters to get their act together.

But the knowledge that he could have hung on and, by doing so, provided time for Colley to muster the support necessary to ensure victory gnaws at him.

He had the strength and the support and the control of the party establishment. And no cabal of backbench rural TDs could have toppled him in 1979.

The factor that would have carried him through is the factor described in the following terms by Dick Walsh in his 1986 book, *The Party – Inside Fianna Fáil:* "Lynch was as tough as he was sympathetic, as tough as you might expect a man who had won six All-Ireland medals in a row was bound to be".

Sean Duignan, concurring, put it this way to me in Dessie Hynes' pub in Dublin in April 1991: "Jack was the toughest of the tough. People talk about Charlie's eyes, but when Jack fixed those eyes of his on you, you could feel the steel . . . "

Official opening of Government Buildings, January 1991. An Taoiseach Charles J. Haughey with his three predecessors – Liam Cosgrave, Garret Fitzgerald and Jack Lynch

26. Jack and Charlie

Sunday, 16 September 1990, was Charles J. Haughey's birthday. He was 65. It was also the day that Jack Lynch came to Croke Park to see Cork achieving an historic "double" by winning the All-Ireland Senior Football Final.

In the Hogan Stand, Jack and Charlie sat just a few feet from each other, each observing a veneer of civility.

An outsider, looking on, would be forgiven for thinking theirs was at least a normal, if not particularly cordial, relationship.

The truth is very different, and much sourer.

The two can't stand each other.

In fact, quiet detestation is an accurate description of their relationship.

And while many of those who know both men think it all stems from 1970, it goes further back.

The truth is that Charlie Haughey never liked Jack Lynch.

He never had much regard for him.

And at times his behaviour, even after Lynch became Taoiseach, was characterised by contempt.

Long after Lynch was gone from politics, Haughey – who was then Taoiseach – regularly railed against some peoples' habit of referring to Jack as "the real Taoiseach".

But there is no love lost on Lynch's side either. I remember talking to another ex-Taoiseach, Dr Garret Fitzgerald, one day about Lynch's failure to hold on to any of the State papers (or to copies made), from his period in office.

Dr Fitzgerald explained that to gain access to them now, Lynch would have to go through the present Taoiseach.

"He won't ever do that of course," remarked Fitzgerald. "Jack wouldn't ask Charlie for a cup of tea."

In cinematic terms, their relationship could be said to parallel that of Gary Cooper and Burt Lancaster in *Vera Cruz.*

Outwardly, they were on the same team, sharing the same goals, promoting the same policies, pursuing the same political objectives.

And, just as in the film, there had to be a showdown.

Cooper against Lancaster.

Eyeball to eyeball, nerves stretched to breaking point.

And just like Cooper, Lynch won.

This happened in May, 1970.

But this was no film. There was real blood involved here, not ketchup.

The stakes were high. Reputations were on the line. So was the control of power. Even, perhaps, the destiny of an entire island, an island of two states, or a nation and a statelet, as some would prefer.

Lynch's behaviour throughout this period totally belies Conor Cruise O'Brien's view that he wasn't tough enough for politics.

"He may have been a tough man on the playing field, but he wasn't nearly tough enough when it came to politics," according to Dr O'Brien.

The truth of the matter is that he took on two of the toughest, roughest and most formidable figures in modern Irish politics – and won.

And when you consider some of the characters we've had in Irish politics, that's saying something.

There may be more substance in Dr O'Brien's view that Lynch showed weakness in allowing Haughey and Blaney to dictate policy on Northern Ireland from August 1968 to May 1970.

"The question which Lynch has never satisfactorily answered is why he appointed Haughey and Blaney to the Cabinet sub-committee responsible for Northern Ireland," says O'Brien.

One senior civil servant put it another way: "Lynch knew the difference between a cactus and a caucus. In a cactus, all the pricks are on the outside, in a caucus, they're inside.

"In other words, he knew who he was dealing with, and he knew it was better to have them inside the tent pissing out, than outside pissing in."

Vincent Browne, in his courageous series on the Arms Crisis in *Magill* (April-May-June 1980) concludes that: "It was the darkest period of his leadership and there is a great deal of evidence that he acted weakly and indecisively throughout."

Dr O'Brien is even more critical.

Yet there is evidence that Lynch bit the bullet when he had to.

And when the full truth of what had happened dawned on him, he acted decisively.

Ever since it has been said that there have been two wings in Fianna Fáil.

Be that as it may, one thing is beyond dispute – Lynch forced the party to come to terms, once and for all, with its one-dimensional nationalism.

From the Lynch-Haughey enmity stems a new perspective on the North and on republicanism. That's the plus factor, and it is a major plus.

The two men are as different in style as they are in temperament, personality and motive.

And the differences have implications which reach far beyond the two of them.

The differences, in fact, determine the methodology of politics, how politics operates in Ireland, how the business of politics is conducted; how, why and on whose behalf power is exercised.

People are frightened of Charlie Haughey, people in high places, people of wealth and status.

Lynch never frightened anyone – except, perhaps, on the playing field.

To many, especially those who have to deal with him, Haughey is a classic Machiavellian.

Haughey loves power, and loves exercising it. He exudes it, relishes it, basks in it. And he uses and applies it with utter ruthlessness.

Lynch never wanted power, and he exercised it uneasily, and sometimes not at all.

"At times of crises, Lynch always gave the impression he'd prefer to be somewhere else," said one civil servant. "Crises pained him, though he was a superb crisis manager. But you had the sense that circumstances forced him to be.

"Haughey, on the other hand, handled crises as though born for them. To see him in action at a time of crisis was something quite special."

A former colleague, Dr Martin O'Donoghue, said Haughey was the best 24-hour politician he ever saw.

Strange as it may seem, one of the best insights into the disparities between the two men can be gleaned from their attitude to, and effect on women.

Journalist Mary Kenny says there is no flirtatious side to Lynch. And I think she is right.

"Jack was always a dear old sweetie, but there is a tough and shrewd side to him as well.

"He is every inch the family man, and when I see photos of him and Mairin I think of Neil and Glenys Kinnock because they are both very much political couples."

After the 1969 General Election – Lynch's first electoral test as Taoiseach – Mary did an interview with him for the *Irish Press* (she and I were part of the team covering that election for the *Press*), and she said he rang up afterwards and was very complimentary.

"I think for a Prime Minister to do that was very considerate."

Asked about differences in attitudes to women and power between Jack and Charlie, Mary had this to say:

"You never felt Jack was flirting with you, and to that extent you could be completely at ease. He was terribly avuncular and incredibly pleasant.

"Charlie, on the other hand, plays the sex card with women, though not in any crude sense. He can be very gallant with women.

"As for power, Charlie obviously loves it, though one always has the feeling there is a sub-text to everything he says and does.

"Jack was uneasy with power, uncertain about using it, but I'm told he had a very tough side to him as well. I think people who said he was honest were right."

Another woman journalist, Mary Kerrigan, isn't so sure about Jack's lack of flirtatiousness, though she was talking about the later Lynch.

She told me of a telephone conversation she had with him, when she rang up to ask him to review *Planning Ireland's Future*, the 1990 book on T.K. Whitaker for the *Sunday Press*.

Mary had to ask him for his address in order to post the book to him. "Number 21 – the same age as myself."

She had the feeling he was flirting with her. But I think his playfulness with "Number 21" was just that, while also conveying something of an old man's longing for his lost youth.

The reaction of Norene Sheehan, an attractive young woman whose work for the National Lottery takes her over most of Munster, is more typical. She recalls being in the West Cork Hotel in Skibbereen, a favourite haunt of Lynch's, having dinner with friends.

Lynch was at another table, but he knew a member of her party and he came over to join them.

"He just sat down and started to talk to us without any fuss, or pretentious introductions. If I hadn't known him I wouldn't have known he was a politician, never mind a former Taoiseach."

Another former team-mate, Paddy "Chancer" Barry, told me he knew of two girls in Cork – one was a judge's daughter, the other was a solicitor – who had a big crush on Jack. But nothing came of it.

"He wasn't interested."

That's only surprising in an age which has come not only to accept but to expect that politics and sex should go together, and that leading politicians should have amorous encounters. We live in a world in which hanky-panky in high places is the norm.

In our age, certainly since the 1960s and the Profumo Scandal and the tales of the womanising in the Kennedy White House, sexual intrigue has come to be regarded as part and parcel of the world of politics.

In Ireland, even in the 1990s, we are still a bit coy about these matters. Sexual affairs or involvements are acknowledged on a wink and a nudge basis.

The contrast between Lynch and Haughey in this regard could hardly be sharper.

Charlie charms the women.

One woman who knows him told me he has the gift of being able to make a woman feel that she is the only person in the room, even when it is crowded.

But his charm is erotically charged.

Lynch too has charm, but it carries no sexual overtones or undertones.

Mary Kenny is surely right when she says women never felt threatened by Jack.

Lynch's charm is avuncular. He makes you feel safe and secure.

Lynch isn't the kind of man who would walk into a radio studio for an interview, spot a lovely girl while in the process, and then send a gofer to ask her if she would like to spend the rest of the day with him.

Haughey would not return from London – as Lynch did in 1979 clearly smitten by Margaret Thatcher.

He might come back and say she was sexy – but that would not have helped her one whit to get her way.

It would matter very much in another sense, but not in assisting Mrs Thatcher or any other woman to get her way with him.

It would with Lynch, because there was a soft, almost feminine side to his character.

That's another key difference between the two men. And it comes down to objectification.

Haughey, in what some would regard as a useful attitude to have if you are a top politician, is able to treat people like objects.

Lynch could never do that.

Ruthless men, men who love power, men who are lured by it and who thrive in the exercise of it, have to be able to de-humanise people.

They wouldn't get much sleep otherwise.

If they have consciences at all, then they are very selective ones. They have to be in the interests of survival.

Lynch has a very well developed sense of morality: an ethic. That sets him apart from Haughey, and also enabled him to do things because he perceived they were right in themselves without regard to party or personal gain.

His appointment of William Fitzgerald as Chief Justice of the Supreme Court in 1972 is an example of this.

So was his appointment of Thomas Finley, who was once a Fine Gael candidate, to the High Court.

So too was his appointment of Tony O'Reilly to Bord Bainne, though he would be the last to claim that he was the first to "spot" O'Reilly's very considerable talent.

In the final analysis, the contrast with Haughey could not be starker.

Cocky, self-promoting and ruthless, Haughey is motivated by a sense of self-aggrandisement and what may turn out to be a spurious sense of historical purpose.

The man who was once likened by the *Sunday Times* to the *Playboy of the Western World*, believes destiny will rank him alongside Eamon de Valera.

Mixing charm and single-mindedness with steely determination and a dour conviction that his vision of Ireland represents and enshrines "the spirit of the nation", he has shown himself to be the great survivor of Irish politics.

He is loved, feared and hated in about equal proportions.

But even amongst those who support him, many have mixed feelings, not least about the way he accumulated his wealth, and his autocratic style of leadership."

The new famous *uno Duce, una voce* remark from the then Fianna Fáil press secretary, P.J. Mara, may have been said in jest, but then many a true word is spoken in jest.

He is a believer – he believes in power and his own right to it and ability to use it.

He is a curious man, a man who both repels and fascinates. And he was always had an uneasy, not to say rumbustious, relationship with the media.

Despite setbacks, or perhaps because of them, the Haughey mythology grows and grows, dutifully fed by acolytes and by a volume such as *The Spirit of the Nation*, which is a 1,000-page collection of his speeches.

This mythology encapsulates a number of beliefs held with varying degrees of conviction by varying numbers of people. These beliefs include (a) that he helped to create the Provisional IRA, (b) that he is an economic wizard and (c) the ultimate pragmatist.

The latter is a belief he willingly fosters himself, having claimed more than once when asked about "ideology" that "I am neither a servant of the Right nor a prisoner of the Left – I am a pragmatist of the Centre".

After his election as Taoiseach for the first time in December 1979, in succession to Lynch, Conor Cruise O'Brien, writing in the *Observer* of which he was then editor-in-chief, said that Haughey was "fonder of women than Irish politicians allow themselves to appear". And he went on: "There is a 'Kennedy' touch about him, including that faint whiff of brimstone ..."

If the gossip is to be believed – and here we get perilously close to the questionable phenomena labelled by Normal Mailer as "factoids" – then Haughey certainly likes the company of women, especially beautiful women.

Wasn't it that knowledge, as much as anything else, that lent the "Charlie sequences" in "Scrap Saturday", the hugely popular radio satire series on RTE, much of its appeal?

And if power, as Henry Kissinger once said, is "the ultimate aphrodisiac", then we all know who those political groupies (and Dublin has some unlikely ones) have as their prime target.

The popular tabloids regularly carry stories about the amorous exploits of political and other figures from around the world. The thought that there may be one such creature in their midst adds spice to life for the Irish, and even evokes in some of them what can only be described as sneaking admiration.

In an article entitled "Champagne Charlie Lives – in Leinster House", Mary Kenny made these pertinent observations:

"Charlie's reputation is that of a womaniser – which has done him no harm at all; although the Irish are supposed to be very puritanical about sex, they are in practice rather tolerant and easy-going. From Parnell to Jeremy Thorpe, Irish public opinion has tended to the view that a chap's private predilations are his own affair, and it is vulgar to draw attention to personal weakness.

"Womanisers in Ireland are characterised as 'a bit of a lad for the women' or 'a right boyo'. Nobody in Dáil Éireann has ever fallen from grace for this reason ..."

Since the "Arms Trial" of 1970, Haughey has made no public utterance of substance on that bizarre episode, other than to say at his first press conference on becoming Taoiseach in 1979 that he would write his own account of it – someday.

Yet because of the events of 1970 when Haughey was dismissed by Lynch and subsequently acquitted by the High Court in Dublin of the charge of conspiring to import arms illegally into the Republic), Haughey is, in the eyes of many Unionists the man who, in the words of Ian Paisley, "assisted at the birth of the Provisional IRA".

Against this, it has to be remembered that when he became Taoiseach he condemned the violent activities of the Provos and their front organisations in the USA. And in 1980 his Government approved a £100 million security package to combat the growing menace of terrorism and subversion in the Republic.

Which brings us to Haughey's reputation as a pragmatist. He believes in a United Ireland, fervently. In this he is different from Lynch. And at the 1980 Árd Fheis he declared: "We must face the reality that Northern Ireland, as a political entity, has failed and that a new beginning is needed."

If he has charm Joan Baez who met him at a Siamsa Cois Laoi concert in Cork, admitted this readily to me, he also has an abiding – some would say consuming – love of power.

In their book *The Boss: Charles. J. Haughey in Government*, Joe Joyce and Peter Murtagh include this telling passage.

"Friends and enemies alike had been mesmerised by his relentless pursuit of power. He was living proof of the usefulness of that dictum that, in politics, one should never resign. He wore his ambition on his sleeve in a totally un-Irish manner, the antithesis of the Lynch type of 'reluctant politician' who had to be persuaded into every office."

The attitude to power is clear. So is the naked ambition.

And that's what separates him most of all from Lynch.

It is here that the real differences are to be found.

And the gulf between them on the acquisition and exercise of power was summarised by a top civil servant who worked with both.

"With Jack you knew where you stood. He was always straight and upfront."

"Charlie was a very different animal. With Charlie you could never be sure ... of anything ..."

During the period 1979-81, there was an uneasy truce between them.

On 16 February 1980, at his first Árd Fheis as Taoiseach and Leader of Fianna Fáil, Haughey spoke of his "three great predecessors, Eamon de Valera, Sean Lemass and Jack Lynch".

Of the latter he had this to say: "Jack Lynch brought us through difficult times with patience and wisdom. His personal qualities endeared him to the entire nation in a way rarely achieved by political leaders".

In the circumstances, it was the minimum that could be said.

Later, in June 1981, during the General Election campaign, there was speculation about whether, and to what extent, Lynch would campaign.

Thirteen months previously he had announced that he would not be a candidate at the next election.

Would he turn out to help Charlie and the Party?

He did, but in a very perfunctory fashion.

On 9 June (two days before polling day) Haughey called a hurried press conference following Lynch's failure to appear at an election rally there in Blarney.

Anxious to dispel thoughts that Lynch might be a reluctant campaigner (he was!), Haughey had hurriedly told reporters: "He is determined to give our campaign his fullest personal endorsement".

That night in the Grand Parade in Cork City, Lynch appeared on the platform with Haughey at the final rally of the Election.

When Lynch said he was standing on a General Election platform for the last time, there was a huge collective groan from the crowd.

When he finished speaking, Haughey told the crowd they had just heard one of the last major political speeches from "Cork's favourite son".

Then he turned to his predecessor and raised his arm in a victory salute.

It was a move Lynch had not expected, but typical of Haughey who wanted no public hint of disunity.

"We are proud and honoured that he is here with us tonight, endorsing our case and supporting us in his wonderful, noble, generous way ..."

That might have fooled some of the people and some of the media.

It didn't fool Jack Lynch.

On 10 June 1981, the *Irish Press* report of that rally carried this passage: "Mr Haughey's warm appreciation of Mr Lynch's services to political life seemed to mark the end of the long-standing hostility between them".

It was wrong. Dead wrong.

An Taoiseach Jack Lynch with Mrs Thatcher (then leader of the opposition)
(Copyright Camera Press)

27. The Folk Hero

In a reference to Parnell, the Professor of Modern History at UCC, Joe Lee, opined that no mature people, political people, ought to rely on heroes to lead them – "that's for a tribe, not a people".

Jack Lynch might not agree, for there is undoubtedly an element of the tribal in his appeal, his popularity, and the public perception of and response to him.

Nowhere was that better or more movingly demonstrated than on the first Sunday in September 1984 in Semple Stadium in Thurles – an historic day.

The apotheosis of Jack Lynch occurred on that day, in a location and at an event which could hardly have been more appropriate, even if he had stage-managed it himself.

The occasion was very special, and the thousands who crammed into Thurles didn't need to be reminded of that fact.

In Tom Dunne's pub (Dunne was a Fine Gael TD), across from the Railway Station, the pints were being lowered, and the sandwiches and crubeens were being passed around long before noon.

It was – as it nearly always is on big match occasions in the town – a largely Cork crowd, Dunne's being a favourite and convenient watering hole.

As always, they were good-humoured, extrovert, colour-bedecked and in fine voice.

Long before the throw-in the smell of victory was in the air. And this would be a very sweet victory indeed.

For 1984 was the centenary year of the GAA, and the Cork hurlers had come to do battle with the men of Offaly in the town where 100 years previously the GAA had been founded.

It happened in Hayes Hotel, which still stands on Liberty Square. And here too there was a carnival atmosphere, with Corkmen and Corkwomen much in evidence, and in good singing voice.

In fact, it's the only time I can remember "The Banks" being sung before the pubs opened!

Overhead the sky was clear, with not a cloud in sight. And in the still empty Semple Stadium, the Tricolour over the stand fluttered limply in a weak breeze.

The setting was perfect: it was an ideal afternoon for hurling.

The hurling would come, and there were moments of magic though overall it was to prove a disappointing Final for such an auspicious occasion, with Cork running out easy winners at the end. If only because this was no ordinary Final, there was more than the usual pageantry beforehand.

As the Corkman said to the Offalyman in Dunne's Bar, "Centenaries don't come every year, boy!"

In the extended pre-match ceremonies, the most memorable moment occurred when the tall, slightly stooped figure of Jack Lynch walked out on to the lush, green sward of Semple Stadium.

Almost as one, the vast crowd rose to their feet.

Here is how Stephen Collins described what happened in the *Irish Press*, 3 September 1984:

"The biggest cheer at the centenary hurling final was evoked, not by the Cork team, or even Offaly, but by Jack Lynch.

"Mr Lynch was called onto the pitch twice at Semple Stadium as part of the celebrations surrounding the centenary final.

"The entire crowd – Offaly supporters as well as those from Cork erupted in sustained applause when Mr Lynch made his appearance as one of the 38 All-Ireland winning captains of the past.

"He was called onto the field again as one of the 15 men honoured with places in 'the team of the century'."

The display of warmth for the former Taoiseach was quite out of the ordinary.

And as the applause died away, Mary Fanning, a good Offalywoman (and wife of the Editor of the *Sunday Independent,* who was sitting next to me) gave voice to the thought that was uppermost in my mind: "There's no doubt about it, Jack is an authentic folk hero".

The display of affection and respect was unprecedented on a great sporting occasion.

It was genuine, it was spontaneous, and it was very moving.

Around me in the stand, the talk was all of Jack, the hurler supreme, and the politician supreme.

Yet this incredible public display of esteem, this demonstration of tribal regard, also revealed the contradictions, some would even say the schizophrenia, of the Irish psyche.

Here was this vast crowd, the epitome of "Middle Ireland", acclaiming a man who had been responsible, in the minds of many, for bringing the country to the very threshold of bankruptcy back in the seventies.

How could this be?

Is it that, having done us proud as a race often in the past, we are willing to forgive our folk heroes the fall from grace when it comes?

Is it that, having entered our collective psyche, and in so doing transformed it, we are prepared to turn a blind eye when our tribal idols, our totem-figures, are shown at last to have feet of clay?

The parallels with Parnell, with which we started out, courtesy of Professor Lee, may be more apposite than we realise.

When he fell from grace in 1890 after the Kitty O'Shea divorce case, it is recorded that the Archbishop of Cashel, Dr Thomas Croke (an erstwhile champion of Parnell and his cause) threw his bust into the dust in disgust.

But the plain people of Ireland never forgot what Parnell had stood for, or what he had achieved.

And when the power-brokers finally deserted him, the people, in their hearts, remembered and gave thanks.

Perhaps so too it is with Lynch. He also was deserted by the powerbrokers. And for a while the new regime around Haughey tried to obliterate his memory, as though Fianna Fáil in the years from the resignation of Lemass to the election of Haughey (1966-1979) had been led and governed by some kind of non-person.

For a time party booklets appeared listing and showing photographs of the leaders – with the exception of Lynch.

In the memorable phrase of one journalist, a blatant attempt was made to "airbrush Jack Lynch out of history".

But the people were not duped. They remembered. And in remembering that day in Thurles, they showed – as an earlier generation had shown with Parnell – that "history" is not just what is written in books, it is more especially what is graven on human hearts.

One other sporting arena – all of 34 years before that historic day in Thurles – was also the setting for another extraordinary demonstration of Lynch's reputation and standing with the general public.

The occasion was the dying minutes of the 1950 Munster Hurling Final in Killarney, with Cork trailing Tipperary by a couple of points.

On the terraces and the sidelines temperatures soared when Cork scored a point, and some of the crowd in their excitement and exuberance spilled on to the pitch, disrupting play.

Cork, sensing a chance to pull the game out of the fire, were anxious for play to continue, believing that they now had the momentum and the initiative.

That, at any rate, was how Jack Lynch saw it. And he intervened.

In an article for the *Irish Press* entitled "No Better Hurler Than Jack Lynch", and written on 11 November 1966 (the day after Lynch became Taoiseach), here is how the late Padraig Puirseal described what happened:

"Round the ground he went, appealing to the exuberant crowd to move back and let the teams get on with the game.

"No greater tribute could be paid to his popularity and prestige with Cork followers and Tipperary followers alike than the way in which those spectators, for all their excitement, did move back at his request. . . "

The game was eventually restarted, and Tipperary went on to win by three points.

But for Puirseal, who had seen all of Lynch's great games for Cork and Munster, "that July Sunday in Killarney – the last time I saw him in the Cork jersey – remained his finest hour".

I heard a somewhat more humourous version of that famous incident in Killarney from a Tipperary man who knows Lynch well – Michael O'Kennedy (who served as Minister for Foreign Affairs in the 1977-79 Lynch Administration).

He told me the story in the RTE studios at Montrose on 23 February 1991, during a break in Andy O'Mahony's 'Sunday Show' where we were both guests.

"I remember the incident well," said O'Kennedy. "And I also remember years later Jack telling me that although he was being praised for his civic behaviour in trying to get the Killarney crowd to behave, the real reason he was so anxious to avoid a disruption was because he had Tony Brennan, his Tipp opponent, in his pocket, and could have won the game for Cork in the time remaining if the crowd hadn't invaded the pitch.... "

We'll never know, but with Lynch you never could tell.

On Friday, 19 December 1980, at the City Hall in Cork, sport also featured prominently when the Freedom of the City – the highest honour his people can give – was bestowed on him.

The Lord Mayor, Alderman Toddy O'Sullivan, in paying a special tribute in keeping with the occasion, perhaps revealed some of the qualities which account for Lynch's unique stature: "Jack Lynch's first appearance in public as a hurler and a footballer revealed very fully his personality. On the playing field he was a clean, skillful and determined player.

"These same characteristics he brought into his public life. In all the high offices he has held, he has always acted with dignified restraint, firmness and, most essentially, with humour and humility ...

"He has always shown his concern for his fellow countrymen and, despite the high offices which he has held, he has never lost the common touch, always remaining one of 'our own'...."

Truly, a folk hero.

Waving to the crowd in Thurles on All-Ireland day 1984

28. A Lukewarm Pluralist

In an article in the prestigious magazine Foreign Affairs in June 1972 the Taoiseach of the day indicated that his Government would contemplate constitutional and legislative change in the South in advance of any negotiations about unity.

"Our aim would be to encourage Northern Unionists to look favourably at our overtures," said Jack Lynch.

Further back, in a keynote speech made in Tralee on 20 September 1969, he had sought to reassure Unionists that in seeking re-unification the aim was not to extend the domination of Dublin.

"Whatever the constitutional setting might be – and we are prepared to explore all the possibilities in constructive discussion – the United Ireland we desire is one in which there would be a scrupulously fair deal for all.

"The Protestants of the North need have no fear of any interference with their religious freedom or civil liberties and rights."

What price unity?

The 1937 Constitution – Dev's creation?

Not then. Not in 1969.

Tackle the whole question of a Constitution *de novo* in the 1990s?

Hardly.

In March 1971, during a State visit to America, Mrs Lynch gave an interview to the *Pittsburgh Post-Gazette* in the course of which she said that should unity occur, Protestants would not have to fear discrimination.

"Our first President was a Protestant," she pointed out.

Then she was asked if recognition of divorce was an example of the kind of legal changes that would probably have to precede unity.

"We don't allow divorce," said Mrs Lynch. "That would have to be changed by referendum of the people. And that's a different kettle of fish. I would be against divorce. My husband would be against divorce."

The referendum, as we all know, took place eventually in June 1986 – and the divorce proposals put forward by the Government led by Dr Garret Fitzgerald were massively defeated.

I don't know how Jack and Mairin Lynch voted in 1986, but by 1991 Jack had certainly had second thoughts about the view his wife said he held in 1971.

"Having regard to the evolution of events over the past ten years, I would now favour divorce.

"Early on, I would not have favoured divorce. But I would now.

"The extent of the problem of marital breakdown is now at a stage where I believe divorce facilities are necessary.

"I have had to rethink my attitude."

And he makes it clear that concern for the children of a second union (involving one or both partners from previous marriages which have broken up) is a prime consideration.

"It is unacceptable to me that these children might continue to be regarded as illegitimate.

"Overall, with the increasing incidence of the break-up of marriage, I believe divorce facilities are now necessary."

He seems to share the view of many now that it is no longer a question of whether there will be divorce in the Republic, but when.

He is also too experienced a politician to know that it won't be easy to push through the necessary changes, even in the 1990s.

He knows that within our society and our culture the forces of what Conor Cruise O'Brien once called "political Catholicism" working against change are still formidable.

The referenda of 1983 and 1986 showed that. The fate of Dr Garret Fitzgerald's constitutional crusade demonstrated the pitfalls awaiting any politician desirous of change, or pushing for change too quickly.

Festina lente might well stand as Lynch's motto in regard to social legislation.

The cautious, conservative side to Lynch showed itself again and again in the periods from 1966-1973 and 1977-79 when he enjoyed real power.

"I would be very critical of his legislative achievements," Michael D. Higgins once told me, when I asked him for an assessment of Lynch.

"He could have introduced a lot of non-cost legislation, but he lacked the vision and the will.

"Modernising social legislation could have been introduced by him, with his personal prestige and his majority in the Dáil.

"People would have worn those changes coming from him, when they wouldn't have from another Taoiseach or party leader."

Family planning legislation is a case in point. Despite his demotic stature and appeal, he vacillated on contraception, saying at one time – in a phrase that has given rise to a fair few laughs as well as serving as the basis for many a *double entendre* – that it was something that should be put on "the long finger".

The story is told that back in 1971, when he was thinking about changing the law on contraception, he was amazed by the number of deputies who insisted there should be no change whatsoever.

"Political Catholicism" was at work again, though the changes which took place in terms of moral practice among the Irish people after Pope Paul VI's highly controversial and divisive birth control encyclical, *Humanae Vitae*, in 1968 might have been more far-reaching than Lynch thought at the time.

Always an advocate of consensus politics, he might well have found in 1971 and afterwards that his backbenchers (the rural Deputies in particular) were paying more attention to the episcopal and clerical lobbies than to their constituents.

In the period from 1966 to 1973 the law on contraceptives was a "pathetic pretence". The appropriate piece of legislation was the Criminal Law Amendment Act of 1935 which made it illegal for any person to import, offer, advertise or expose for sale any contraceptives.

Meanwhile, the Pill was being prescribed by hundreds of doctors and sold by hundreds of chemists knowingly as a contraceptive to thousands of patients who were buying it in the knowledge that it was a contraceptive.

The theory was that it was being prescribed and sold to women who had irregular or heavy menstruation. This was all a charade.

But it was a charade which caused Lynch no problems. It has been unkindly said that because he himself had no family, he did not regard family planning legislation as a priority issue.

Thousands of others did, but the charade continued until the historic Supreme Court decision in 1974 in the McGee case.

By then Lynch was Leader of the Opposition, but appropriate family planning legislation had still not been prepared by the time he was back in power in 1977.

In choosing his Cabinet, Lynch appointed the rehabilitated Haughey as Minister for Health and Social Welfare. And it was the latter who – having met privately with the Catholic Bishops – piloted through the Health (Family Planning) Bill in July 1979 in an attempt to tidy up the "free for all" situation which ensued in the aftermath of the McGee case.

The new legislation permitted the importation and sale of contraceptives by licensed pharmacists and health boards. Within the terms of the Act, however, contraceptives could only be sold to married people on the basis of a prescription or authorisation by a registered physician.

It was the "ridiculously restrictive nature" of that legislation which led to it being described as "an Irish solution to an Irish problem".

Some years later, Michael D. Higgins put a different slant on this. He said Haughey, who saw Lynch as a very devious man, believed the Taoiseach had put him into the Department of Health and saddled him with the family planning legislation because he (Lynch) believed it was a "no-win" situation.

"Haughey's boast that this was an 'Irish solution to an Irish problem' was really a euphemism for saying: 'He set a trap, but I didn't get caught!'"

Whether that is so or not, the fact remains that Lynch dragged his feet on this and other social legislation.

As far as the 47 women who travelled on what became known as the "contraceptive train" from Belfast to Dublin in May 1971, their protest, as Mary Kenny emphasised to me later, was as much against the Lynch Government as against the Catholic Bishops.

Today, as he looks back on his period in office, one senses a twinge of regret.

Getting him to admit this, or to articulate the reasons for it, is not easy.

It remains an unspecified regret, but at its core, I am convinced, is a nagging realisation that he could have achieved a lot more, that a policy of *festina lente* might not always have been appropriate.

This mustn't blind one to the fact that Jack Lynch was a conservative Taoiseach, a very orthodox Catholic – by the standards of the fifties rather than the sixties – and a man with a reverence for Eamon de Valera, and all the latter's works and pomps.

This is particularly evident in relation to the 1937 Constitution, which was Dev's creation.

Even now, despite all that has happened, he is unclear about the need for an entirely new document.

His sparse comments on this lead one to believe that he sees a new Constitution as a consequence of unity rather than as a vehicle by and through which unity might be facilitated.

He sees the need for tampering with the 1937 document, for amending sections of it. But he does not appear to be prepared to follow the example of the present Leader of the Progressive Democrats, Desmond O'Malley (for whom he has great regard), in calling for the adoption of an entirely new Constitution.

O'Malley argued at his party's 1991 annual conference that the present Constitution was a major impediment to liberal, progressive ideals.

There is no reason to believe that Lynch shares his desire for a new Constitution which would reflect Unionists' concerns, would provide for divorce and allow unequivocal participation in a united Europe.

Piecemeal reforms to meet specific circumstances, yes; starting all over again *de novo*, no. That would appear to be Lynch's position.

But even so harsh a critic as Dr Conor Cruise O'Brien has acknowledged the evolution of Lynch's thinking.

In constitutional terms, this was manifested very clearly in 1990.

On 1 March that year the Supreme Court issued a ruling in the McGimpsey case which took a lot of people by surprise.

The Court ruled that the constitutional claim to Northern Ireland was one of legal right, rather than simply a political aspiration.

One of those taken aback by the Supreme Court's adjudication was the former Taoiseach, Jack Lynch.

Two months earlier Lynch himself caused widespread surprise when he pronounced in public on the constitutional claim to the North.

The occasion was a seminar organised by the Irish Association for Cultural, Economic and Social Relations. The date of the event was Saturday, 5 May 1990 – ideal for the Sunday papers!

And, sure enough, the following morning, Lynch's remarks provided the lead story in the *Sunday Press,* the *Sunday Independent* and the *Sunday Tribune.*

"Lynch Calls for an End to State Claim on the North" said the *Tribune*, getting to the heart of what he had said the previous day in Buswell's Hotel, Dublin.

"Would it not be worthwhile considering again an amendment of Article 3 along the lines put forward two decades ago . . ?"

Lynch was referring to the All-Party Oireachtas Committee set up in August 1966 under his predecessor, Sean Lemass, to review the constitutional, legislative and institutional bases of Government.

In its Report published in December 1967 the Committee (which Lemass, after retiring as Taoiseach, joined at Lynch's behest) recommended that Article 3 be replaced as follows:

"The Irish Nation hereby proclaims its firm will, that its territory be united in harmony and brotherly affection between all Irishmen."

In his address to the seminar, Lynch adverted to the possibility of talks on the future of Northern Ireland (this was the initiative of Peter Brooke, Secretary of State for the North), and intimated that reform of Articles 2 and 3 might be part of that process.

He said the Unionists always regarded these Articles as a threat, and the Supreme Court ruling would have the effect of reinforcing this "alleged threat".

He had an additional reason for advocating change. "If the IRA feels that the Supreme Court's interpretation of Articles 2 and 3 could give them any legitimacy in their campaign of violence, then by all means we should change them.

"I believe that to do so would in no way dilute our desire for reunification, and I believe that to give an indication of our purpose along these lines could open the way for peaceful dialogue and reconciliation."

A fortnight later we met in Cork and discussed, among other things, the Supreme Court judgement and his reaction at the seminar.

"I still believe that Articles 2 and 3 are no more than an expression of a sincerely held desire for unity. That, I believe, was the intention. They had no legal import and, above all, were no threat against Unionists.

"The Supreme Court has imported a legal imperative, as against a political aspiration, into Article 3 in particular.

"At the seminar I said, well, if that is the case, if we must accept – as we must – the Supreme Court interpretation of the law, then let us change it along the lines suggested in 1967.

"I never felt from day one that these Articles should have that legal implication.

"Above all, what frightened me was that the IRA could take comfort from this and try to use it to justify what they are doing. . . "

There was, and still is, no evidence that he favours scrapping the 1937 Constitution and replacing it with a new one.

But at least he has moved beyond the position he held in the mid-seventies when he expressed disappointment at the Unionist reaction to the removal of a section of Article 44 (deleting the reference to the "special position" of the Catholic Church).

That referendum took place on 7 December 1972 when Lynch was Taoiseach.

"This initiative was completely ignored in the North, as if of absolutely no consequence . . .

"I appreciated then that it was futile making any constitutional changes in advance of unity, and that any further changes should be made in an All-Ireland context," he told *Magill* magazine in November 1979.

An editorial in the New York paper the *Irish Echo*, implied that Lynch, by and through the comments he had made at the Irish Association seminar, was contributing to "a revisionist history" which was attempting to "put a benign face on the partitioning of Ireland".

Understandably, this brought an angry response from Lynch.

He claimed, justifiably, that the editorial distorted the import of his speech.

That aside, he is a revisionist and, *pace* Dr Conor Cruise O'Brien, an important one.

O'Brien's hostility to Lynch is difficult to understand, though his attitude has mellowed over the last few years.

Lynch has almost single-handedly brought about the reshaping and redefining of Fianna Fáil's concept of republicanism.

And his brand of *'realpolitik'* has compelled a major rethink on attitudes to the settlement of the "national question".

That's revisionism in action.

The pity is that Lynch's revisionism is limited and selective.

Unlike another Taoiseach, Dr Garret Fitzgerald, his concept of Church-State relations is pre-Vatican II rather than post-Vatican II.

His concept of pluralism and the need for a pluralist society during his years in power was lukewarm at best, vapid at worst.

And what he had in terms of demotic appeal, he lacked in social vision.

To say that he squandered the greatest electoral majority in the history of the State may be overstating it.

But he missed great and, some would say, never to be repeated opportunities.

Certainly, no leader is ever again likely to enjoy his prestige or his massive public support of the 1977 period.

If it wasn't a squandered mandate, it was certainly a grossly underutilized one.

And history won't forget that.

29. Jack and the PDs

With the dissolution of the 21st Dáil on 21 May 1981 Jack Lynch's career in politics came to an end.

But did it really end then and there?

Lynch had signalled his intention to quit almost exactly a year previously.

On 15 May 1980 – it was a Thursday – a special meeting was held in the Fianna Fáil rooms in the Grand Parade in Cork to consider the new constituency boundaries recommended by the Constituency Commission.

Lynch chose the occasion to announce that he did not propose to stand for re-election to Dáil Éireann at the next General Election.

He specified two reasons for his decision: (a) the need for Cork to be represented by a younger man, and (b) in order to give adequate time to the party organisation in Cork to place candidates to the best advantage in the redrawn constituencies.

The decision was not unexpected, and Lynch was following the pattern of his predecessor, Sean Lemass, who also retired from active politics after stepping down as Taoiseach.

It had been generally anticipated that Lynch would only remain in the backbenches for the life of the 21st Dáil, and would not seek to retain his seat after that.

The timing came just five months after his resignation as Taoiseach.

The heading over my own front page story in the *Irish Press* on 16 May 1980 read: "Jack Lynch to quit Dáil".

So Jack had effectively bowed out of Irish politics.

But had he?

Was this really the end?

It seemed so.

And in a formal sense it was so.

Whether he would have gone if Colley had defeated Haughey in the contest for the leadership of the Party must remain a matter of speculation.

Over the next three or four years, the unresolved tensions of the period from 1970-1977 continued to surface within the Party.

The dissatisfaction with Haughey was deep-rooted, and his failure to secure an overall majority in the three General Elections of 1981-82, prompted some of his opponents to move against him.

The man chosen to spearhead the "heaves" against him was Des O'Malley – the man appointed as Minister for Justice by Lynch after the clean-out of 1970.

The "heaves" failed and after his famous "I Stand By The Republic" speech on 20 February 1985, and his refusal to vote with Fianna Fáil in a Dáil division on family planning legislation, O'Malley was finally expelled.

The date of his expulsion was 26 February 1985.

Within 10 months O'Malley had established a new political party – the Progressive Democrats.

That party came into being on 21 December 1985, dedicating itself to "breaking the mould" of Irish politics.

And to this day the belief persists in some quarters that O'Malley was given aid and comfort throughout by Jack Lynch.

The fact that O'Malley had been joined in the PDs by other such "Lynchites" as Bobby Molloy, Mary Harney and Pearse Wyse gave ammunition to those who wished to perpetuate the notion that Jack was involved hand and glove with Dessie.

And in February 1985 Lynch himself had played into the hands of his enemies by giving an interview on the RTE Radio News at 1.30 in which he made a stout defence of his political protegé.

This interview took place just hours before the meeting at which O'Malley was expelled (the vote was 73-9), and it was the view of a number of deputies that Lynch's intervention ended whatever slim chance remained of reaching a compromise.

In the course of the interview Lynch described O'Malley's epic Dáil speech as one of the best ever made in the House.

"He fearlessly, very courageously, portrayed his concept of Republicanism, a concept that would find an echo in the hearts and minds of most real Fianna Fáil supporters and members throughout the country."

Although Lynch, very properly, stood aloof from the internal moves to topple Haughey between 1982-85, there can be no doubt that he would have been very happy to see O'Malley as Taoiseach.

He never made any attempt to hide his admiration for O'Malley, just as he has never made any attempt to conceal his regard for Dr Martin O'Donoghue.

Indeed, he said O'Donoghue was one of the "best brains" ever to have served the country, after Haughey had abolished the Department of Economic Planning and Development, and banished O'Donoghue to the backbenches.

This was Lynch just being himself – loyal to his friends and former colleagues.

It was in character, but also open to misinterpretation, or in danger of being misconstrued.

This was especially the case in February 1982, when O'Malley threw down the gauntlet to Haughey for the first time.

Lynch made a statement in which he said Dessie was right to allow his name to go forward before a meeting of the Parliamentary Party as a nominee for Taoiseach.

The challenge fizzled out, and afterwards Lynch had to deny reports that he helped organise O'Malley's campaign to wrest the leadership from Haughey.

In particular, he had to refute suggestions that he attended meetings at the home of Seamus Brennan, TD, to plot Haughey's downfall.

The former Taoiseach said quite categorically that he played no part in organising O'Malley's challenge.

Then he added: "I make no secret of the fact that, as is evident from published statements from me in recent years, and in the one I issued after the Parliamentary Party meeting, I would favour Des O'Malley as Party Leader and would wish to see him as a future Taoiseach."

He may have given comfort to O'Malley, but there was no question of his having given aid.

But it wasn't until December 1985 and the founding of the PDs that the rumours that Lynch was backing O'Malley, were really given legs.

The day after the formation of the Progressive Democrats, Lynch wished the new party well, and said that Fianna Fáil had "finally lost two of its most able deputies".

He went on: "The Progressive Democrats will bring a new dimension into Irish life to which Des O'Malley and Mary Harney have a great deal to contribute ..."

It did not go unnoticed, however, that O'Malley felt it necessary to make a statement specifying that Jack Lynch had not helped to establish the new party.

On 22 December 1985, he said: "After deciding to go ahead with my plans, I called the Lynch home and told Mrs Lynch my intentions. Mr Lynch was not there."

Later, on the RTE 'This Week' radio programme, O'Malley denied that Lynch had advised him against forming a new party.

He said he did not ask Mr Lynch for support, as he felt it would be inappropriate as the former Fianna Fáil leader was now retired from active politics.

"He wished me luck," he added.

Nearly a year after the PDs came into being, there was even speculation in some papers that Lynch might join the new party.

Was it ever a realistic proposition?

Could the man who idolised Eamon de Valera turn his back on the party Dev created, and which he himself took over?

Some of Lynch's friends and former colleagues would undoubtedly have been delighted to see him among the ranks of the PDs.

The presence of the elder statesman would have been a great boost.

But his ties to Dev, above all (though, unlike Dev, Lynch was free of zealotry), cancelled out any faint urgings he may have felt to throw in his lot with O'Malley, Molloy, Harney, Wyse, and the others.

The likelihood of Jack joining the PDs was always a non-runner.

And today Jack himself remains adamant that he never had "any hand, act or part" in the setting up of the PDs.

Jack Lynch in the Berkley Court Hotel at the inaugural dinner of the Flex trust in honour of the late P.V. Doyle (L to R Mairin Lynch, Anne Roche (daughter of P.V. Doyle), Jack Lynch, Mrs Margaret Doyle and her daughter Bernie Gallagher)

30. Jack-in-The-Park?

Jack Lynch could have been a candidate for Áras an Uachtaráin in 1990. And wouldn't that have created a most interesting situation?

If the circumstances had been slightly different, Lynch could have been persuaded to allow his name to go forward as a candidate for the Presidency in 1990 under the Fianna Fáil colours!

More than at any time since his resignation as Taoiseach in 1979, he was ready to run for "The Park".

Isn't that ironic?

Isn't it doubly ironic given all that happened?

Imagine the scenario if Lynch had been the Fianna Fáil candidate. Imagine what would have happened.

For starters, Fianna Fáil would have kept their "unbeaten record" in the Presidential stakes.

Brian Lenihan would still be Tanaiste and Minister for Defence, and he and his family would have been spared the controversy and the strain of the "Duffy Tapes", and the trauma of defeat at the polls at the hands of Mrs Robinson.

Most of all, he would have been spared the indignity and the hurt of being fired from the Cabinet by his "old friend" Charlie Haughey.

On top of all of that, the party itself would have been spared the disappointment of losing, and the inevitable and painful soul-searching which this led to.

The strains imposed on the Coalition with the Progressive Democrats as a result of the part played by the latter group in the sacking of Lenihan would also have been avoided.

And the main beneficiary of all of that would have been none other than the Taoiseach, C.J. Haughey, whose leadership of the party in the post-election situation was again called into question.

How ironic!

And to think that Jack Lynch could have been the means by and through which all of that could have been avoided.

Would Lynch have been a candidate if the summons had come?

The answer, I believe, is "yes" – in the right circumstances.

Abandoning his long-held attitude that he had no interest in the Presidency, Jack Lynch indicated to me in 1990 that he would consider running.

"But I would want a contest," he added, significantly.

"If I went, I'd want a contest," he repeated. "I wouldn't want a walk-over."

Urging him to go, I said: "It would be a fitting end to your career".

He glanced at me, thought for a while, and then replied: "They said that about Dev too . . ."

It was the first time in 11 years that he responded positively (albeit in a guarded fashion) to a question about the possibility of his being a candidate for Áras an Uachtaráin.

On all previous occasions, he has been quick to dampen down any speculation that he might go forward.

The other irony is that on this one occasion, when he could have been coaxed, he was never asked.

And I think the signs were there this time that he was adopting a new approach – for those with the eyes to see.

In the past it was different. In the past he was asked no less than three times to go for the Presidency.

It was never on; not then.

Those approaches came from within Fianna Fáil.

In 1990 approaches were made again from those who wanted Jack to go for the Park.

These included some members of the Progressive Democrats.

One or two voices urging him to run also came from within the Fianna Fáil ranks – but nobody at the top showed any interest.

One of the most significant of all voices which urged Jack to stand was that of Dr Conor Cruise O'Brien.

In an article in the *Irish Independent* on Saturday, 26 May 1990, headed (shades of the World Cup!) "Give It A Lash, Jack", Dr O'Brien, whose hostility to Lynch has puzzled many people, urged him to run.

"He would be hard to beat, would he not, as a Presidential candidate, were he to be a candidate at all?" Dr O'Brien wrote.

He revealed that the thought came to him when he encountered Lynch at a public meeting in Buswell's Hotel, Dublin, on Saturday, 5 May.

The meeting was organised by the Irish Association - a body concerned, broadly speaking, with North-South relationships. The subject under discussion was Articles 2 and 3 of the Constitution, as these now stand in the light of the Supreme Court's decision of 1 March 1990 in the McGimpsey case.

The discussion was divided into two sessions. The first, discussed the legal aspects. The second, dealing with the political aspects, was chaired by Lynch.

And Dr O'Brien was impressed.

"As chairman, Mr Lynch gave a short, thoughtful speech, which was generally considered a most useful contribution to the discussion.

"He told the history of the Dáil Committee which had studied the question of these Articles, in the late sixties, and had come up with a recommendation for amendment.

"He said that, after the events of August 1969, his Government had felt obliged to shelve that recommendation. Looking back on it now, he felt some regret over that decision. He now believed that Articles 2 and 3 should be amended: the process of getting them amended was a delicate one, and should not be rushed, but amendment there should be . . . "

This sufficiently impressed Dr O'Brien to set him wondering what Jack Lynch was doing at the meeting, when he was supposed to be retired.

"Answer: maybe he isn't really retired. Supplementary answer: maybe he's thinking about the Presidency. He was making a public appearance in the role of an Elder Statesman. And who could be more suited for our Presidency than an Elder Statesman?"

Dr O'Brien admits it was just a hunch, though at the time he thought it might turn out to be right.

"And President Lynch would be a credit to us all."

I think his hunch was right: all that was needed was an invitation to run.

The encouragement to run had come from others before Dr O'Brien put pen to paper.

Euro MEP, T.J. Maher, a sound man without a political axe to grind, had said a month earlier that the presence of Jack Lynch in Áras an Uachtaráin would be good for the country.

And on 1 May 1990 Jack Roche, a respected Fianna Fáil member of Cork County Council, called on the party to approach Lynch and request him to become the FF nominee for the Presidential election.

Cllr Roche stressed that Lynch would be an excellent candidate for the Presidency, and would have little difficulty in being elected in view of his widespread popularity.

Picking up on this, an editorial in the *Cork Examiner* said:

"The man who signed Ireland's Accession Treaty might find it more difficult to turn down a public approach from Fianna Fáil to return to public life in a non-political role, especially at such a momentous time in European and world affairs".

Evidence that the Presidency was very much on the mind of the former Taoiseach can be gleaned from remarks he made at the inaugural meeting of the Philosophical Society at Trinity College, Dublin, on 5 November 1990.

He told the Society he believed a case could be made for changes in the Constitution affecting the powers of the Presidency, and the method of nomination for election to the office.

He said the President, who is the guardian of the Constitution which guarantees the fundamental rights of citizens, must be a person of integrity, and have the experience and ability to exercise such an important role.

Changes in the method of nomination were also necessary, he added.

"I believe it would be useful to consider the setting up of another inter-party committee specifically to consider these matters, that the committee might be required to refer its report back to both Houses of the Oireachtas for debate and decision, following which the Government of the day could bring forward proposals for legislation."

There is little doubt in my mind that if Cllr Roche's suggestion had been taken up by the Fianna Fáil party, Jack Lynch would not only have been a candidate in 1990, he would now be in Áras an Uachtaráin, for, as the *Examiner* said, this man "once described as the best loved politician since Daniel O'Connell, would be a virtual certainty to be elected".

As things turned out, it wasn't to be.

But it will remain one of the tantalising "might have beens" of the 1990s.

An Taoiseach Jack Lynch with President Nixon in 1971(copyright Camera Press)

31. A One-Dimensional Man?

It was my second time with a VIP in Suite 213 of Fitzpatrick's Silver Springs Hotel in Cork. On the first occasion – during the two Michael Jackson concerts at Pairc Uí Chaoimh in Sept 1989 – I was interviewing singer Kim Wilde.

We talked politics then as well – feminist politics and the issue of sexism in the pop/rock business.

Now I was going to talk politics again, but politics of a very different kind. On this second occasion I was in the company of one of our leading politicians and statesmen, Dr Garret Fitzgerald, a man whose discursive approach to politics is of a different order to that of Ms Wilde.

In the spacious surrounds of the suite on the afternoon of 4 February 1991, I was reminded momentarily of the lovely Kim as the former Taoiseach took off his shoes and settled back into a comfortable armchair.

Now Garret began to talk about Jack.

It's worth remembering that there is a bond of friendship between Fitzgerald and Lynch which is very unusual, given the history of antipathy between Fianna Fáil and Fine Gael.

They are easy in each other's company in a way which could never be true of Lynch and Fitzgerald's predecessor Liam Cosgrave, and which would be unthinkable in terms of Fitzgerald and Lynch's successor, Charlie Haughey.

The fact that Fitzgerald now regrets the famous "flawed pedigree" remark he made in the Dáil when opposing Haughey in 1981 doesn't really change anything.

His view of Haughey – much the same as Lynch's – remains unchanged today. And a fair clue to the nature of that view is contained in the fact that neither Fitzgerald nor Lynch would approach Haughey (as they would be required to do) to gain access to the State papers for their respective terms of office.

"Are ex-Taoisigh constitutionally entitled to have access to such papers," I enquired of Garret, knowing that when I was talking to him he was still working on a book dealing with his period in Government.

"It has never been clarified," he replied, in the unconcerned frame of mind of one who took steps from day one in office to have everything that crossed his desk copied.

"Charlie said if I wanted anything to let him know," added Dr. Fitzgerald. "But I wouldn't want to be under a compliment to him."

In Lynch's case where, astonishingly, he has kept no copies of any State papers at all, the matter of access is much more serious.

He has never shown any inclination to put the matter to the test, and has never commented one way or the other about it. Lynch, I suspect, regrets that he didn't make a move to get at his papers while Fitzgerald was Taoiseach. And that too, would be indicative of the bond between them.

In his book *Garret – The Enigma*, published in 1985, Raymond Smith goes to the core of that bond when he writes: "So too with Garret Fitzgerald, who admired Jack Lynch for his courage as he had admired Sean Lemass for his pragmatic approach to industrialisation and economic growth in the sixties".

Now at my behest, as we settled down in Suite 213, Garret turned his thoughts to the "real" Taoiseach.

A little earlier in the hotel's impressive Convention Centre, Dr Fitzgerald had spoken in a light-hearted fashion at a Publicity Club of Ireland lunch about his time in politics as a Senator, a TD, a Minister and as Taoiseach.

I wanted to hear his thoughts – again – on another Taoiseach.

In March 1989 – in response to another request from me (I was preparing a series of articles on Jack Lynch for the *Cork Examiner* at the time), Dr Fitzgerald met me in the office he uses in the redbricked Department of Finance building across Kildare Street from the Dáil and also discussed Lynch's strengths and weaknesses.

Since Dr Fitzgerald's work on his book had taken him through the Lynch Years, I wondered if in his ruminations he had revised any of his earlier assessments of Lynch.

The frivolity of his lunchtime performance was over and done with. This was serious stuff; this was Dr Fitzgerald, academic, economist, journalist, politician and statesman, in his element.

"I never thought in my meetings with Jack prior to 1966 that he had the qualities of leadership which would take him to the very top in politics.

"He seemed too conscious of his own inadequacy for high office. It was something he talked about openly when I first met him in 1961 in a ministerial capacity. And that kind of thing can be a serious failing in a politician."

In a 1989 interview, Dr Fitzgerald had this to say: "I think his modesty and his reluctance to go for the top office were genuine.

"When I met him first in the early sixties, when he was Minister for Industry and Commerce, I was struck by his extreme modesty. He deprecated his role as Minister, and suggested it was only because of the lack of talent around that he could possibly be Minister.

"But there is also something very interesting in the fact that at every stage he deprecated his own talents, and appeared to have no great ambition, and yet always ended up moving up the hierarchy from one post to another, and eventually became Taoiseach.

"It is rarely that people achieve eminence through being modest about themselves, yet Jack Lynch managed it."

Today Dr Fitzgerald still finds, in pondering that, a certain fascination.

As he himself has stressed, what would more than likely prove a fatal flaw in most politicians, did not appear to hinder Lynch at all. And it may also have contributed to his extraordinary popularity with the common people of Ireland.

Dr Fitzgerald agrees. But he remains adamant that another facet of the Lynch persona which was evident in the sixties did prove a sizeable handicap.

"It seemed to me from our first meeting in 1961 that he was very uneasy, very uncomfortable about his place in Fianna Fáil. He was unsure of himself. After all, there was no family connection with Fianna Fáil.

"I felt that he felt he lacked the kind of traditional links with the Party which Neil Blaney, for instance, had. And for a long time this left Jack in a situation where he felt he couldn't take on the likes of Blaney.

"He did in the end, of course, though we may never know to what extent his hand was forced in this regard."

Political commentator John Healy had also focussed on this back in 1979 when he said Lynch's problems as a Leader had been "compounded by his reluctance to deal with the challenge of 'Blaneyism' when it manifested itself in the closing days of the sixties".

Dr Fitzgerald also blames Lynch for the overbearing attitude of the Civil Service which the Coalition Government, led by Liam Cosgrave, ran up against when they took over from Fianna Fáil in 1973.

"The natural resistance of the Civil Service to innovative policies, whose effects cannot always be foreseen, had been broken down before and especially during the Lemass years.

"But by the time we came into office in 1973, the old attitudes had been reinstated, which leads me to believe that during Lynch's first terms as Taoiseach (1966-73) the Civil Service had not been policy driven or policy-directed.

"We ran up against that, and we had to strive, along with everything else, to make up the ground which had been lost during Jack's time in office.

"Lynch was, in many ways, a very lucky politician. It is possible to argue that he benefitted from the economic policies of Sean Lemass and the period of 1966 to 1973 saw tremendous economic growth created, I would contend, by the momentum which has been initiated by Lemass.

"Then in 1973 Lynch was gone out of office before the first great oil crisis, so he escaped responsibility for that. And when he came back in, in 1977, the economy, thanks to our endeavours, had entered a new and healthy phase again. All of that is, from his point of view, good fortune. I throw that out as a hypothesis. And I think it is worth testing."

But what of 1977 itself and the economic consequences of Fianna Fáil's historic electoral victory?

Dr Fitzgerald scratched a shoeless foot and smiled wryly. You could almost see the lights flashing in the micro-chips of his economist's brain during its rapid-fire calculations.

"The results of all of that were disastrous for the country and, as I said to you on a previous occasion, we have been picking up the pieces ever since.

"In a sense, Jack was lucky here too, because he has never really carried the can for the 1977 Fianna Fáil Election Manifesto. The blame today attaches to Martin O'Donoghue. That in itself is not unjust, because he was largely responsible for the Manifesto. But it could never have gone ahead without Jack's approval. Yet, by and large, he has escaped the backlash. It's another example of Lynch's good fortune."

The Manifesto, of which O'Donoghue as Lynch's economic guru was the principal architect, is a document which has since become one of the most contentious ever issued in Irish political life.

But were its effects as disastrous as some commentators claim?

And what of O'Donoghue's defence of the Manifesto, most notably in an article entitled "Irish Economic Policy 1977-79" in the Autumn 1990 issue of *Studies?*

"Martin is terribly defensive about it. We all make mistakes, though, mind you, this was a mistake of some considerable magnitude.

"I thought first when I heard that Lynch was bringing in O'Donoghue as a special adviser that he would be good for Lynch and Fianna Fáil. It was clear that Lynch needed someone on the economic front whose advice he could trust, someone whose advice would not be tainted by narrow party considerations.

"I felt O'Donoghue would fulfil that role for Jack. He was a good, quantifying economist. But he went political. I didn't think that would happen. But Martin went political, and I think that distorted his judgement."

Garret is in no doubt that the 1977-79 period marks the nadir of Lynch's career.

"It started with the election. And the irony is that they would have won anyway without doing some of the things they did, like abolishing rates.

"If they had done polls themselves – and I don't know whether they did or not – they would have known they were going to win in any case.

"One of my abiding memories of that election is of a scene in the RTE television studios when the outcome was clear. I can recall the horror on Seamus Brennan's face as the size of the Fianna Fáil majority was becoming evident.

"He knew, just as Jack himself did, that a majority of that size could only mean trouble. And that's how it turned out. It may seem strange in political terms to say it, but Jack didn't want a victory of this magnitude. It was only storing up trouble for the future, and he knew that. That kind of majority is as much a handicap, perhaps more so, as an advantage."

While readily admitting to a personal fondness for Lynch – "we have always got on well together" – Dr Fitzgerald, in his reassessment, is less sure nowadays of his former opponent's political stature than before.

"In the main, circumstances have been kind to him."

When Lynch resigned in December 1979, Fitzgerald paid a tribute to him, in the course of which he praised the service he had given to the Irish people through his leadership of Fianna Fáil and the Government.

"Amongst his many major achievements was his successful leading of Ireland into the EEC.

"Since 1969, in particular, when the Northern Ireland crisis broke, he has consistently sought to ensure that moderation prevails, and has promoted policies of reconciliation.

"In victory he was modest, in defeat generous, and throughout his political life a sincere patriot."

It was fair, and it was sincere.

And it still stands today.

But is there more or less to Jack Lynch than meets the eye?

Is it a case of what you see is what you get, or are there hidden layers?

What of the view, expressed from time to time, that there is a hidden dimension to Lynch, a side that very few know?

Garret didn't hesitate.

"Is there another side to him, is he a very complex character? Or is he just as many find him – a one-dimensional man?

"Maybe that's just the plain truth."

32. Assessments

Bad news travels fast. For Jack Lynch in 1979 it came in a double dose, and from his own backyard as well. On November 7 the Taoiseach left on an eight day State visit to the USA. The next day, as he prepared for a visit to The White House and a meeting with President Jimmy Carter, the bad news began to trickle through.

The White House meeting was less than an hour away, but the news from home was so dispiriting that the Minister for Foreign Affairs, Michael O'Kennedy, who had accompanied the Taoiseach, refused to break it to him. That thankless task fell to the Government Press Secretary, Frank Dunlop.

What Dunlop told the Taoiseach effectively determined a decision which was to lead to an adjustment in Lynch's resignation plans. Those plans had been formulated earlier in 1979 after a long talk between Jack and his wife, Mairin.

For months the party had been restless, and Lynch was tired. "Psychologically, he was preparing to go," said a close aide. January had been chosen, though only Jack and Mrs Lynch knew that, as she straightened his tie before leaving for The White House.

He knew there were stirrings of dissension among his backbenchers, though he underestimated it. In June of 1979 the Party had not done well in the elections for the European parliament; the economy was stagnating, and the feeling that Lynch had lost his way was growing.

On August 27, with plans for the visit of Pope John Paul II being finalised, Lord Mountbatten was killed when his boat was destroyed by a bomb, and 18 British soldiers were killed in an ambush near Warrenpoint. In London on September 5, after attending Mountbatten's funeral, Lynch had talks with Mrs Thatcher. Anglo-Irish relations were under strain.

Then four days later, Síle de Valera, TD, made a speech at the annual Liam Lynch Commemoration at Kilcrumper near Fermoy, which was seen as a challenge to Lynch's leadership. Behind the scenes, power-broking of the highest order was underway. The cracks were beginning to appear.

In his book *Hiding Behind A Face*, Stephen O'Byrnes describes the bad news Dunlop had to convey to Lynch: "On Thursday, 8 November 1979, when the voting stopped, the politically impossible had happened. Fine Gael won both seats. Jack Lynch had been mutilated in his own backyard."

The "mutilation" referred to the loss of two by-elections in Cork City, where Liam Burke took the seat, and in Cork North-East, where Myra Barry triumphed. The by-elections had been occasioned by the death during the summer of two TDs – Fianna Fáil's Sean Brosnan, and Labour's Pat Kerrigan.

O'Byrnes takes up the story: "For Fianna Fáil the by-elections were a disaster. Jack Lynch had left for a scheduled visit to the United States before the results materialised. He was shaken by the outcome, and described it as a serious mid-term rebuff.

"He promised a Government reshuffle in the New Year. But many of his backbenchers were not prepared to wait that long. The heave against Jack was on . . . "

Those two results effectively transformed the political situation. Fears for their own electoral survival drove government backbenchers to desert the man who had pulled off the great triumph of 1977. And Charlie Haughey was about to become the political beneficiary of the backbench revolt against Jack Lynch. The end was in sight.

The two pivotal dates in Jack Lynch's political life are 1970 and 1977. During the seven years which separated them, he reached the apogee of his career, a career which spanned one of the most turbulent and crucial periods in modern Irish life.

In any barometer of that career, the dates mark the high and low points. And if it seems strange to say that 1977 – the year of the unprecedented 20-seat Fianna Fáil majority – was ultimately to be the low point, it cannot be overlooked that the real results of that Election spelled economic disaster.

This is disputed by Lynch himself, and by Des O'Malley, who worked closely with him at the time, as well as Martin O'Donoghue, the chief architect of the Manifesto.

As a close aide said: "That's all very well now, but at the time nobody objected to the free lunch . . . "

Even as he savoured the historic victory, Lynch remarked to a friend that a majority of 20 seats in the Dáil carried with it as many risks as advantages.

And within two years he would ruefully acknowledge that he was right, though in a way which even he could not have foreseen. Backbenchers were in revolt, and the clock was ticking. Afterwards he would say "they couldn't stand the heat in the kitchen".

There was more to it than that. He himself was showing signs of being a "burnt-out case". He had visibly aged. The stresses and strains of 13 very difficult and sometimes turbulent years had taken their toll.

They had been 13 of the most critical years in Irish politics leaving a legacy of huge plus factors, and equally huge minus ones.

Looking back Lynch would single out Ireland's accession to the EEC in January 1973 as "a major achievement". In the referendum of May 1972, more than 82% of those who voted agreed with Lynch that our destiny should lie in a direct link with other countries of Western Europe.

The immediate benefits were obvious – significant increases in agricultural prices (by as much as 50% in beef and dairy produce); guaranteed prices for our farmers, tariff-free entry to the markets of other EEC States and regional and social funds.

Overall, Ireland has fared well from the European connection. The Community is neither the disaster some predicted it would be at the time of entry, nor an easy answer to all our problems. It does, however, provide a new context in which to see and solve those problems.

Lynch would also attach considerable importance to the decision in December 1978 to join the European Monetary System (EMS) – "breaking the link with sterling" – a decision still regarded by some historians and economists as double-edged.

It was a decision, according to Joe Lee, "impelled by the search for cheap money and cheap discipline".

The "downside" of the Lynch story – as Dr Garret Fitzgerald contends – is undoubtedly the "cost" of the 1977 Election. Critics say it was "bought" by a manifesto which proved ruinous (Dr Fitzgerald claims it did the equivalent of 25 years economic damage in five); economic mismanagement, and the lack of a coherent social philosophy.

This has always been the problem with and the puzzle about Lynch. A child of the northside of Cork, where there was widespread poverty during his boyhood, he brought none of the customary working-class fire or revolutionary zeal to politics.

In a perceptive essay in *Ireland 1945-1970*, Professor John A. Murphy offers this analysis of the former Taoiseach: "Lynch had no clearcut political philosophy, and lacked Lemass's vigorous and innovative temperament. It does not seem unfair to say that he personified the party's development as it moved into the late 1960s, standing for nothing in particular except a kind of affable consensus".

Former Fianna Fáil TD, Flor Crowley – no great admirer – chose a sporting metaphor to express the same thing: "Lynch was a counterpuncher; he reacted rather than initiated".

Labour Party TD and former Chairman, Michael D. Higgins, who liked Lynch as a person, says his great failure was his inability, through lack of social vision, to "use" the huge 1977 victory in a reforming manner.

"Modernising social legislation could have been introduced by him, with his personal prestige and his majority in the Dáil. People would have worn these changes coming from him when they wouldn't have coming from another Taoiseach or party leader."

Maurice Manning, lecturer in politics at UCD, says that "Jack Lynch's greatest weakness as a political leader was that he too often gave the impression of not really wanting to use the power which he had.

"He appeared to be over-cautious in his exercise of power – more concerned with orderly continuation of the *status quo,* as careful as any civil servant or lawyer of precedents and procedures, of reacting to events rather than seeking to innovate, to cause them; of being a man without any clear vision of the society he wants, of having no real passion for reform or change."

When the end finally came – he announced his resignation as Taoiseach and leader of Fianna Fáil on 5 December 1979 – Lynch quickly moved to dispel any notion that he might be interested in the Presidency. "I have ruled it out completely," he said at an impromptu press conference in the Victoria Hotel in Cork just nine days after resigning. It was still his stance up to 1990, when he showed signs, for the very first time of having second thoughts.

There remains, of course, the final and very gracious tribute from Liam Cosgrave, who was Taoiseach when Lynch, in Opposition, came to be known as "the real Taoiseach".

Looking for a parallel to describe Lynch's enormous appeal (this was the day Jack resigned as Taoiseach), Cosgrave said he was the most popular Irish politician since Daniel O'Connell.

These are his exact words: "He is widely respected for his personal qualities, and the personal popularity he achieved was unrivalled by anyone since Daniel O'Connell. This was a measure of the high esteem and general regard for his character and integrity." With that there is no arguing.

An Taoiseach Jack Lynch and Mairin Lynch and the Indian Premier Mrs Indira Gandhi in 1968 (copyright United Press International)

33. The Lynch Legacy

The year was 1969, the place Monaghan, and the occasion a General Election. Among the group of reporters following Jack Lynch was a mini-skirted Mary Kenny, who admitted to having a "crush" on him.

"Are you a republican?" a heckler shouted at Lynch, as Mary Kenny furiously scribbled notes.

"I am," the Taoiseach shouted back.

"But are you a socialist?" the heckler demanded.

"I am," replied the Taoiseach, looking him in the eye. "I'm a republican socialist."

"Bedad," said the heckler, "you have me bet."

It may have been good repartee, but the answer was only half right.

Lynch was no socialist. Indeed, it would be claimed later by prominent members of the Labour Party – which had vowed to make the "seventies socialist" – that he had created a "Reds-under-the-bed" scare during that campaign to scuttle them.

That he was a republican was indisputable. "The fundamental basis of any republican movement is the supremacy of the people," he stated in 1976 – a definition which the Provisional IRA treats with deadly disdain.

In 1985 he issued a credo which has yet to win universal acceptance on this island: "I have never believed that it was necessary to carry a gun to be a republican".

Winning overwhelming, if not total, acceptance for that (not least within his own party: the 1971 Árd Fhéis, remembered now for its boisterous scenes, saw the last real challenge to him), will be an essential feature of Jack Lynch's enduring legacy.

When in November 1966 he was chosen, at the age of 49, to succeed Sean Lemass, it is fair to assume that that decision was made with little or no regard for Northern Ireland. It would be another two years before the situation there began to unravel in a most unpleasant way.

Yet the decision by the Fianna Fáil party that November was to have vitally important consequences for Northern Ireland, and for all our perceptions of its "troubles".

It should be emphasised that those consequences were benign – a view still not shared by some (both within and outside of Fianna Fáil), despite all that has happened.

But the matter goes beyond parties – fundamentally, it has to do with morality and freedom; it has to do with our understanding of who we are as a new century beckons, and with how we view our history, and the lessons we draw from this.

The advent of Lynch to the top political post marked a change, at least in this sense – he was the first Taoiseach in the Republic who was not involved, who had not been a participant in, the terrible years from 1916 to 1923, from the Easter Rising to the end of the Civil War.

Lynch was the first Taoiseach who had not been earlier in his career a "gunman".

All the others were, including Eamon de Valera, to a greater or lesser degree. They were certainly products of, upholders of, or creators of a "gun culture".

Lynch was not. Whether he would have been in different circumstances is another matter.

He, therefore, served as a kind of dividing line, a kind of "border" or demarcation, between leaders who were, in part, the creators of, and were in turn created by that terrible time (1916-1923), and who were accordingly and inevitably limited, circumscribed and inhibited (trapped, if you prefer) by the imperatives of that time.

Lynch was free of those – which is more than can be said for some of his contemporaries, even younger than him – though again how much of that is due to chance or accident or to temperament and conviction is beside the point.

What matters – and this is where the imaginative possibilities open up – is that from 1966 onwards (and some will consider it ironic that Lynch's succession to the post of Taoiseach should occur in the 50th anniversary year of the Easter Rising) we were in a different era.

It was the era of the first post-revolutionary Prime Minister.

"We can be sure that Lynch sincerely wished to continue consistently, the pragmatic policies of Lemass, the primacy of politique over mystique," emphasised Dr Conor Cruise O'Brien in an influential article entitled "Shades of Republicans".

Ireland had a man at the top who was able to see things differently, who possessed a different perspective, albeit an imperfect one.

What Lynch saw was that we are "trapped" by our "official" history. He was aware that history is used and abused for political purposes; he knows history can be turned into ideology to prop up slogans and catch-cries, to underpin and legitimise myths, and to score political points.

What he tried to do in relation to Northern Ireland and the mythology of "The Republic" was to show that the justification for violence was facile, and that the willingness to resort to violence lurked just beneath the surface in the most unlikely places – not least within his own party.

"Lynch had to face crisis after crisis in those years, and he reiterated Fianna Fáil's determination to seek reunification by peaceful means, constantly dissociating his party from the men of violence," affirmed Professor John A. Murphy in *Ireland in The Twentieth Century*.

He was aware of – and reacted against (up to a point) – what one might call the "refrigerator" or "deep freeze" version of history – the idea that only one version is pertinent, and that that version is frozen and fixed for all time.

He failed, in that we still have the problem of violence which is politically motivated, on the surface anyway. We still have the unresolved problem of Partition and how we should regard it whether we should find a way of living with it, or whether we should press for its abolition.

But one could also argue in another sense that he succeeded up to a point. It comes down to a kind of head count here. He may have influenced a lot of people. There is every reason to believe that he did.

He may have prompted people to look again, to think again about our history and whether we are its slaves or its makers, to look again at our notion of who we are and where we want to be as the final decade of the twentieth century ticks away.

Lynch perceived (though, sadly, he did not fully explore or follow through the implications) that what was said and done in 1916 need not be binding on us or normative for this generation.

He challenged the conventional wisdom of "republicanism" – the "romantic" version in whose name all morality can be cast aside. And he understands that either we are moral beings or we are nothing.

The moment we concede that one human life is "expendable", in the name of history or ideology or politics, is the moment in which the very texture of our lives as moral beings becomes radically altered.

We have not yet as a society fully accepted this, or its crucial importance to a civilised society. Yet to the extent that its acceptance is greater and more widespread now than it was 20 years ago is due, in no small measure, to the persistence, the courage and the steadfastness of Jack Lynch.

He has expressed it with muted elegance himself: "If I feel that I have done something to diminish the feelings of bitterness and antagonism that pervade the two communities in the North and between North and South, then I think my contribution as Taoiseach will have been worthwhile".

Nowadays, he is no longer in politics, he is no longer an actor on the political stage. But, using another theatrical metaphor, we can say that the "play" we are all currently in was in part scripted by Lynch, and so, to that extent we are still in "the Lynch years".

They have been, in many respects, bleak, distressful years, overshadowed by the tragedy in Northern Ireland. But the histories of the future, official and otherwise, will record that Jack Lynch chose to ride the tiger (of violence), and to tame and control it rather than give it its head.

For that, all of us ought to be grateful.

To those who were his bitter opponents, both within and outside of Fianna Fáil, Lynch today is the "forgotten man" of Irish politics.

It is no exaggeration to say that the Party is run today as though he never existed.

If one wished to be unkind, one might look to the pre-Gorbachev Soviet Union for a parallel and describe this as a kind of "Stalinist exclusion" – no photographs, no busts, no memorials. Kill the image, expunge the memory, promote a kind of collective amnesia among the Party faithful.

Of course, it is all futile. History is bigger than men or parties. It has its own cogency and its own laws. And Jack Lynch is firmly wrapped in its embrace, his place in its pantheon secure despite the begrudgers.

The plain people of Ireland are not easily fooled. They made him a folk hero – first on the playing field, and then in the political forum.

And they haven't forgotten. He remains a folk hero, living proof that "good guys finish first".

Over the years, in sport and in politics, many tributes have been paid to him.

On a personal level, perhaps the simplest, most endearing, yet profound tribute comes from Con Houlihan of the *Evening Press:*

"Jack Lynch is a man who never lost the run of himself".

Jack and Mairin Lynch

Jack Lynch

Select Bibliography

Arnold, Bruce, *What Kind of Country: Modern Irish Politics 1968-1983* (Cape), London, 1984

Bishop, Patrick & Mallie, Eamonn, *The Provisional IRA* (Heinemann), London, 1987

Boland, Kevin, *The Rise and Decline of Fianna Fáil* (Mercier), Cork, 1982

Brown, Terence, *Ireland: A Social and Cultural History 1922-1985* (Fontana), London, 1985

Coogan, Tim Pat, *Ireland Since the Rising* (Pall Mall), London, 1966
The IRA (Pall Mall) London, 1970

Cooney, John, *The Crozier & The Dáil: Church & State 1922-1986* (Mercier), Cork, 1986
EEC in Crisis (Dublin University Press), Dublin, 1979

Cronin, Sean, *Washington's Irish Policy 1916-1986* (Anvil), Dublin, 1987

Cruise O'Brien, Conor (ed.) *The Shaping of Modern Ireland* (Routledge & Kegan Paul), London, 1970
States of Ireland (Panther), London, 1974

De Paor, Liam (ed.) *Milestones in Irish History* (Mercier), Cork, 1986

Doig, Alan, *Sex, Money and Scandal in British Politics* Westminster Babylon (Allison & Busby), London, 1990

Dorgan, Val, *Christy Ring* (Ward River), Dublin, 1980

Downey, James, *Them & Us* (Ward River), Dublin 1983

Fanning, Ronan, *Independent Ireland* (Helicon), Dublin, 1983

Farrell, Brian, *The Founding of Dáil Eireann* (Gill & Macmillan), Dublin, 1971

Hickey, D.J. & Doherty, J.E., *A Dictionary of Irish History 1800-1980* (Gill & Macmillan), Dublin, 1980

Horgan, Tim, *Cork's Hurling Story* (Anvil), Dublin 1977

Joyce, Joe & Murtagh, Peter, *The BOSS* (Poolbeg), Dublin, 1983

Kennedy Kieran A., (ed.) *Ireland in Transition* (Mercier), Cork, 1986

Lee, Joseph, *Ireland 1912-1985: Politics and Society* (Cambridge University Press), Cambridge, 1989

Leigh, David, *The Wilson Plot* (Heinemann), London, 1988

Lord Longford, *Peace By Ordeal* (Sidgwick & Jackson), London, 1972

Lynch, Jack, "Speeches and Statements" (Government Information Bureau), Dublin, 1971

Lyons F.S.L., *Ireland Since the Famine* (Collins/Fontana), London, 1973

MacArdle, Dorothy, *The Irish Republic* (Corgi), London, 1968

Manning, Maurice, *Irish Political Parties – An Introduction* (Gill & Macmillan), Dublin, 1972

Murphy, John A, *Ireland in the 20th Century* (Gill & Macmillan), Dublin, 1975

O'Donnell, Jim, (ed.) *Ireland, The Past Twenty Years: An Illustrated Chronology* (Institute of Public Administration), Dublin, 1986

O'Malley, Padraig, *The Uncivil Wars: Ireland Today* (Blackstaff), Belfast, 1983

O'Leary, Cornelius, *Irish Elections: 1918-1977* (Gill & Macmillan), Dublin, 1979

Perry, Keith, *Modern World History 1890-1990* (Heinemann), London, 1990

Ryle Dwyer, T. De Valera: *The Man & The Myths* (Poolbeg), Dublin, 1991
Charlie (Gill & Macmillan), Dublin, 1987

Smith, Raymond, *The Quest For Power* (Aherlow), Dublin, 1986
Garret: The Enigma (Aherlow), Dublin, 1985
The Greatest Hurlers of Our Time (Sporting Books), Dublin, 1986

Walsh, Dick, *The Party: Inside Fianna Fáil* (Gill & Macmillan), Dublin, 1986
Des O'Malley: A Political Profile (Brandon), Dingle, 1986

White, Barry, *John Hume: Statesman of the Troubles* (Blackstaff), Belfast, 1984

Whitelaw, William, *The Whitelaw Memoirs* (Headline), London, 1989

Whyte, J.H., *Church and State in Modern Ireland 1923-1970* (Gill & Macmillan), Dublin, 1971

Young, Hugo, *One Of Us* (Pan), London, 1990

Other Best Sellers from Blackwater Press

No Problem – To Mayo and Back
By
Ann Lenihan
Price £5.95

For The Record
By
Brian Lenihan
Price £6.95

Day of Reckoning
By
Michael Keating
Price £5.95

Gillian: A Second Chance
By
Veronica Staunton
Price £6.95

Who's Who in Irish Politics
By
Jim Farrelly
Price £9.95

Manchester United
By
Stephen McGarrigle
Price £4.95

From Parnell to DeValera (A Biography of Jennie Wyse Power)
By
Marie O'Neill
Price £7.95

My Life in Football
By
Frank Stapleton
Price £6.95

All the above publications are available in leading bookshops or direct from the publisher: 8 Airton Road, Tallaght, Dublin 24.